CHOOSING HAPPINESS

STEPHANIE DOWRICK

CHOOSING HAPPINESS
LIFE & SOUL ESSENTIALS

In collaboration with
Catherine Greer

JEREMY P. TARCHER/PENGUIN

a member of Penguin Group (USA) Inc.

New York

JEREMY P. TARCHER/PENGUIN
Published by the Penguin Group
Penguin Group (USA) Inc., 375 Hudson Street, New York, New York 10014, USA •
Penguin Group (Canada), 90 Eglinton Avenue East, Suite 700, Toronto, Ontario M4P 2Y3,
Canada (a division of Pearson Penguin Canada Inc.) • Penguin Books Ltd, 80 Strand,
London WC2R 0RL, England • Penguin Ireland, 25 St Stephen's Green, Dublin 2,
Ireland (a division of Penguin Books Ltd) • Penguin Group (Australia), 250 Camberwell Road,
Camberwell, Victoria 3124, Australia (a division of Pearson Australia Group Pty Ltd) •
Penguin Books India Pvt Ltd, 11 Community Centre, Panchsheel Park, New Delhi–110 017,
India • Penguin Group (NZ), 67 Apollo Drive, Rosedale, North Shore 0632, New Zealand
(a division of Pearson New Zealand Ltd) • Penguin Books (South Africa) (Pty) Ltd,
24 Sturdee Avenue, Rosebank, Johannesburg 2196, South Africa

Penguin Books Ltd, Registered Offices: 80 Strand, London WC2R 0RL, England

Previously published in Australia in 2005 by Allen & Unwin
All material written by Stephanie Dowrick copyright © 2005 by Wise Angels Pty Ltd
All material written by Catherine Greer copyright © 2005 by Catherine Greer

Most Tarcher/Penguin books are available at special quantity discounts for bulk purchase for sales promotions, premiums, fund-raising, and educational needs. Special books or book excerpts also can be created to fit specific needs. For details, write Penguin Group (USA) Inc. Special Markets, 375 Hudson Street,
New York, NY 10014.

Library of Congress Cataloging-in-Publication Data

Dowrick, Stephanie.
Choosing happiness: life & soul essentials / Stephanie Dowrick; in collaboration with Catherine Greer.
p.   cm.
Includes index.
ISBN 978-1-58542-582-2
1. Happiness. I. Greer, Catherine. II. Title.
BF575.H27D69   2007   2007027933
158.1—dc22

Printed in China
1   3   5   7   9   10   8   6   4   2

This book is printed on acid free paper. ∞

Book design by Nada Backovic

**THIS BOOK IS FOR MY DAUGHTER,
KEZIA DOWRICK**

There are three things that last forever: faith, hope and love.
But the greatest of them all is love.
1 Corinthians 13

We all live with the objective of being happy;
our lives are different and yet the same.
Anne Frank, *The Diary of Anne Frank*

How many people are genuinely happy? I don't mean happy because
they've just met the man or woman of their dreams, or because they've got
a new car, or a new house, or the job they've always wanted. I'm talking
about being inwardly happy. I'm talking about having a wellspring of inner
joy and peace. . . . How many people do you know like that?
Tenzin Palmo, *Reflections on a Mountain Lake*

Happiness is not simply a feeling or emotion;
it is a connection to the world, a realization of one's place in it.
Mark Kingwell, *Better Living*

Contents

Introduction

Stephanie Dowrick

Most books tell a story and almost every book also has a story.

The story of *Choosing Happiness: Life & Soul Essentials* began almost three years ago. Or even a decade ago when, despite having much more enthusiasm than talent, I began to take group classes in gospel singing. That singing life evolved into being part of a community choir called the Honeybees, a group which eventually included a Canadian woman called Catherine Greer.

At the time she joined the choir, Catherine was still relatively new to Australia, where I have been living since 1983. Because I have moved country several times during my adult life, I was sensitive to her settling-in issues, which were compounded by her being a new mother. We talked. It emerged that I am a writer. She began to read my books.

None of this is so unusual. Writing has been my primary occupation since I came to live in Australia. In fact, coming to Australia was propelled in part by my decision to leave behind my career as a publisher, and as Managing Director of The Women's Press in London, in order to focus on writing and psychotherapy, rather than publishing.

By the time Catherine and I met, I had been writing for almost twenty years. Because my subject matter is ordinary life, and how we might live it with more-than-ordinary awareness and appreciation, I already knew that in transition moments especially, when they are more than usually open and ready, some people can and will respond to my books passionately as well as positively.

I don't take this for granted. In fact, I am quite sure that it's this level of response that has sustained my writing life. So when Catherine told me how much she was appreciating the books, I was delighted but not especially surprised. What did surprise me, however, was the depth of attention she was giving to them. Quite quickly I realized that Catherine was the kind of reader every writer hopes for: someone who reads for content, certainly, but who is also engaged with questions from her own life as she reads. Before we began to talk in depth about the books, and long before we began to talk about the project that evolved into this book, Catherine was allowing herself to "read" her own life and experiences from a broader perspective, using my books as her catalyst. And not only was she reading and thinking, she was also making changes that she believed were enhancing her life in new and very welcome ways.

Over several months, Catherine continued to feed back to me glimpses of the practical effect the books were having on her life. She was seeing things differently; she was responding to life more confidently. She was making choices more easily. She was feeling lighter and happier.

Her passion for literature, and her training in reading books closely, meant that she was also sensitive to the art of writing, to how information is conveyed as well as to the content. That breadth of appreciation made those conversations enormously rewarding for me. They allowed me to see the span of my books freshly. And because she was talking so openly and honestly about her life while she was also talking about my books, I began to know Catherine better and to trust her instincts.

At some point in this dialogue—fitted between songs at choir practice, or occasional phone calls in the midst of two extremely busy, overcommitted lives as working mothers—Catherine made a fairly startling request. Many people, she asserted, would be or could be as supported by my work as she had been, but might see themselves as too busy to read an entire book from cover to cover. Her generation particularly, Catherine suggested, had become used to wanting and getting information in highly focused, highly accessible chunks. They wanted depth. They needed depth. They were hungry for depth. But they wanted it fast. Was it possible to provide depth—at speed? Was it possible for me to present some of what I had researched and discovered through my psychotherapy training, and years of writing, workshops and teaching, in a more concentrated, episodic form?

Was it possible to give readers the essentials of what I believed to be the most useful principles and actions, psychologically and spiritually? And could I do it in such a way that this would go to the heart of people's lives as they ran, sometimes breathlessly, between work, love, family responsibilities, social concerns, public demands and private dreams?

Holding this book in your hands, you will know that the answer was, eventually, yes. But the journey turned out to be more complex and richer than I could possibly have imagined.

When Catherine put this idea to me, I was intrigued. My own two beloved children were becoming adults. I know and admire the generation younger than Catherine's, and was well aware that in this information age the ways in which knowledge is shared are at least as crucial as what that knowledge is.

The possibility of reaching out in new ways to new readers was attractive. Yet I was also aware that over my many years of speaking publicly, readers often present me with copies of my own books to sign that have copious notes in the margins. Those readers, too, who have in part loved my earlier books because they are more leisurely and internal, might, I thought, also welcome a book that reviewed the more familiar essential questions while also moving on to new territory.

A different format would give me a chance to look very directly at the most persistent issues and questions that run through our lives. I would need to be clear and direct about what was and is most useful. Yet I still also have the instincts of a novelist. Some things need to be said indirectly; some things can only be said indirectly. *Choosing Happiness* had to be spacious enough to allow that. (Sometimes you will get a far more useful "answer" through seeing your situation differently, or being guided to ask yourself the right questions, rather than having someone like me tell you what you "ought" to do or think. On some of our key issues, one size does not fit all. This book respects that.)

I also had to be sure that there would be enough really new learning so that I could bring energy and dynamism to the project. I write for my own sake, as well as for yours. Whatever drive you have to understand your life better, I share. As I write, and you read, I am aware that we are in this process of seeking and learning together.

These years of writing, of personal therapy and training, of working as a psychotherapist with individuals, of running workshops and spiritual retreats for groups, as well as writing my newspaper column and broadcasts, have not diminished my appetite to know more about the ingredients of a worthwhile life. I, too, want to know more about the essentials: what makes us kinder, more thoughtful, happier; what makes us more forgiving, tolerant and courageous; what makes us content, more easily delighted, more passionate, more engaged.

What's more, I was acutely aware that despite the deluge of information made available over the last couple of decades (some of it very good), by every available measure levels of stress, anxiety and depression are rising. Relationship breakdown is also accelerating and loneliness is on the increase, even (and perhaps especially) among people who seem to have "everything." "Everything" might include high levels of education, work success and financial security. These rewards are substantial. People make extraordinary sacrifices to achieve them. Nevertheless, for many people they are not enough.

Whatever our background, culture or race, what rewards us most powerfully and consistently are the most deceptively simple abilities of all: the ability to be kind, to live enthusiastically and creatively, to appreciate and understand experiences different from our own, and to sustain a sense of inner stability and trust even in unwelcome and difficult situations.

Those are the abilities that, bit by bit, moment by moment, choice by choice, create a life of happiness. But however "simple" those abilities may be, they are frequently elusive—even in the face of our best intentions. We need guidance and encouragement, many of us, in finding our way back to those abilities, looking at them freshly, and valuing them by learning how to live them.

We are also rewarded when we know how our minds work, how our thoughts and attitudes drive our emotions, reactions and behavior, and how our values and presence (not our status) affect and even shape the world around us.

The promise of this book is very direct. You can be happier. Through your choices, you can also bring greater happiness to the people around you. You can lift other people's spirits—and your own. Understanding and using your power to choose, discovering what your strengths are, giving new value to your insights and experiences, cultivating a genuine sense of respect, appreciation and consideration for other people, you grow not just in happiness but also in inner stability, trust and confidence. And, perhaps unsurprisingly, you lose much of the self-consciousness, self-focus, anxiety and even depression that can haunt and limit you while your strengths are unknown to you, while you remain a stranger to yourself or while other people remain mysterious, or painfully out of reach.

The way the contents of this book are delivered is just as direct. I am genuinely confident that you can learn actual skills that will enhance your capacity for happiness (joy, contentment, peace of mind, stability) and also make an immediate and substantial difference in the way you respond to complex, difficult or painful situations. "Happiness" then ceases to be limited by your ideas of what's immediately pleasing. In fact, it becomes less and less exclusively about pleasure (as lovely as that can be), or about things going your way, and it becomes more and more a way of living that can also and very honestly encompass the times when things do not go right or well.

Learning to live with greater self-responsibility and awareness of choice is already uplifting. But recognizing that you can be a positive influence on everyone around you takes your life—and your perception of what happiness is—to an even finer place. When you have room in your mind and heart genuinely to care about the welfare of other people, your own life comes into balance. We are social beings. We don't become "better" without also "doing better" in our interactions with other people. We cannot, I believe, lift our lives in isolation. We do it by practicing kindness, thoughtfulness and compassion. Being kind to ourselves and other people *because we can* (and not because we should, or because we will get a prize or eternal reward for doing so) is our greatest freedom. It also leads directly to our greatest and most reliable experiences of happiness.

And it is from that place of confidence, peace of mind and happiness that we can also more readily tolerate and bear the other less welcome emotions: the uncertainty, grief and sorrow, the losses and disappointments, even the tragedies that are inevitably part of a complex life.

Following this Introduction is a short section suggesting ways to use this book. But I want to say here, too, that the structure of this book reflects my awareness that the deepest learning is frequently circular. What's more, it has to engage your emotions and imagination, as well as your rational, analytic mind. This is a book for both sides of your brain!

Key themes and topics appear then reappear. This is not only because many of you won't be reading this book consecutively but also because each of us makes sense of things in our own way. I may have written about a theme—let's say it's giving others the benefit of the doubt—in three or four contexts. However, it's not until you suddenly "see" how it would transform *your* Friday sales meetings, or how it would make it possible to enjoy dinner with *your* partner's difficult sibling, or how you could manage when *your* teenager walks in with a new tattoo, that this idea falls into place, bringing not just insight, but also choices.

My books were a significant catalyst for change in Catherine's life. And Catherine was a significant catalyst in the writing of this book. She believed in the need for this book; I was inspired and sustained in my writing by that.

During the research and writing processes, we had countless discussions about what "the life and soul essentials" really are. The differences in our lives were at least as fruitful as any similarities. In her role as public "reader," Catherine also asked many specific questions, some of which appear here. This is an aspect of the book that I like very much. They reflect Catherine's own courage and drive to understand. But, more generally, they mirror the potent dialogue that exists between the writer and her readers, especially in books as personal as this one.

Catherine's explicit questions—and my answers to them—form only a small part of the book, but they are central to it. Some of her questions or concerns that didn't make it to the page provoked entries. Yet, as my work progressed, I was also increasingly mindful of the many marvelously varied people I have worked with psychologically and spiritually over the years, or met at workshops, or simply listened to with real interest in a quiet moment.

The questions that Catherine is asking here reflect her own circumstances. But the readers that I held in the forefront of my mind as I researched and wrote the entries come from highly diverse backgrounds.

If this book is to be the friend, the companion, the quiet counselor, the cheerleader and supporter I want it to be, then you need to find your place here. You need to feel at home, welcomed, understood and totally safe.

So, I want you to know this.

Whatever your age, whatever your personal and social circumstances, whether you are single or married, gay, heterosexual or celibate, whether you have children or feel like a child yourself, whether you are successful in your career or biding time or retired, whether you believe in the Divine or not, whether you feel ready for greater happiness or not, I have had you in my mind. No, more than that—as I have written it over hundreds of hours in my peaceful writing room at home as well as in the bustle of my office, I have had you in my heart.

This book is for you.

Introduction

Catherine Greer

Every reader has a story. This is mine.

When I arrived in Sydney eight years ago, I was newly thirty, newly married and suddenly immersed in a culture both like and unlike home. After four months of exploring the city, I started a career as an advertising copywriter and searched for friends, hoping to re-create both the professional life and close relationships I had left behind in Canada. Eventually pregnancy and parenthood arrived, and I was ecstatic. I wanted so much to be a mother and I was committed to being at home full-time. I fell in love with our wrinkly baby son. But, like many first-time parents, I was completely shocked that parenting was such hard work, especially with a baby who never seemed to sleep. My life had taught me that it was important to be upbeat and I knew that I should have been happy, but I didn't feel that way. Somewhere in all the changes I had lost myself. I was completely dislocated in Australia. I didn't have any idea what I wanted. I was afraid to assert myself or listen to my own inner authority. I needed almost constant reassurance. And yet, I had "everything": faith, family, career and lifestyle.

The truth was, like many people, too often my emotions were running my life. My moods and even my most routine thoughts would often derail me. When that happened, I would look to other people to soothe and reassure me. I would assume that "if only" this or that happened, I would be happier.

That's where I was when Stephanie's books found me. Despite taking many classes in psychology during my undergraduate degree, I had never read books like Stephanie's before. I honestly didn't think I "needed" them. I assumed that I was living my life as best I could, that all my *feelings* were just who I was: quite pessimistic, a real worrier, a bit hard on myself. I realize now that I had very little understanding of the general principles of psychological well-being and was lacking a whole set of practical skills that I needed to navigate my life. In fact, when

I started reading Stephanie's books, my overwhelming question was "Why don't I know these things?" "Why aren't we taught these skills?" I couldn't believe the extent of what I didn't know—despite years of university education and some fairly substantial life experiences.

Stephanie's books expressed some timeless truths and, even more importantly, they gave me practical skills to go out and live my life with greater confidence and awareness. Her writing showed me— upfront and without apology—that regardless of our circumstances, happiness and gratitude really can be a choice. But her message was far deeper than that. That life can be challenging and still be precious. That it doesn't have to be frightening to learn more about ourselves; in fact, the insights will often bring peace of mind and greater security—and many more choices. That self-knowledge will help us deal with challenges, hurts and even raw grief.

I *knew* this but I didn't understand it. Instead, I somehow believed in the world I was teaching my young son about: that life should be pretty much fair and reasonable, that all the people in your world will try to love you, and that if you behave well and ask nicely, you will get a treat.

When I think about it now, perhaps that's where I was—in the childhood of my understanding of the world. Every conflict and even some disappointments left me bruised and unsure. And, like a child, I didn't have the psychological skills and resilience I needed to cope well with the demands of an adult life. Despite my life experiences, education and professional skills, I didn't know how to make good decisions. I wasn't able to reassure myself. I assumed I had to give space and credence to every thought that ran through my mind. I didn't know that I could "try on and borrow" the strengths I admired in others. I constantly reduced people to one-word labels, conveniently ignoring their complexity and inconsistencies while being totally understanding of my own. And outside the small circle of people I loved or the charities I supported, I rarely considered others.

As I read and reread Stephanie's books, I started learning. I thought about what I wanted most—to be less fearful and more optimistic. I wanted to *understand* that the world was complicated (and many times would not be "fair") and in spite of that, I wanted to know that I could choose to live with optimism, happiness and hope.

So, I started asking Stephanie questions. And she answered them. She tells me it's brave to share my questions with readers of this book but really, I feel that it's just honest. *This is what I don't know. This is what I want to know. Can you give me some skills to get there?* And she did.

Reading Stephanie's answers to my questions gave me what I think of now as "psychological breathing room." I experienced the relief of being encouraged to step back a little, to look at myself with some gentleness and understanding, and almost paradoxically, to be free then to focus wholeheartedly on others. It was as if Stephanie's answers—and all the entries she was writing between those answers—gave me space, and led me, step-by-step, from knowing who I am to knowing and appreciating others more.

Of course I asked many more questions than those that appear here. And there has been so much learning that it's hard to encapsulate briefly. It comes in waves, and I know that *Choosing Happiness* will be one of those bedside books that I will dog-ear, pick up and read sections of for years to come. Even with the most powerful ideas, I seem to need constant reminding.

Overall, I learned to think about my life and myself far more constructively (and lovingly). To do that, I had to observe my thoughts and moods, sometimes challenging them, sometimes dismissing them, and sometimes discerning the truth behind the emotion. As I did that I began to feel happier, more in control, better prepared to meet challenges, more relaxed, and less self-focused. I know now that I am in charge of my thoughts, and that it's my thoughts about events (rarely the events themselves) that hurt me. Now I look at my thoughts from different perspectives—sometimes humor ("What? Another MAJOR catastrophe and it's only 8 A.M.?"), sometimes self-encouragement ("at *least* as much as an under-twelves soccer coach gives to his team" as Stephanie's *The Universal Heart* reminds me), sometimes forgiveness ("It's okay—I did the wrong thing but I can start over right now."). Casually but consistently, as I build a new habit of kindness toward myself, I work on correcting my thinking, not wasting thoughts on past hurts that can't be undone.

I use this skill of "right thinking" constantly to improve my self-confidence and my relationships. In our marriage, our problem-solving has changed from expecting that my husband will reassure me and "make me feel better" to soothing myself. This change alone lets us move so much more quickly into quality conversation, where we can solve problems together or just relax and have fun. I think now about all those hours spent running around in emotional circles, and how much better we use our time together just because of this one simple change: *I am not my thoughts. I am not my moods.* Thoughts come—both positive and negative—and they go. I don't have to *believe* all of them or give them space in my head or my heart.

I've also learned (*really* learned) that other people are as inconsistent and complex as I am. It is so easy to label and dismiss people, to assume that my son is "shy," the waitress is "rude" and the client is "difficult." Somehow it gave me the illusion of control, of security. Of course I was often wrong and my judgments were limiting for me and other people. Now I pause and reassure myself that it's not possible for me to know everything, and that I certainly don't know anyone else's motives! It's giving people the benefit of the doubt, but it's also more than that: it's becoming mature enough to realize that other people are, like me, inconsistent, complicated, and usually trying to do the best they can given what they know.

Working with Stephanie has also reminded me to give the people I love the best of me and not, as my friend Janet jokes, the "unplugged version" they usually get. Even though this seems obvious, it's hard. I take so much for granted. I have a tendency to rush into family shorthand: giving orders instead of speaking respectfully, not really marveling at the amazing gift of my husband and children. So I've taken on board Stephanie's suggestion of acknowledging them every time they walk (or crawl!) into the room, just taking a few seconds to *look* at them, say hi and smile. A small change that generates a lot of love: these are the skills of awareness and presence that Stephanie writes about often.

As a copywriter who works from home while my children sleep (theoretically), family and work are closely connected. I chose this arrangement because my deepest value is to be available for my kids, especially now when they are little. During the production period of this book, I was pregnant and gave birth to my second son. It was my first real foray into the world of mothering, child care and serious work, and it has made me more compassionate about other mothers' choices. Sometimes it was very hard. It forced me to address my perfectionism and pride and to balance my needs with my children's. Thankfully, I was in good company. Stephanie's writing reflects her own experiences as a mother, as well as a psychotherapist and writer. With her words running through my head, I looked at my priorities and choices creatively. Stories at night were important for my older son; going somewhere educational and stimulating every single day was not. I learned to accept the trade-offs and value my choices.

Now as I move forward, one thing is certain: I feel confident about applying the skills from Stephanie's books to all my relationships, both personal and professional. I am learning how to understand that all people want the same care and respect I want, and are as complicated and inconsistent as I am. I am learning that thoughts and feelings come and go and that not all of them have to be believed. I can make perfectionism—or any other quality—work for me and not against me. I see that everything has a trade-off, that life cannot be ordered around, but that it's important to act in good faith and do the next right thing anyway.

The truth is, when I started thinking about Stephanie's ideas and writing my questions for this book, it took all my intelligence, perception and self-knowledge to grapple with the biggest question of all: *how do I live my life like it matters?*

That's the question *Choosing Happiness* answers.

How to use this book

Speed-reading

This is a book written and designed to give you a wide choice of entry points. I would love you to begin with the Introduction so that you get some sense of its evolution. But after that there are almost as many entry points as there are individual entries.

A single entry may be all that you will need to read (at least for the moment). In fact, as the book grew I envisaged you reaching toward it for psychological or spiritual "first aid" in large and small cases of emergency. ("Ah, the life and soul *essentials*!") Using the descriptive titles of the entries, or the Smart Index as your guide, you should easily find what you are seeking.

What you seek out first may be the entries that offer the specific skills and strategies you most urgently need. These are intended to be as useful in your workplace as at home, and in your dealings with your six-year-old as with your best friend, peers or parents. They offer ideas in areas as various as how to listen; choosing values; soothing yourself; forgiving yourself and other people; how to be more encouraging and less critical; how to respond rather than react; how to limit aggression, anger and competitiveness; how to be more generous (and why this benefits you); how to get over hurts and difficulties; how to think about love, sex and other people; how to detach from unhelpful moods and emotions; how to think more creatively as well as positively. They also deal very specifically with some of the tough issues of our time: loneliness, depression, anxiety, uncertainty, fear, resentment and aggression.

They (and the many entries like them) *are* the essentials, the psychological and spiritual "basics" that can make such a profound difference as to whether or not you feel in charge of the life you are living. They are also what you need to know in order to lead a decent, self-responsible and *enjoyable* life.

But I see this as a book for your less urgent moments also.

These entries can help to sustain the lifelong journey that you are taking toward greater self-understanding and care for others. So, although each entry is at least somewhat self-sufficient (which makes this very different from my other longer books), they do also lean together and gather momentum. Moving from one entry to the next, you will certainly notice how the book as a whole encourages you to see your entire life, and life itself, with renewed appreciation.

The book opens with a clear focus on you, on your choices, goals and values, on your self-confidence and self-respect. It then moves on to encourage in very practical and feasible ways greater and more rewarding engagement with other people (people in general; then those closest to you). Finally, it takes you toward considering an inclusively positive attitude to life.

Moving through the book in this way, with diversions back to reread as feels right, you will experience, I hope, that this is a book not just for reading but for interacting with, talking back to, engaging with as your actual life meets these ideas.

Circling and landing

Because this is a book that only some of you will be reading consecutively, there are some repetitions as key ideas appear in different guises in different places.

I won't apologize for this. Even if you are reading the book page by page, my years of working with people in psychotherapy and my own psychological and spiritual journey have demonstrated to me that often we need to come back to an idea a number of times before it "works" for us or becomes our own.

Choice, self-responsibility, care for others; living consciously and respectfully; doing your best; being your best; trust, peace of mind, forgiveness, creativity and courage as well as happiness are just some of the themes that I return to many times, knowing how crucial they are in all kinds of situations.

And I return many times also to those themes that are harder to define but that make such a profound difference as to whether or not we think life is going well: how to grow in awareness; how to limit our emotional "bad habits"; how to relieve our suffering; how to like ourselves more (and accept others less critically); how to see that thoughts create feelings; how to deal with negativity—your own and other people's; how to encourage, coach, inspire; why it is possible to make change once you recognize a pattern; how to borrow the strengths you need and make them your own; how to know and use your mind.

These rich themes are rarely unpacked in a single moment. The more clearly you recognize them, the easier they are to bring home.

Learning in different ways

Shaping this book, and talking about it extensively with Catherine and other colleagues, I was also very aware of how differently we each learn, read—even think. (You may be visionary in your thinking or strategic; you may be highly emotive, literary or literal. You may be able to critique, but not provide insight or solutions. You may want information—or simply inspiration.)

Providing enough variety within these pages to meet those thinking styles has been challenging. And fun. But it takes me to a more serious issue still.

We are, globally, more highly educated than ever. We pride ourselves on our levels of training and expertise. We can source information on virtually any topic. Yet even the most intelligent among us can make the same basic mistakes repeatedly when it comes to getting along with other people; the most well educated can be at a total loss to understand why they feel so dissatisfied, critical and empty; the most brilliant thinkers can fall helplessly into depression or despair.

In her introductory remarks Catherine speaks for many people when she says, "Why didn't I know these things?" by which she means the key insights that make a difference to the way we live, think about ourselves and value and interact with other people.

The short answer is that many people believe that the kind of learning this book offers is so "natural" or basic that it should not demand their conscious attention. It's also true that many people are uncomfortable looking inward for answers, rather than relying on other people's experiences. And there is also, still, a tendency in many people to trivialize their emotional education, even when they (or the people who love them) are living at the mercy of their moods and feelings.

Perhaps it is also true that people fear selfishness, and confuse self-knowledge with self-absorption or self-obsession, despite strong evidence that the person who trusts and knows herself is also most free to pay close and meaningful attention to the world outside herself.

Outer and inner action

The entries that offer no explicit practical insight may be among the most useful of all—even to the "left-brainers" (action-oriented, strategic thinkers). These are the entries where I point to another way of "seeing" and sometimes (but not always) invite you to take this further, often using the basic skills of journal and "free" writing as your key tools.

At first glance, you might recoil from the idea of writing a few lines in a journal. Or you may consider it odd to write a letter to yourself or risk your time on a seed meditation.

Yet, my many years of experience have taught me this. *For you to have choices, your life must have depth. Living at the surface of things, you will remain vulnerable to every passing setback and disappointment. Your instincts will be limited and often your judgment will be impaired.*

"My understanding of the fundamental laws of the universe," said Albert Einstein, "did not come out of my rational mind."

Finding the courage to go beyond the obvious and familiar, you will come to know yourself in new ways and perhaps feel new respect for the information that springs directly from your lived experience. You will feel safer internally. And you will quite unself-consciously respond to other people at greater depth.

Journal writing: a whiteboard in miniature

Journal writing, or "free" writing in a journal, is the most effective way that I know to go beyond the most obvious and familiar thoughts that clutter your mind. Your journal can be a pile of papers placed in a folder. It can be a beautiful book, tailor-made for discovery. The physical object is less important than understanding that this kind of writing engages your more creative side (we do all have one!) but is also key to clarity across every area of your life.

For those of you who are more used to writing company reports than a journal, I would suggest that you think of your journal as a whiteboard in miniature.

Let this be the place where you brainstorm freely. I have taught journal writing to literally thousands of people. I know that writing things down unself-consciously and without censorship lets you "see" your own thoughts and get some vital distance from them in ways that ruminating never can. It also clears the space for new thoughts to emerge. And it anchors new insights, making them real.

Seed meditation

Just days ago I reread the wise saying that *you cannot solve a problem with the same mind that created it.* Using seed meditation, you bring to any problem or issue a fresh "mind," even if it seems to be dressed in the same old self.

Here's how to do it.

Take a sheet of blank paper. Write down in the center of it the word or phrase you are focusing on. It could be a value you want ("tolerance"); it could be an issue that is causing you problems ("feel ignored"). Circle the word or phrase, then close your eyes and just hold this word in your mind. When associations arise, however odd, write them down, encircling each one, and linking it to your "seed" with a single line. This exercise is also very whiteboardish in style. What makes it different, however, is that between each burst of uncensored, brief writing, you go back into your internal world. You let your mind drift. You relax your body. And you don't *try.*

When your page is covered with your inner associations, or half an hour has passed and your page is still a blank, leave the seed meditation alone.

Rest.

Like journal writing, this is an opportunity to quiet your judgmental mind and open yourself to a more spacious and fruitful way of thinking.

You may want to repeat this process several times, using the same word as your "seed." Gradually your powers of lateral and creative thinking will "wake up" along with your awareness. You will bypass habitual ways of thinking; you will see the situation differently. You will also experience that you can observe your thoughts and that thoughts are not inevitable. Again you will see the resource of your own inner world differently, making yourself available to the most satisfying kind of learning of all: that moment of discovery that no one but yourself can give you.

You can use journal writing or seed meditations to explore any of the ideas in this book. Don't limit yourself to the relatively few times that I make an explicit suggestion.

Notes & quotes

We write ourselves reminders for many things. Why not for the qualities we need through our day? It can be laughably helpful to find out how different a situation looks when you see it as an opportunity to practice your quality of the day. Because most of us are creatures of habit, we slip back into old patterns fast, especially under pressure. Someone is rude to us. Aren't we fully entitled to be rude back? Yet our Post-it note reminds us that good humor was the order of the day!

Writing the word down creates a promise to yourself: "This is my quality. I will practice it in my own way."

I am also a collector of other people's inspirational thoughts. Some appear in these pages. Hunt out your own. Join the community of people willing to be inspired—and perhaps to inspire.

Smart Index

The Smart Index is key to the emergency services offered by this book, as well as being a great resource for browsers. This is Catherine's inspiration and it lets you hunt and find not only the explicit words on any page but also the implicit themes that drove the writing on that page. You might, for example, look up "anxiety" or "loneliness" or "creativity" and find yourself directed to pages where those words don't occur (as well as where they do occur). Nevertheless, there will be something on that page that gives you insight—and greater choice.

Dipping plus

Many people dip into the books they trust, sure that the page they open will say something of special relevance. *Choosing Happiness: Life & Soul Essentials* lends itself beautifully to dipping. However, I would love you to do a little more than dip.

Opening a page, reading a paragraph or two or just a line, read it as though it has been written today, for your situation. Then take a moment or two to let yourself know what meaning those lines have for you at this moment in your life.

In fact, circle back to the journal. It is through noting what those lines mean for you that they will come alive. Let yourself see how they can support you and in what situations. Doing this, they become *your* lines. I can think of no better way to use them.

Enjoy.

Trust who you are

CHAPTER ONE

TRUST YOURSELF AS A SOURCE OF HAPPINESS

You have the power to choose your own happiness. People, situations, events outside yourself will affect you. But no one can give you happiness.

You may try to find all kinds of things outside yourself that will reassure you that you are happy—or keep unhappiness at bay. But even the most substantial of them will be short-lived.

Romantic love, family, work success, friends, interests, status and wealth can certainly affect your well-being. They may, for many years, save you from the need to look harder or further. Yet sometimes even in the midst of "everything," you may have a feeling that "something" is missing.

A happy person can have everything that the world regards as important. But someone can also have all those things, and not be happy. What makes the difference?

Inner trust makes the difference, I believe, not trust only in what the world can see, but in who you most fundamentally are: a being of intrinsic value, with everything else "adding on."

This not only makes it possible to experience happiness; it also makes it possible to go on believing in happiness (connection, contentment, optimism, peace of mind) during the times it is out of reach or even out of sight.

EVERYTHING YOU NEED

You already have the strengths and qualities that you need.

Yet, if your life is anything like mine, there will be times when you overlook or forget this, when your strengths seem obscured by self-doubt, anxieties, fears, disappointments or losses. But those strengths remain. While you are living, where else could they go?

Think about them like the sky that never ceases to be blue, even when there are clouds covering it; or like the mountain that is still present, even when dense fog keeps it hidden.

Trusting yourself, and looking at your life from a more engaged and compassionate perspective, you will become more and more familiar with how to meet the world, and what it asks of you, using those strengths.

You will experience how this settles and stabilizes you from the inside out.

You will experience how this quite naturally brings peace of mind, clearer choices and greater happiness. And how it changes the way you view other people and see the physical and social worlds around you.

This book speaks directly to your strengths and qualities. It invokes and develops them. It helps them—and you—to come fully alive.

EVERY DAY IS A NEW DAY

I have found it almost absurdly helpful to recognize that whatever stage of life I am at, I have never been here before.

There are many things that I have learned in the decades that I have lived so far, and some of them I can now put to excellent use. But if I am tempted to give myself a hard time because I don't think I am dealing with a situation as well as I "should," it is extremely encouraging to remind myself that this is a brand-new moment in my constantly unfolding life. And, in fact, recognizing it as a new moment is the best possible way to save myself from offering a stale or habitual response.

It is also very useful to know that for most people—women and men alike—the decade of the twenties is spent looking outward primarily. This is the decade when you are establishing your sense of yourself in the world, finding out what really matters to you (and what doesn't), and how other people perceive and affect you.

However, even as that decade proceeds, and certainly in the decades that follow, it is invaluable to know that other people's reactions, values and experiences are only ever part of the picture. You also have a core sense of self that you can develop and rely upon.

It is the development of this inner sense of self that makes you much less vulnerable to feeling controlled or pushed around by other people. It makes you less dogmatic and controlling; it eventually makes you less needy of status and other people's admiration, or less inclined to "opt out" as a gesture of despair. It lets you assert yourself appropriately and, more often than not, make decisions that genuinely reflect your own principles and values and what you stand for. It is also this inner sense of self that wakes you up to notice and value everyone around you and to see how deeply and inevitably your own happiness is linked to the happiness of other people. *And how you can affect that.*

YOUR LIFE IS YOUR MESSAGE

A couple of years ago I had the experience of visiting the Mahatma Gandhi ashram in Ahmedabad, a city in the state of Gujerat in the north of India. It was the first day of my first visit to India and after traveling for more than twenty hours I was exhausted and enchanted in equal measure.

The ashram is quite extensive but remains simple and modest. It certainly doesn't obviously reflect the extent of Gandhi's reputation as one of the great peacemakers and inspirational figures of the twentieth century. Yet perhaps that modesty is entirely appropriate.

One of the walls displays a key saying of Gandhi, in his own handwriting. It reads: "My life is my message."

This is no less true for you or me than it was for Gandhi.

Through your attitudes, beliefs, thoughts, words and actions, through everything that drives your choices and decisions, you write and reinforce your "message" on a daily basis.

This message runs in three crucial directions:

+ You are guiding *yourself* as to what is possible.
+ You are guiding *others* about what is most important to you (how they should see you; what they can expect from you).
+ You are affecting and influencing the *environment* around you.

WHAT YOU PAY ATTENTION TO GROWS STRONGER IN YOUR LIFE

What follows is an extremely simple insight that literally has the power to change your life. It also brings back power to where it belongs: with you.

You shape your life through the power of your own attention.

Whatever you pay attention to (think about, dwell on, talk about, worry or obsess about) will increase and multiply and absolutely affect who you are becoming.

+ *If you constantly think about what frightens you*, you will become more fearful.
+ *If you constantly think about how unfair life is*, you will see more and more around you to support this point of view.
+ *If you believe that your life will be bleak and blighted*, that's how it will feel.
+ *If you believe your life is worthless*, your choices and behavior will reflect that.
+ *If you feel entitled to be angry*, you will find more and more to be angry about. And you will become increasingly skilled at the many ways there are to be an angry person.

Equally, if you pay close, conscious and purposeful attention to what is positive, hopeful, supportive, uplifting and encouraging, then your life and sense of self will inevitably express that.

This doesn't mean that I believe that every factor in your life is the manifestation of an inner thought. On the contrary, there will always be crucial social and genetic factors, as well as cultural and economic ones, over which you have little or no control. Nevertheless, you do have the power to choose what to cultivate in the inner garden of your mind. Whatever your circumstances, you can direct your attention to what will most positively affect your attitudes and actions.

Nourish your life

Nourish your mind, spirit and your soul with at least as much attention as you give your body. What you take in—what you pay attention to—will closely reflect the quality of what you can give out.

Remember happiness

Your personal attitudes and values, your moment-by-moment choices, will lift your spirits or dash them far more effectively than anything outside yourself.

Happiness cannot be found by "hoping for the best." It is found by claiming the best of who you are; recognizing your inner strengths and capabilities—and bringing them to life even when old habits would hold you back.

There is more to life than facing and getting over obstacles. In one of the greatest lines ever written, Sufi poet Rumi reminds us: "The soul is here for its own joy."

WHERE TO START

Trust in yourself flows from self-knowledge.

Self-knowledge is not something to acquire before you get serious about living. Nor is it something that will ever need your constant attention. (Thank heaven!)

Self-knowledge is best acquired while in the thick of living. You might even forget it for months or years on end. Nevertheless, you are alert as your life unfolds.

This entire book supports you to know yourself and other people better. But this is where to start:

+ *Observe your impact on other people.* Put yourself in their shoes. See yourself from their perspective. Listen to yourself. Know what your moods are and how inevitably they will affect everyone around you. When you don't like what you see, change it.

+ *Listen carefully to your stories.* How you describe other people's impact on you, what you emphasize, what you keep harking back to, whether you think other people have more power over your life than you do: these stories shape your character, temperament and sense of what's possible. Know what your stories are. Then discover how powerfully they are affecting you—and that a switch in attitude can bring a different "ending."

+ *Know what your strengths are.* Know what especially challenges you. Assume that both strengths and obstacles have lots to teach you.

+ *Find out what matters to you.* What do you talk about most persistently? Where are you giving your time, money and attention?

+ *Notice what makes you happy*, what makes you feel genuinely excited and alive, what inspires and moves you, what daunts and fascinates you. Allocate your time accordingly.

+ *Notice what affects your moods negatively*, what thoughts are driving your fearful thinking. Moods are driven by thoughts; not the other way around.

+ *Experience how much you can learn from your mistakes.* This saves you from repeating them (and some just like them). It also allows you to be much less fearful and defensive.

28

◆ *Let yourself learn from other people.* Appreciate their separate reality, and also what you can learn from them.

◆ *Get to know the contents of your inner world:* your dreams, hopes and wishes; how you interpret situations; what you dwell on.

◆ *Assume there is always more to know.*

What did you learn today?

Most of us are unused to thinking in fresh ways about our lives. Habits of thought rule us. This is what makes us feel stuck and limits our choices. It may even make us feel much more helpless than we are.

You will be abundantly rewarded by spending just a few minutes each day or evening reflecting on the question, *"What did I learn today?"* And maybe, *"What surprised me?"*

You can use the practical list above as a prompt. One day you might learn something about your impact on others; another day it may be an insight about what makes you happy and how you are allocating your time.

Don't discount small insights; sometimes they make the greatest difference.

HOW DO YOU SEE YOURSELF?

The deepest beliefs you have about yourself express themselves in countless ways.

They write their story across your face and body. They emerge through your eyes. They are lived out through the friends you choose, the values you identify with, the risks you take, the work you do, what your passions are, what you believe in and give your time to, how and whether you value your existence.

What qualities do you most value about yourself?
What qualities do you most want to claim and express?
What makes you feel most alive?
What habits or patterns are you ready to leave behind?
Does anything hold you back from being fully yourself?

A trusted friend?

You may choose to explore these questions with a trusted friend, giving each other complete attention, and sharing precious listening time equally.

You may prefer to use your journal as your trusted friend, taking just one question at a time and giving yourself space to pause and reflect, as well as write.

WHAT WILL YOU FIND?

Many intelligent, thoughtful people are afraid to know themselves.

They may read books like this one, turn for help to a range of psychotherapists, or talk about themselves and their "issues" fairly compulsively. Yet the challenge of self-knowledge eludes them. Things go on happening "to" them; disasters pile up that they feel helpless to affect; their moods swing between extremes, and their emotional intelligence trails far behind their potential.

The most common reason is that they are afraid their opinion of themselves might sink with greater knowledge: that "knowing more" might mean more to dislike—or more "to work on."

In fact, the opposite is true.

Self-knowledge is not "issues" or "problems" focused. Self-knowledge lets you find your strengths and develop them. It lets you recognize your passions and embrace them. It lets you see what's tripping you up and how you can learn something from it. It lets you live in the present, rather than the past.

Building trust from the inside out, self-knowledge frees you from the prison of self-absorption and the pain of constant self-questioning.

It lets you rest on solid ground.

NO ONE KNOWS YOU BETTER
THAN YOU KNOW YOURSELF

You have no greater asset than your own experiences.

As my daughter, Kezia, said to me recently, "No one knows you better than you know yourself. 'Putting on' other people's opinions of what you should or shouldn't do, or about who you are, is like sending someone else out to buy a pair of shoes for you. They may know what your size is, but they could never know from the outside how the shoes feel on your feet."

Nothing could have greater truth. Yet it is so easy to discount that. It's so easy to forget, ignore, or dismiss what we know.

Often when we are in a tight spot emotionally we do the headless chicken thing: running around in diminishing circles asking one person after another what *they think we should do*. Doing this, we are acting out our assumptions that other people know more about our lives than we do. Perhaps we trust them more than we trust ourselves. And we are certainly telling ourselves that their insights and experience have more value than our own.

They do not.

You are the only person witnessing your life at every moment. You are the only person experiencing your life from the inside out. **No one knows you better than you know yourself**.

Valuing what you know, you shift your center of gravity from outside yourself to inside yourself where it belongs.

This doesn't mean you won't continue to be interested in what other people think; you will be. But you will value their views and opinions differently.

And you will certainly value yourself—and your treasure-trove of experiences—differently.

WHAT YOU GAIN BY UNDERSTANDING YOURSELF BETTER

Understanding yourself better, you will know that it is you, and not someone else, who is making your crucial life choices.

Understanding yourself better, you will know what your strengths are—and how to use them.

Understanding yourself better, you will be slower to judge some situations as "bad," others as "good"; some as "welcome," others as "unwelcome." You will see how much you can learn from every situation. You will also see how powerfully your own beliefs and attitudes influence events.

Understanding yourself better, you will see that what happens to you matters less than your own reactions. This is wonderful because you always have far more choice and control about your reactions than you do about "what happens."

Understanding yourself better, you will feel less vulnerable, less fearful. Your sense of stability will come from what you know and trust about yourself rather than other people's highly subjective opinions.

Understanding yourself better, you will feel much less pushed around by your moods and the thoughts that drive them.

Understanding yourself better, you can't help but understand other people better also. You will be less dependent and more appreciative. You will take both praise and setbacks far less personally. You will accept your own complexity and contradictions—and accept that same reality in other people's lives.

Understanding yourself better, you will be much less inclined to see yourself as a victim of past events or other people's lack of kindness. Where you have suffered trauma or hurt, you will be more inclined to get the support and professional help that you need to heal, reconcile with your own situation, and gain whatever insights you can from all of your many experiences.

Yourself and other people

"Understanding yourself better" will quite naturally allow you to look more closely at how your emotions and especially your behavior affect other people. It might include asking yourself, "What do I want to achieve in this situation? What 'message' is my behavior giving to other people? Do my actions match and reflect my intentions?"

Watch the things you "didn't mean to do" or "didn't mean to say." Often it is those slips that are most revealing. Allow yourself to learn from them.

Your chance to choose

Value your own experiences. Learn to ask, "What experiences have I got through in the past that would help and support me in this situation?"

Value your own strengths. Learn to ask, "What's needed here? What would make a positive difference? What can I bring to this situation?"

THE SELF I AM AND THE SELF YOU SEE

CATHERINE: I'm thirty-eight and like most people my age, I've gained some hard-won self-knowledge through the years. Still, one of my most painful experiences is the inconsistency in how I feel about myself compared with how I appear to others. I know that I have some fairly substantial abilities and talents, yet often I hide them, retreat into girlishness or cheerfulness, and, in the process, refuse to "step up to the plate" or challenge myself.

When my behavior doesn't reflect my real abilities, I sell short my own intellect and inner authority. *I'm aware of this*, and don't understand why I continue to do it. It isn't serving me well, but there must be a pay-off in it or I would behave differently!

How can I develop the courage to be more authentically myself, to trust the self I know on the inside and dare to express it to others?

STEPHANIE: In those few lines, Catherine is asking *many* questions, none of them small!

My hunch is that the "splitting" she describes between the way she feels on the outside and the way she feels on the inside is far more common than she may guess. Many people whose achievements are awesome nevertheless feel empty, insecure or "unreal" on the inside. This was a key theme that drove the writing of my book, *Intimacy and Solitude*. I, too, felt that way. I knew from the inside out how easily "splitting" could feed feelings of disconnection, depression and even despair.

If your "outside" is very different from your "inside," how can you trust other people's admiration or even love? You want to be loved for "yourself." But who is that self? Can she be known? Can she be trusted? *Is she lovable?*

"Splitting" usually starts in childhood. We learn instinctively that life is easier if we behave as the world (the people around us) wants—and not as we feel. This is especially true when the feelings we have are painful or outraged. The pressure to hide our true selves can be intense.

"Girlishness" and "cheerfulness" made life easier for the people around Catherine—or so she believed. Those behaviors may even have made life easier for her. Less is asked of a girl than a woman; certainly less is asked of girls who hide their talents, abilities and authority.

But now, at thirty-eight, Catherine is feeling healthy boredom with the old ways. She has outgrown the masks. She is ready to be herself.

Nevertheless, the behaviors that go with the masks are very familiar to her. And the pay-offs—being liked, not inviting envy or power struggles—matter to her.

Because I know Catherine, and have come to know her much better through our work on this book, I am confident that people would not only like her "real self," but even find that real self *easier to be around.* When we are "ourselves," we give other people unconscious permission to be "themselves." Communication can move to a deeper and far more rewarding level. And in fact, much of the time—perhaps more often than she realizes—Catherine is already fully "herself" and communicating in exactly those ways.

So the challenge she identifies is perhaps less one of finding new behaviors than of *extending the authentic behaviors that she already has, even into tense or difficult situations.* (I suspect those will be situations where Catherine is afraid of being judged by people to whom she has attributed lots of power.)

Extending rather than changing herself, she will also discover that the courage she believes she needs *can be found as she dares to act more courageously* even if the old fears are present. In other words, she doesn't need to find courage in order to make change. In fact, my experience is that the contrary is true: as we make whatever change is needed, we also gain courage.

Risking being herself even in vulnerable situations, Catherine will inevitably feel different. She may feel exposed and awkward for a time. She may even have to sacrifice a little of the old pay-off (being "liked") in order to risk being liked more by some and less by others—and *not taking this as a measure of who she is.* But her gains will be considerable.

At whatever stage your life has reached, it takes a great deal of energy *not* to express who you really are; to deny your inner authority; to draw your sense of reality from an outside world in which you are sometimes false.

Love matters here, too. And self-love and self-acceptance matter most of all.

If you find yourself feeling disconnected between how you feel and how you believe you are seen, it helps to know that the person you really need to love more, and accept less conditionally, is your own self. Risking that you can trust and care for *all of who you are,* and that you can be *your own inner* "authority figure" as well as expressing your authority in the outer world, a crucial shift takes place.

Your inner reference point—like Catherine's—comes back to where it belongs: with your own self.

Expressing your authority and authenticity in the outside world then becomes secondary. Your sense of "wholeness" and consistency becomes remarkably easier.

You don't have to be brave in advance

I cannot emphasize too strongly how freeing it was for me to discover that I didn't have to be brave *before* making the changes I needed to make; or *before* facing situations that were tough or distressing.

Doing what needs to be done, facing a situation in the best way you know how, "borrowing" the behaviors that will best support you: these *are* acts of courage. And they bring courage with them.

It also helps to know that mistakes are rarely fatal. As you risk behaving more authentically—or more in line with your values—you may fall down many times. This matters far less than learning as you go—and rising up again.

All change is small change

Small but significant changes can be achieved by using your ideals or intentions as a reference point, increasing your awareness of choice.

"What do I want from this situation?"

"How do I want to behave?"

"Is this in line with my values?"

"How do I want to affect or influence this situation?"

These are all action-oriented questions that are simultaneously clarifying and encouraging. "Taking charge" like this promotes a more secure sense of self, and the trust and affection that come with it.

Noticing comes first

When you need to make a change, "noticing" is the first crucial action. This is already an empowering step. Having *noticed*, you can ask yourself, "How is this limiting me? What change am I ready to make? How do I intend to do it?"

Your greatest teacher

Your own life experience is the greatest teacher you will ever have. As with any teacher, however, you must be willing to pay attention—with all your senses.

LOOK FOR PATTERNS

To gain self-knowledge, it can be far more useful to look for patterns than to pay too much attention to an individual experience.

Patterns are far easier to identify than isolated events or responses.

Patterns let you know that you are responding less to whatever is going on outside yourself and more to your own habits and assumptions.

- ✦ What do you most commonly tell yourself as you walk into an important meeting?
- ✦ What do you expect when you open an e-mail from your boss?
- ✦ How do you react when someone asks you to do something you don't "feel like" doing—or when they criticize you?
- ✦ When you meet someone with whom you might possibly get involved, do you always tell yourself how unlikely it is that things could work out well?
- ✦ If someone is rude to you, or doesn't return your call, or discounts something you believe is important, do you tell yourself how little they think of you?
- ✦ Are you constantly defending your actions in your own mind? ("If she hadn't been so rude to me I could have easily . . .")
- ✦ Do you feel taken by surprise when things go really well?

Once you recognize a pattern, it loses the power that it had while it was still unconscious.

CHALLENGE A FAMILIAR PATTERN

Once you see that a pattern of behavior is not getting the results you want, it makes good sense to change it.

Start with the outcome you want. And the strengths you need.

Check if you are already achieving this in some other area of your life. If that's the case, "borrow" the behaviors you already have. ("Upfront" in the office? Be that straightforward at home. "Fun" at the pub with friends? Let your kids enjoy that, too. "Thoughtful" to your neighbors? Try it with your difficult sibling. "Patient" with your friends? Give yourself the opportunity to be patient with your co-workers.)

Sometimes you need to be more creative, visualizing how someone you admire would deal with the situation. Let yourself "see" in detail what qualities they would use. Now "borrow" those qualities. (Perhaps you have every right to be furious with a friend who has, once again, let you down. Your ideal person would be patient, but would also be unafraid to raise the issue at an appropriate moment. If they can do it, so can you.)

Often it's enough to tell yourself, "I can react less defensively and more creatively. Here's how I am going to do it."

A fresh and more creative response is always energizing. It makes you feel good about yourself and better about the situation.

THE POWER OF PRESENCE

Your wit, beauty, talent and riches are lovely. And probably other people enjoy them too. But **what matters most is your gift of presence**.

Presence is what will remain longest in other people's minds when they think about you. It is what will eventually determine whether you affect them positively or not.

Be aware of what your presence brings to other people. Stand in their shoes.

✦ Listen to the tone of voice you use when you speak to others.

✦ Be honest about your moods. Other people sense these before you have spoken a single word. *Nothing is more powerful in its effect on others than your mood (and the thoughts that drive your mood).*

✦ Recognize how like others you are in the fundamental things—however different your outward self may be. Know that what affects, hurts or pleases you will affect them in almost exactly the same ways.

✦ Let yourself remember how a brief kindness "makes your day." Free yourself to be kind to other people. Recognize your power to do that. And *be kind to yourself also.*

YOU ARE RESPONSIBLE
FOR YOUR OWN HAPPINESS

Other people can and will profoundly affect your happiness. None more so than the people closest to you.

And you will affect their happiness also.

However, no one but you is responsible for your happiness. (I wish that sentence could be neon lit!)

It is fair to expect that other people will treat you well. When they don't, it's crucial to act decisively on your own behalf. What is less fair—in fact, unreasonable—is expecting that other people should "make you happy" even in the face of your persistent unhappiness.

Taking back that expectation, you unburden them. And you bring the power to determine what kind of life you will be living back to yourself, where it belongs.

Free from fear

Happiness leaps into existence from a positive attitude to life. Not just to your own life; to life itself. With that comes a priceless set of freedoms: from fear, anger, hatred, resentment, jealousy and envy. Happiness cannot exist in the presence of those emotions. And those emotions lose much of their power in the presence of a positive mind.

What a *relief*.

WHEN THINGS GO WRONG (AND THEY WILL)

The idea that you are responsible for your own happiness can seem brutal. Life is not fair. We don't all get dealt the same hand. Even the best of us can be thrown badly when things go wrong. I know that I feel far from great when either of my children or someone else close to me is suffering, or when there is news of yet another world or local disaster. My mood can plummet; I can feel overwhelmed and afraid.

Nevertheless, even in those tough times, I have choices about my response. I can collapse—or hold relatively steady. I can meet the situation from a fearful place or I can ask myself that vital question, "What does this situation need?" Or, "What does this *moment* need?" This "wakes up" my inner strength. It makes my fear less powerful. **I am paying attention to the strengths needed**. I am also holding on to a bigger picture than I can access when I am overwhelmed by distress.

Where it is the suffering of other people that drives my unhappiness, I have to make some tough decisions. If I allow their unhappiness to flood me, I am much less help to them than when I can be with them in their unhappiness without allowing it entirely to overtake me. This does not mean that I am less loving or empathic. On the contrary, it can be the most loving response *not* to fall into the same place where they are. This is of course hardest when you truly love the people who are suffering. But here your steadiness is needed even more. The analogy would be taking off your life jacket so that you both drown, rather than keeping yours on to help the other person stay afloat.

When the distress is really tough or long-term, I often have to move through several layers of response, noticing that I am afraid or outraged, then dealing with those feelings—sometimes by simply accepting them and not berating myself for them. More often, again, by asking myself what the situation needs.

I also pray. And I visualize anyone concerned (including myself) moving through these difficulties and restored to happiness. I give myself plenty of time to see them in my mind's eye well, happy, even radiant. I do this slowly and in detail. This may not help them; it certainly helps me. (I believe it helps them too. But that's another story!)

As helpful as any part of that process can be, however, I want to add a word of caution. In my experience, there isn't a timetable for moving through fear to equanimity. I believe that we need to be extremely cautious about making judgments about how we *ought* to be coping—especially in the face of a major setback. Self-righteousness can so quickly creep in when we are judging someone else's situation, and self-blame when we are judging our own.

Serenity is another word for happiness

Very often what destroys our happiness or peace of mind is something relatively trivial, an inconvenience or disappointment rather than a tragedy.

Participants in the powerfully effective twelve-step programs like Alcoholics Anonymous say the Serenity Prayer daily: *God grant me the serenity to accept the things I cannot change; courage to change the things I can; and wisdom to know the difference.*

Serenity is another word for happiness. It is the most powerful antidote possible for frustration, pettiness, rage and self-pity. It builds inner strength and stability; it "grows" character.

We gain serenity when we make a clear distinction between what is important and what is not; what we "have to have" and what we could actually do without; what warrants a "fuss" and what does not; what really hurts and what hurts our pride or ego; what will cause lasting sorrow and what will be, a day from now, entirely forgotten.

THE CHOICE IS YOURS

Through your choices, you can certainly become happier. You can also bring greater happiness to the people around you.

Some people are naturally optimistic, open and easy-going. They (and the people around them) are the lucky ones. But there are countless moments of choice when you could lean in one direction or another: opening your mouth to say those mean words or closing it; making a damning comment or an encouraging one; looking at what's wrong or at what's right; taking your bad mood out on other people or getting over it; focusing on what's depressing or on what's strengthening and uplifting. Those choices are yours.

Your power to choose

This book is full of ideas to support your well-being and happiness. But beyond anything that I could share with you, something else also needs to happen. *You have to make a choice.* Or, perhaps more realistically, you have to make a series of choices. You have to choose to live your life with greater trust and confidence—and not just when things are going well. It's rather old-fashioned to talk about will. But there is no other word quite as useful here. In taking responsibility for your own happiness, you are waking up your will to be happy. This is an incredibly powerful decision that will have resonances across your entire existence. It doesn't mean that you will be inanely cheerful from this day forward. It does mean that happiness (trust, inner confidence and well-being) can become your basic stance. In the countless moments of choice, you will choose to pay attention to the positive rather than to the negative; to what is possible; to what is connecting; to what is uplifting; to what is fair and just—even "good."

When genuine difficulties arise—and they will—you can then meet them from a far less depleted place. You may also be able to circumvent some of them altogether, or see them as part of the "big picture," rather than feeling overwhelmed by them. This choice too is yours.

MISTAKES AND OPPORTUNITIES

Until you have some idea of what drives you, what matters to you, and what makes you "you," then you will make all kinds of common social and psychological "mistakes." You will make them repeatedly. And you may feel helpless in the face of them.

These familiar "mistakes" include all the "shadow" or disowned behaviors that your conscious mind is eager to overlook, rather than look into.

✦ Refusing to take responsibility for the effect of your emotions and actions on other people.

✦ Obsessing about tiny details and losing sight of your life's bigger picture.

✦ "Blaming" other people for the choices you have made and the life you have created.

✦ Assuming that other people are thinking your thoughts ("I know he thinks I am fat and ugly") or feeling your feelings ("She's never liked me").

✦ Talking incessantly about what other people are doing "to" you (or failing to do for you).

✦ Repeating the same error of judgment over and over again without recognizing yourself as the common denominator ("I'm unlucky with love").

✦ Idealizing other people's lives while discounting your own (the gossip magazines depend on this!).

✦ Feeling disturbed and distorted by powerful emotions (jealousy, envy, rage, bitterness) that you sincerely believe are "caused" by other people.

✦ Transferring feelings from the past (especially about authority figures) to fellow adults in the present. Responding to them as though you were still the child, not the much more powerful adult that you now are.

✦ Letting people down, failing to meet commitments, saying the "wrong thing," doing all the things "you didn't mean to do."

A simple lack of self-knowledge can also see you losing out on joy, pleasure and genuine opportunities. Not knowing who you are, it is also difficult to stand up for what you want.

Out from the shadows

Any pattern of behavior or response loses much of its power to entangle you once you recognize it.

You can then review other more positive alternatives; you can also see much more clearly what you can control and affect, and what you can't.

Value feedback from other people. Sometimes it lets you see what you are doing in new and useful ways.

ALL YOUR EXPERIENCES CAN
TURN TO GOLD

Experience turns to gold when you know how to reflect on it, use it, learn something from it—and move on.

Valuing what you can learn from your own experiences, nothing is ever wasted.

You learn from everything when your eyes and heart and mind are open. Sometimes it's the unwelcome experiences that have most to teach you. These are the experiences that push you to grow up; that test your judgment; that force you to assess more honestly how you are affecting other people, and what you are expecting from them.

Learning something of value from the tough times (even if it's only, "I won't need to do that again!"), has two brilliant outcomes:

✦ You can stop beating yourself up about them—or finding someone else to blame.
✦ More wonderfully still, you can leave the experience behind—and move back into the present moment where life is continuing.

When the experience is one of sadness

Grief and sadness, loss and disappointment, also offer lessons about life's complexity and value. But take your time. Allow yourself to feel those genuine emotions, and to gather new insights, at your own pace, as they emerge.

HOW TO REFLECT

Experiences are valuable in themselves. They create your life! But they become more than doubly valuable when you know how to reflect on them, learn what you need, and move on.

Reflecting shouldn't be confused with ruminating, where you are endlessly going over and over the same ground without gaining insight or relief. ("How could I . . . and when he . . . and I should have . . . if only . . .")

Reflecting means focusing, daring to go a little deeper than usual, looking at a situation with curiosity, interest and a dash of distance. Sometimes it's achieved in a few moments of quiet thought; sometimes in a conversation with a trusted friend or loved one. Your journal can also be an ally here, letting you reflect in your own way and at your own pace.

These questions can help:

+ What's familiar here? (Is this a pattern?)
+ What were my intentions in this situation? What was I hoping for or wanting?
+ What actually happened?
+ How might this have looked from the perspective of whoever else was involved?
+ What can I see now that I didn't then?
+ What would I do more of—or less of—another time?

Write down in your journal whatever insight you have gained, no matter how modest. Then literally "close the book" on it. And waken to a fresh new day. Remember that a journal or notebook entry can be just a few lines—yet still be fresh and invaluable.

THE COMMON DENOMINATOR

You are the sole common denominator in every relationship and every situation that creates your life.

Are you aware how you are driving or influencing those situations?

> If you have already had three husbands and they were all "disappointing," *perhaps there is something that you should look at.*
>
> If you leave every job within a year, because "nothing ever works out," *perhaps there is something that you should look at.*
>
> If "no one" can be trusted, or "everyone" asks too much of you, *perhaps there is something that you should look at.*
>
> If you never have any money, or have lots of money but feel as though you never have any money, *perhaps there is something that you should look at.*
>
> If none of your dreams are in danger of coming true, *perhaps there is something that you should look at.*

You are the sole companion you will have at every waking moment of your life.

Are you good company, especially for yourself?

> *Be aware* what you pay attention to; how you fill your time; how you nourish your mind; how you engage with the world around you; how enthusiastically you welcome each new day.
>
> *Be aware* what you identify with most strongly; what gives your life its shape, meaning and purpose.
>
> *Be aware* what you are giving to others; what gifts from your own existence you are sharing with others on a daily basis.

THE BIG PICTURE

It takes many of us years to discover how fiercely and even obsessively we focus on tiny details in our lives—and how rarely we stand back mentally to look at the big picture. **Yet no single event, no matter how massive or overwhelming it feels, is all of who you are**.

When you find yourself caught in a trap of your own making, remind yourself that whatever it is you are worrying about is only ever part of the big picture of your life.

Look down on your life from the vantage point of an eagle.
Think about where you have come from, what you have already learned—and where you are going.
Acknowledge what resources you already have.
Ask yourself gently if you need help and how you will ask for it.
Remember tough situations that you have already survived; what you learned; what you gained.
Let yourself see how the situation will look six months from now. Remember some dramas from the past that once loomed large, and are now mere pinpoints in your history.
Appreciate the scale and depth of your life's journey: the complexity of it, the richness of it, the uniqueness of it.

The attention that you give to the details of your life will always be enhanced when you are also able to see and appreciate the more spacious picture of your existence.

What can the eagle see?

Looking "down" on your life in this way (guiding your own inner meditation) is best done with your eyes closed and in a state of physical relaxation. And without interruptions.

Keep your journal close by. When you have an insight you want to hold on to, jot it down. When you feel ready to stop, briefly describe the experience, including the feelings you had while doing it. ("Noticed it was hard for me to look at . . . but once I persisted, then . . .")

You may also want to explore one or two of the questions above in your journal—but give yourself time to find out what the eagle can see first.

YOUR EFFECT ON OTHER PEOPLE

Gaining self-knowledge, you find that other people are never out of the picture. From the moment of your birth, you have been discovering who you are *in relation to other people.*

Chances are good that you are fairly preoccupied with how other people treat you, what they think about you, how they behave toward you.

Seeking self-knowledge, you need to look with at least that same amount of interest in the opposite direction.

Observe how you affect other people.

+ Watch and learn what "works" and what doesn't.
+ Listen closely to your tone of voice as well as to what you say.
+ Stay aware of your body language; it speaks volumes.
+ Value your capacity for *restraint* as much as for action.
+ Recognize the power you have to influence other people positively: to lift their spirits, encourage them, listen to them, show your care and concern even for a few moments.
+ Exercise positive choice.

This will profoundly benefit you as well as everyone around you.

YOU ARE NOT THE CENTER
OF THE UNIVERSE

There's real irony in the fact that many of us who are highly skilled at self-blame and self-criticism, and perhaps think rather too little of ourselves, are nevertheless easily seduced by the belief that if something goes wrong *we must have caused it* or it is "about" us.

> Your friend is late for lunch. *"She doesn't care about me."* Or did her bus fail to arrive?
> Your boss criticizes your work harshly. *"I can't do anything right."* Or is he projecting his own bad temper?
> Your lover is quiet and withdrawn. *"He thinks I'm boring."* Maybe he has a lot on his mind; none of it about you.

Simply reminding yourself that *"Not everything is 'about' me"* can be powerfully soothing. It is also true.

THE WORLD BEYOND OURSELVES

Too little self-knowledge doesn't only affect your own life and relationships; it also drives many of the most familiar social catastrophes caused at least in part by too little self-awareness, self-respect, restraint and self-control. These can vary from the major conflicts that continue to rage around our world to the nasty moment in a meeting when two colleagues turn on one another like sworn enemies.

Perhaps that's why the philosopher Socrates—and countless philosophers who have walked in his footsteps—was so adamant that we need to know ourselves (and own up to the effect we have on others).

We help create a peaceful world when our own minds are peaceful. We help create a generous world when our own impulses are generous. We help create a happier world when we recognize our power to treat other people well and kindly.

The more clearly we can see our own inner conflicts, contradictions and inconsistencies, the less harm we will cause by projecting them onto other people.

The more clearly we can see our strengths and aptitudes, the more delight we will have in living—and the more positively we will influence and affect other people.

Self-awareness gives our own lives stability. It also allows us to give the best of ourselves to other people.

Self-knowledge isn't selfish

Some people shy away from self-knowledge because they believe it is so natural it shouldn't need their attention.

Others shy away because they are afraid—with good reason—that it may lead them to becoming self-absorbed or even narcissistic.

So it's wonderful to know that in a lovely paradox, typical of human behavior, genuine self-knowledge and self-awareness lead you away from self-absorption and not toward it.

The reason for this is simple.

When you feel comfortable about who you are, you will be less obsessively concerned with yourself—and what other people think of you. You will be freer to pay them more attention.

Becoming familiar with your own complexity, you will also be freer to give others the benefit of the doubt. And to see your "part in things," rather than seeing the world as black/white, right/wrong, good/bad. Your attitudes will soften and broaden. Life itself will become more of an adventure than a struggle.

TRUSTWORTHY FOR OTHERS ALSO

You cannot control how other people will perceive you or interpret your behavior. (Though you will often wish that you could!) In all kinds of situations people will respond to their internal assumptions, rather than to who you "really" are.

You will be less vulnerable to the effects of this when there is a steadiness and consistency within your own life and behavior.

The following sets of questions are well worth considering. Share them with a close, trustworthy friend. Or explore them in your journal. You may want to explore them one set at a time. And keep returning to the same set until you feel satisfied with what you have discovered.

Who is the most trustworthy person I know? What qualities does that person have? How do I see them lived out? Do they have any qualities that I want to develop within myself?

Does my behavior show other people that I am trustworthy? Are there any changes that I need to make?

Am I a trustworthy friend, parent (or adult child), spouse, partner or worker? Can my colleagues trust me to think about their interests as well as my own? Can my family trust me to think about their interests as well as my own?

Can I be trusted to be relatively reliable in mood and reactions? Do I value that kind of trustworthiness in other people? If people know they can rely on me to be even-tempered and generous-minded, how would this support my relationships and the way that I experience myself?

KNOW WHAT'S *RIGHT* ABOUT YOURSELF

It's all too easy, I suspect, for you to name what's "wrong" about yourself. Our powers of self-criticism are usually highly developed; our powers of encouragement and self-encouragement often trail far behind.

This dramatically affects our relationships with other people which are often marred or even destroyed as *we project onto them our worst feelings about ourselves*.

To value your own life, and to learn what it means also to value other people, learn to focus on what's right about yourself.

Do this consciously and consistently.

Feeling more confident in your ability to support and encourage yourself—and learning to focus on what lifts your spirits and makes you feel good—you will be much less vulnerable to resenting other people's happiness or to feeling jealousy or envy. As you feel increasingly good about yourself, this will ease and support all your relationships—especially your relationship with yourself.

What's "right" about you?

What's "right" about you will include your talents and strengths, your physical capacities, your psychological gifts (good humor, trust, courage), but also some more subtle qualities. For example, you may be the person that others turn to when they have problems. You may be the one who is able to come up with useful strategies at the eleventh hour when your office is in crisis. Perhaps you are the one who is always able to serve a meal beautifully or whose garden looks wonderful all year round. Maybe you see the good in other people or can make them feel included and relaxed.

It is so easy to overlook what others appreciate about you or to discount and dismiss what you could appreciate more about yourself. Yet getting to know your strengths in this way, you are far less likely to fall into the trap of devaluing yourself if someone else is unkind— or if something in your life goes badly wrong.

If you are not sure what's "right" about you, try this variation on the seed meditation.

In the center of your page put your own name and also the name of someone who knows and appreciates you. Thinking about yourself from their perspective, note all of the qualities that they can see in you.

Follow the seed meditation format: write spontaneously and without censoring; reflect with your eyes closed; write again. Continue this pattern for at least twenty minutes.

You may want to continue this several times: thinking about people in different areas of your life and looking at yourself from their perspective. My experience of doing similar exercises with people is that this can help make them feel more actively appreciative of those other people, as well as of themselves. There is often a great deal of tenderness and self-acceptance that's released once we come into a more appreciative relationship with ourselves.

What's right about your day?

Let yourself be positive about each day, as it comes and goes again.

Take care that when you are discussing your day with friends or family that you select and emphasize what went well, what you appreciated and enjoyed, and what you found stimulating, amusing or touching. Let the negatives of the day go.

Don't ignore small details. Often it's the smallest moments that genuinely "make our day."

TALKING TO AND ABOUT YOURSELF

Words have vast power. This power goes on resonating long after the speaker has fallen silent, especially within the echo chamber of your own mind.

Listen carefully to yourself.

Notice how you talk to and about yourself.

You cannot lift your spirits or feel delighted by your own existence as long as you are describing yourself in negative terms, criticizing, haranguing, replaying "mistakes," or even using litanies of "slave words" like "have to," "must," "should," "can't," "won't."

The words inside our minds are every bit as important as the words we use to other people; maybe more so as they are harder to escape.

Watch them. When a change is needed, make it.

The way you talk about other people also says everything about how you feel about yourself. Speak about other people positively also—for your own sake.

Trust what you know about yourself

Use this essential reminder: "I *can* trust myself. Other people's opinions are driven by their needs and emotions—not by magical insights about my worth."

MAYBE HE WON'T CALL

We give away almost everything when we give other people the power to decide whether or not our lives have value.

If he thinks I am beautiful, *perhaps I am.*
If she thinks I am clever, *maybe it's true.*
If you love me, *perhaps I could feel lovable.*
If this works out, *I will finally be happy.*

So much power is given away to ordinary flawed human beings who probably don't want it, don't know they have it, and anyway know far less about us than we know about ourselves.

Love and work are the two areas where we risk most.

You don't get the job. Or you had the job, but you have been retrenched. This doesn't feel like a blow to your ego only. It feels as though your entire self has been rejected.

You meet the fabulous new person. They promise to call. They don't. Or you are a few months or decades into the relationship and they end it. You feel, you are, "shattered."

It asks a great deal of you to see that the other person's actions may have very little to do with you. They may not even be "about" you or caused by you. Even when they are related to who you are, and to your behavior, there are always other causes and conditions at play. But even that is not the point.

The point is that when someone else's actions or decisions undermine your entire sense of self ("I can't live without him"), *you have given away your power.*

You need to take it back. With love and persistence, you need to assure yourself that *whatever other people need to do, your life has intrinsic value.*

This doesn't mean you won't feel hurt. You may even still feel devastated. But you won't feel demolished. **On top of the pain of loss, you won't be adding the suffering of self-blame.** You won't need to make the other person "bad" for hurting you. And you will be building self-knowledge and even self-confidence ("I am still the same person"), rather than destroying them.

LONELINESS

There are few aches worse than that of loneliness.

So much comes with it: shame that you feel alone (sometimes even when you are in company); desire that you wouldn't be alone; fear that *this is how it is* and that you will be alone forever.

Loneliness eats at our self-respect, and undermines self-love. It is one of the most widespread forms of suffering, and one of the hardest to speak about. Loneliness isn't solitude. In solitude you are not alone; you are with your own self.

When it's loneliness that you are feeling, you experience a sense of being distanced from yourself, distrustful that you can help yourself, unsure of what you have to give or how you might receive what other people could possibly be offering.

It can help to know that loneliness of this kind, even of the worst kind, is a very human thing. Perhaps in villages or towns where people all know who you are and where you came from there is less loneliness. But often in those idealized situations there are also strong pressures to conform. You can be lonely for who you really believe yourself to be, or for who you want to be, even in the midst of familiarity and social plenty.

Sometimes your loneliness is like a dark mood: difficult to bear while it's present, but you know that it will pass.

Sometimes it marks a transition: from a busy day at the office into an empty house or apartment. Once the time of transition is over you settle into solitude, rather than loneliness.

Sometimes the loneliness is another word for grief: you are lonely for someone who has come and gone, or perhaps for someone longed-for who never came. (You might be lonely for the partner you never had or the child you couldn't have—as much as for a child, parent, partner or friend who has gone away, is far away, or has died.)

When loneliness seems to have taken up lodgings in your life, it is always worth seeking help. You may be much more lonely than you need to be because you are also depressed. This will be especially true if going out to be with people feels false or empty, or if it's hard to enjoy yourself even when you are in good company and not alone.

Estrangement from yourself, feeling adrift from your own life, rejecting your own strengths, telling yourself that "nothing matters" or that "no one cares" are strong indications of depression. Help can be effective: both therapy and appropriate medication can make a significant difference that then gives you the energy to look more effectively at the root causes of your loneliness and to change the behaviors that reinforce your sense of being alone.

We are social beings. Wanting companionship, stimulation, care, affection and interaction with other people is a very normal desire. Most of us underestimate how deeply other people want this. And when we are feeling low, we also underestimate how many people struggle to get their needs for closeness met.

We are also spiritual beings. This doesn't mean that we all long for a relationship with the Divine, but many of us long to feel part of something greater than ourselves; to know that our lives have meaning. When this is making you restless there are many paths to explore, books to read, teachers to guide you. Sometimes it is not until we feel sufficiently lonely that we begin to see what we are lonely *for*.

Taking initiatives can be the hardest thing to do when you are feeling unsure of yourself or demoralized. Yet those are also the times when your own positive initiatives are most necessary.

LONELINESS: THE WAY OUT

These strategies will help.

Take and make every opportunity to socialize—even when it seems relatively unpromising. Rather than telling yourself that you are always the one to call your friends to make arrangements, accept that many people have little or no initiative. Be grateful for whatever initiative you have—and extend it.

Spend time with people in situations where the companionship is secondary to what you are sharing: community activities, all kinds of classes, voluntary work, group travel, spiritual fellowship and paid work all fit this category and can be powerfully effective. You may need to make more overtures and take more risks than is initially comfortable. You may also need to accept the imperfections of other people without too much judgment getting in the way. "A good enough day is good enough!"

Let yourself receive what others can give. "I can take this in. This may not be perfect but it feels pretty good." Often when we feel self-rejecting, we push away what we want most. In every situation that you find yourself, focus on making other people comfortable. It gives you a welcome break from worrying what they are thinking of you. It's also a good way to be kinder and more accepting of yourself.

If you are seriously concerned that you are difficult to like, or socially awkward or inept, take this concern to a counselor or therapist. Friendships are every bit as important as any other kind of relationship. They deserve the same thought and attention. Social skills can *be learned. Self-acceptance* can *be achieved.*

If you are in an intimate relationship and feel lonely this is a relationship issue that needs urgent attention. Your intimate relationship can't be required to meet all your needs, but when there is little or no positive communication happening—or you feel "unmet" or "unseen"—this is a tremendous barrier to personal or shared happiness. Professional help can bring difficult issues into the open in a safe way and allow significant positive change.

Cultivate a sense of curiosity and adventure about everything new that you try. It may not be exactly what you are looking for, but it may be an unexpected stepping stone.

Engage with the physical world outside yourself more consciously and intensely. Your sense of your inner world changes as you recognize that you are part of this physical universe as well as the social universe that we all share. Sometimes this can be combined with a social activity: learning to dive or to rock-climb, participating in bush regeneration, or joining a walking club or communal garden.

Know what you enjoy most about your own company: do more of that. Some of it will become delightful all over again when your sense of choice and variety is resurrected.

Don't hesitate to give yourself small treats because "it's only you." As well, consider who might enjoy some of those treats with you. Offer what you would like to receive.

Call on your inner wisdom

Look at your situation from the vantage point of a wise friend. Rather than identifying with your loneliness ("I'm a lonely person. I feel unloved"), switch your emphasis.

With the warmth you would make available to someone else, look at your own situation compassionately and creatively. Perhaps there are opportunities you are missing, old griefs or fears that need understanding and resolving, patterns that have become stale?

You could try writing to your lonely "self" in the guise of your wise "self." My suggestion is to write out a question but *not to seek an immediate answer.* Let it come to you in its own time.

These questions can help:

What habits are keeping me more isolated than I want to be?
What sources of friendship or companionship could I develop?
What is it that I would like to offer more freely to other people?
How could I become an even better companion for myself?
How will I care for my spiritual needs on a regular basis?

A STRANGER TO YOURSELF

Whatever the external circumstances of your life, your sense of aloneness or loneliness will always be worse when you feel emotionally and spiritually distanced from *yourself*. (This frequently drives depression, lethargy, cynicism and meaninglessness.)

This can happen very easily when you are too busy or distracted to take care of your inner world and your quieter needs. If you are constantly focused on demands or entertainment that are happening "outside" yourself, your inner world may come to feel parched.

At those times even good company does not substantially change the "alone" feelings. What's needed is a willingness to turn inward and ask questions as basic as, "What am I needing right now for my heart and soul?" Or perhaps you could ask yourself, "What am I neglecting?" In my experience, the answers usually come very quickly.

This process rewards you twice over. It lets you know how to take better care of yourself; it also reminds you that even when you feel very low, your inner world remains a vital resource for you.

It may be that you are avoiding looking at your inner needs because you suspect this is likely to involve making outer changes. That kind of avoidance is totally understandable, but it takes you nowhere (sorry!). Whatever outer changes are needed—perhaps resolving a conflict with another person, working a little less (or complaining less about your work), perhaps spending less time with people who don't have your best interests at heart—the benefits will come fast from initiating them and seeing them through.

Choosing to act positively on your own behalf brings you back into a healthy, inwardly supportive relationship with your own self. It inevitably lifts your spirits. And, as a bonus, other people will, quite unconsciously, also respond to you with greater ease.

HOW TO SOOTHE YOURSELF

It's hard to trust who you are when you also feel pushed around by your own moods and emotions.

Knowing how to soothe yourself radically increases self-trust. It also lets you know that whatever arises, *you can deal with it.* You may not always deal with it brilliantly or immediately. But it need not devastate you.

"Soothing yourself" is a skill that is easily learned but must be practiced. It literally switches off the "fight or flight" response in your brain that produces a racing heart, limited thinking, tense muscles, sweaty hands, sleeplessness and even panic, anxiety and depression. It brings you to a different level and quality of brain function where you can see the situation with a little distance and cope with it far more effectively.

Trust yourself that "switching to soothe" is possible. *Here's how.*

Recognize the symptoms of panic, anxiety or mounting fear. You will feel them in your body. **Know that you are capable of "switching to soothe."** Tell yourself as often as you need to, "I can deal with this." This powerful message will affect you physically as well as emotionally. It doesn't matter that you don't yet know *how* you can deal with it; what matters is that you will. While you are telling yourself "I can deal with this," you are not also able to rehearse how awful it is, how hopeless you are, how frightful and disappointing life is.

Write down what the issue is. Putting it "out there" on a piece of paper makes space in your mind. It also gives you a little distance. Describe it in as few words as possible.

Ask yourself, "Does this need my attention now?" Often when you are in a panic, you are least creative and effective. If the matter isn't urgent or is still going to be hideous in a week, switch your attention to something else. Give your mind something else to chew on. Your mind can only think about one thing at a time. What you move your attention to may need to be much more stimulating than watching TV. Moving your body also helps. Switch from "victim" to "problem-solver" posture. Sit up straight. Breathe deeply. Put your shoulders back. (Your mind will immediately benefit.)

Know that as long as you are in a panic, your thinking will be distorted and so will your reactions. Take your time. *Focus on calming yourself first,* and only then on dealing with the issues or problem.

Sometimes you need to get some physical distance from what's worrying you. You won't take the problem with you if you tell yourself that you are in the process of dealing with it. Do something that is physically demanding. Digging your garden, walking briskly, swimming, cooking: what the activity is will be less important than taking action, changing your environment and, with that, your thoughts and feelings.

If your mind keeps taking you back to the same issue, just repeat the same steps: "I can deal with this"; writing down the problem; switching your attention; doing something physically demanding. Also remind yourself that you will put your most creative self to work as soon as you feel more physically and emotionally at ease. Boredom with repeating the same steps can actually be helpful.

What you are feeling may be a genuine emotion like sadness. Let yourself feel the sadness without the panic or self-blame ("I shouldn't be feeling this. I will always feel like this.").

Remind yourself that whatever you are feeling, it will pass. Even if you are thrown by a genuine tragedy, the acute stages of grief, disbelief and rage always pass. But often what we panic about is anything but tragic; it can be extremely soothing to acknowledge this.

When you are feeling less distraught, look again at your piece of paper. Do you see the problem or issue differently now? If so, write it out again. Now ask yourself, "Who is the wisest, cleverest and kindest person I know?" (You don't need to know them personally.) Once you have identified who that person is, ask yourself, "How would they deal with this?" Do not underestimate the power of your own imagination. It is your imagination as much as the events themselves that have produced those powerful symptoms of stress or anxiety. Harness that same imaginative power now to support you and to see what needs to be done—if anything. Write down what you imagine their answer would be. The insights you are looking for will be helpful, kind, supportive and manageable.

Know that some problems are not going to be solved; they will only be outlived. Recognizing the truth of that can also be oddly soothing.

Notice how severe a problem looks and feels when you are hungry, exhausted, overwhelmed or stressed. Use your panic as an invaluable "alarm bell" warning you to pay more attention to your life as a whole. Ask yourself: *What extra stress is happening right now in my life? What would help me deal with this stress? Who could I talk to about this? How have I got through this kind of tough time before?*

Remind yourself that whatever is happening is not all of who you are; nor is it how things will always be.

"I can deal with this"

Sometimes all that is needed is for you to remind yourself with quiet conviction, "I can deal with this," rather than focusing on what's disturbing or wrong.

CALM THE INNER CHATTER

However raucous, chaotic or disappointing your life may feel at any given moment, I can say with absolute confidence that **your deepest nature is still, silent and stable**.

There are many ways to experience those qualities for yourself, to quiet your inner chatter and develop your awareness of your deeper self. (And you don't need to have conventional beliefs about "God" or be a "spiritual person" to do so.)

Meditation is the most powerful way to discover and experience your inner stillness and stability. These methods are also helpful:

+ Prayer, inspirational reading, singing, chanting
+ Allowing yourself to become absorbed in nature
+ Mindfulness (close awareness of what's happening right here, right now)
+ Guided meditation
+ Calling up an image of stillness to counteract constant thought
+ Focusing on qualities and values
+ Creating positive intentions
+ Writing a letter to your inner wisdom
+ Valuing and creating external stillness and silence.

Instant calm

This is a meditation that I use when I need an image of stillness to counteract exhausting, incessant internal chatter.

I simply imagine the blue-green ocean, with sand swirling through the water. As the sand settles to the bottom of the ocean floor, I imagine my "busy" thoughts also settling, lying down, taking a rest and giving me the rest I need.

As my thoughts settle, I let my awareness expand. Continuing to watch the water imaginatively, I see how calm it has become. Then, as the water becomes completely still, sunlight strikes it and the water itself becomes infinitely light.

The world changes when you change

Opening to your deepest sense of self, it will seem quite natural to find the world a place of greater enchantment and profound interest.

You will also see the violence, tragedies and cruelty; but you will react to them differently. You will discover your power to make a small but significant difference.

THE ULTIMATE GIFT

I was well into adulthood before I "got it" that this life of mine is an incredible gift. And that it may be perfect exactly as it is! Up to that point—and there have been lapses since—I was quite preoccupied with all the (many) things that are wrong with me.

Whatever vision of perfection I might have had certainly didn't fit any life that I could recognize. It's not that I was entirely ungrateful for my life. In fact, some aspects of it I valued highly. Nonetheless, I paid far more attention to what was wrong than to what was right. I believed that what was wrong needed my attention. Perhaps I unconsciously believed that what was right could take care of itself.

Two sets of events changed my perspective.

First of all, I came to terms with how finite this life is.

Working in psychotherapy with people who were dying, and experiencing the deaths of people close to me, I could not help but gain a different perspective on life.

I came to see that each day is a gift, not for what we can "do with it," but for what it is. Many people express the view that it is not until they know they are dying that they live fully and truthfully, focusing on what's important and discarding what's not. But the reality is we are all dying. Our death may be days away; it may be decades away. But there's no avoiding it.

Understanding how very precious life is, and seeing for myself how fiercely and tenderly people cling to life when they know how little time they have left, I also realized that like any love, our love for life soars when we allow it to become unconditional.

What this means to me is loving life even when it's not following my orders, wishes or desires; loving life even when it feels massively unfair, unsafe, disappointing or tragic; *loving life even when I am not getting what I want from it.*

I don't think most of us realize, unless we are fortunate enough to be dying consciously, how *conditional* our love affair with life really is; how much we complain and how offended we feel when we don't get what life "owes" us.

Unconditional love for life means, to me, entering life fully. Taking it all on. Saying yes to everything: to the suffering *and* the compassion;

to the crassness *and* the wisdom; to the brutality as well as the radiance and beauty; to the disappointments and the triumphs.

Of course I welcome some things more than others; of course I am concerned with keeping myself safe; of course I want to do my bit for kindness and goodness and beauty. But loving life only if or when it gives me what I want would keep me from being real.

What also made a difference for me was attending some Buddhist classes and retreats and reading many books by Buddhist teachers. I am not a Buddhist but over the last twenty years or so I have gained so much from these teachings in particular:

+ This gift of life is precious. *My gift of life is intrinsically precious.* (So is yours.)
+ Human existence is precious.
+ The chance to reflect upon the big questions is precious.
+ *Every* life offers a constant repertoire of opportunities to become happier and wiser. Taking up those opportunities is precious.

My study and reading in more recent years has shown me that there are teachings within all the world's faiths that reveal how precious each life is and that we can worry less about who we are. A famous passage in Luke's Gospel (12:24–27) points to this:

Consider the birds: they neither sow nor reap, they have neither storehouse nor barn, and yet God feeds them. Of how much more value are you than the birds? And can any of you by worrying add a single hour to your span of life? If then you are not able to do so small a thing as that, why do you worry about the rest? Consider the lilies in the field, how they grow: they neither toil nor spin, yet I tell you that even Solomon in all his glory was not clothed like one of these.

But for many Westerners, including me, those insights were buried for too many years beneath other more widely taught ideas about sin, guilt, unworthiness and insufficiency that continue to carry tremendous psychological power to wound and damage.

Our deep sense of being "wrong" or unworthy of love, our distrust of our own strengths, our ability to hurt ourselves and other people are all born from a lack of awareness and trust that our lives are precious: *that life itself is infinitely precious.*

And when I forget? I don't need to beat myself up for my shortcomings or blame myself. I just have to remember.

Gratitude changes everything

Set aside your cynicism for a month or so. Wrap it in a neat cloth; place it in a drawer.

On a daily basis, for 28 days, write by hand: "My life *as it is* is a precious gift."

Silence the arguments. Give gratitude a chance.

Appreciation may be enough

Gratitude for life as it is challenges many people. "How will I improve, grow, change if I am satisfied?" they ask.

Sometimes appreciation *is* the change. And little else is needed.

LOOKING FOR LOVE

As adults, our greatest challenge is to relearn love. And to *remember ourselves as a source of love.*

It's not that we don't know how to love; we do. **Love is our original nature.**

Spend ten minutes with any child who has not yet learned self-consciousness and you will be dramatically reminded that each of us comes into this life with an infinite capacity to give and receive love. So crucial is this that when love is withheld or blocked from human children, they die. They die emotionally; they may die physically.

As adults, our need to give and receive love—to live lovingly—is still that great. But by adulthood most of us have become incredibly confused about what love is, where and how it is to be found, and what we must do to "deserve" it.

The terrors that drive our fears and addictions (to drugs, alcohol, gambling, overwork, sex, abusive relationships, personal and global violence) are themselves driven by outrage about love's absence. *We know that something essential is missing.* But as so many songs have reminded us, we go looking for love in all the wrong places.

To rediscover love (and the happiness that comes with it), we need to relax rather than strive! We need to drop some of our defenses. We need to be much less "conditional" about who deserves love and who doesn't. We need to appreciate it whenever and wherever we can. And, most crucially of all, *we need to learn to love ourselves.*

We cannot love other people and truly love this glorious gift of life if we have forgotten how to love ourselves.

Zen teacher and renowned writer Thich Nhat Hanh, says, "Your capacity for loving another person depends entirely on your capacity for loving yourself, for taking care of yourself." Without that capacity, we will go on asking our loved ones to compensate us for what we are not prepared to do for ourselves. That's a thankless task and perhaps also an impossible one.

If you have forgotten how to love yourself, you will probably ask (or demand) too much of other people.

You want them to love you. But often, when someone tries, you push them away, punish them or trivialize them. Or you take refuge in fantasies that their version of love isn't right and that a better version is waiting in the wings.

Love from other people can be immensely healing, uplifting and sustaining. *But it's never enough.*

To reclaim our inheritance of love, we need to bring love (vitality, engagement, freshness), or perhaps gentleness and faithfulness, to everything we do. And we must dare to love ourselves.

The unbroken loop of love

It is impossible to grow more self-loving without also loving other people and life more.

It is impossible to know and trust yourself more without also finding it much easier to know and trust other people.

AFRAID OF SELF-LOVE

The greatest and most profound of love's absences occurs in relation to ourselves.

There is no expression of love that we are more afraid of than self-love. Confusing it with narcissism (and fearing narcissism), we reject even the idea of it. Yet without loving your own life, without feeling joy and gratitude for your own existence, without knowing how to accept everything that you are, without knowing how to treat yourself tenderly and with good humor and encouragement, you starve yourself of the energy needed to love and accept other people.

What narcissism is

Narcissism is the opposite of self-love.

In the absence of self-love, narcissists have no energy for anyone but themselves. They are preoccupied by their own internal reality, not freed by it. Only their own needs and experiences have any real meaning for them. When you enter their world, you are assessed as more or less "useful." This is why narcissistic people can be so charming, and then so ruthless. They see you only in relation to themselves. Your separate existence doesn't move them. As long as narcissism has them in its grip, they are prisoners of fear, not of love.

THE PROBLEM WITH SELF-LOVE IS . . .

Our resistances to self-love are often fiercely held. They express pain and prevent healing. Opening to love is no small thing; opening to love yourself is a profound and courageous thing.

"There are already far too many people in love with themselves." The people you are thinking of are probably self-obsessed (or even selfish). This isn't love. Love, by its very nature, displaces fear and separation. It opens us, makes us more alive, joins us to the best parts of ourselves and allows us to respond to the best in others. When someone is self-centered, they are suffering from too little love, not too much.

"Can't you call it self-respect rather than self-love? Or maybe self-esteem?" Self-respect is also a vital quality. And it never exists without self-love. Self-esteem has value too but there's a lot of judgment and ego-anxiety around it. Your self-esteem could rise or fall depending on circumstances which have nothing to do with love. You might "get" more self-esteem doing a deal that isn't even honest. As you shift your awareness from your ego and personality to a larger vision of yourself, and as you learn to marvel at the gift of life that's yours, "love" becomes a less troubled word; and the practice of love—in every direction—becomes inevitable.

"I know all my faults. It's hard to get a positive view of myself in the face of them." You have probably paid a great deal of attention to what you are calling your faults. Has that changed them? Are you happier? Encouragement of strengths is far more effective than denigration of faults. This is true in raising children. It is also true in continuing to raise ourselves.

"I think I need to be tough on myself to make any progress." I guess this depends what you see as your destination. Paying attention to your faults (being tough on yourself) is something you already practice. How far has it taken you? Seeing your faults, understanding the trouble they cause other people as well as you, then deciding what you can do about them, can all be done in a spirit of encouragement and even enthusiasm. Those are other names for love.

"I suffer from depression. A lot of the time I hate myself." Do you know how to be stubborn? Use that—and a dash of curiosity. Your knowledge of love already lives inside you. It is obscured for the moment by more recent emotional patterns, but it is still there. Encourage its re-emergence by translating love practically: into "appreciation," "kindness," "self-respect," "friendliness" and "consideration." Practice one of those qualities every day, extending it to others as well as to yourself. Value the smallest opportunities and know that looking out for them already shifts your mood and lifts your spirits.

"Books like yours are self-focused." Some books in this area of psychological and spiritual development are highly self-focused. The best are not. In my own work I take a very consistent view that we become all we can be only through learning to treat other people thoughtfully and well. Self, others and life itself is the trinity of love that I espouse.

"My church teaches that selflessness is what's needed in our society." Your church is right. However, we cannot offer genuinely loving service to others if we don't see ourselves as a source of love! Or if our vision of love excludes ourselves. That makes no sense. Christ's message is to love others (our neighbors) as we love ourselves. His teaching assumes that we are capable of self-love *and* of extending our concept of "self" eventually to include all living beings. That teaching is universal. Only fear and an absence of forgiveness obstruct love. Outgrow those obstructions and love will flow.

"My children are teenagers now and have become painfully self-critical. It breaks my heart." It breaks my heart, too. Our culture is competitive, cruel and critical. Those attitudes are fear-driven and profoundly unloving. However, it is possible to counter them by consistently loving your children and all other human beings for *who they are*—and not for what they do or how they perform. Just as important is to show through example that you value yourself and your own life; that you do not disparage yourself or treat yourself disrespectfully. Demonstrate through the way you live that you believe in the transformational qualities of love. Live joyfully! This may not seem "enough," but it will powerfully affect them. And support you.

"I need to make some real improvements before I can get a handle on self-love." Start now. And start with kindness. Just ask, at any moment of choice, "Is this kind?" And act accordingly. As your thinking changes, so will your behavior and feelings.

"My life feels meaningless. It's hard to love it." A meaningless life is hard to love. Broaden your horizons. Give time, attention, interest, kindness, consideration and concern to the people around you, to your community and to your own passions and interests. Don't wait to "feel like it." Engage with life. Pause to see the beauty that is everywhere. If you don't have any interests, think hard about the people you most admire. What do you imagine that they are doing that you are not? Do those same things.

"Self-love is easy when things are going well." Everything is easy when things are going well! That's why it's good to build up your strengths and insights in the good times. But it's the tough times when you need love most. Trust that it's always waiting. Remember then what you already know. Deal with the situation *and yourself* lovingly.

LOVE YOUR BODY (SILENCE YOUR COMPLAINTS)

Your body is not something to control, manipulate, torment and complain about.

Many of us have, from adolescence onward, cultivated a habit of ingratitude toward our bodies. We focus on perceived faults, deficiencies, drawbacks, comparing them unfavorably to absurd notions of physical beauty that have little to do with good health and physical strength and ease.

Know that it is impossible to cultivate high-minded notions about living positively and to leave your body out of the picture. Accepting and loving your body is crucial to good health.

- Take time to appreciate what is precious and alive about your body, no matter how far from "ideal" your body shape may be.
- Be aware how your attitude toward your body reflects your gratitude for your gift of life.
- Be aware that there is no meaningful distinction between mind and body; treat them as two aspects of the same whole.
- Value the health and strength of your physical being.
- Explore what treats you would like to give your body (a massage, a long walk, adequate rest, nourishing food, fresh air, an easy day).
- Keep in focus that *peace of mind* supports your physical existence beyond anything else.

Listen to Andrew Steptoe (and your heart)

Common sense tells us that happiness has a powerful effect on our physical well-being. A study completed in 2005 by scientists at University College, London, confirmed this, citing better cardio-vascular health as well as lower rates of type II diabetes and hypertension. The British Heart Foundation's Professor Andrew Steptoe reported: "It has been suspected that happier people may be healthier both mentally and physically than less happy people. What this study shows is that there are plausible biological pathways linking happiness with health."

YOU ARE NOT A ROBOT

As the demands in our external world grow more frantic, many of us treat ourselves like robots.

We make demands on our physical well-being and emotions that we would consider outrageous if someone else were doing this to us.

We ignore warning signs of tiredness, hunger, strain and stress. We live dissociated from almost everything around us—including our own bodies and well-being.

Sometimes we want to do this. We have specific goals and tell ourselves that only a superhuman effort will let us achieve them. This may be true. And it may not be harmful if it doesn't become a way of life. Where it *is* a way of life, we might need to rethink our attitude. After all, who's doing the choosing?

Your body can be a tremendous ally here.

Tuning in to your body, recognizing when it's screaming at you for attention, discovering what relaxes and restores you, *pacing yourself*, broadening your horizon beyond your next deadline, you may find that you can work at least as effectively but far less harmfully.

Let your attitude toward yourself soften. As you become more human, you will feel more secure and trusting—of yourself *and* of the people around you.

BEING, NOT DOING

CATHERINE: My Canadian mother came to Sydney for a visit recently, and because she's so helpful, her time in our busy household was a real blessing. In many small but joyful ways, Mom reminded me how to care for my family and myself—all without saying a word. When she sliced vegetables and made noodles for chicken noodle soup, her cutting board looked like a Picasso. To entertain a suddenly grumpy grandson, she spent hours making Easter bunnies out of scrap paper and crayons. When I mentioned I felt cramped in our home, she wiped all the windows clean, letting the summer light back into the rooms. And every night, after caring for us, she cared for herself by taking a bath.

After my mother left, I found the large flat seashell she used as a soap dish, discovered one afternoon on our local beach. I tucked it away in the bathroom cabinet, but the memory of Mom, each night smelling vaguely of flowers in her white-and-blue nightgown, remained.

When autumn and the cooler weather came, I decided to try it myself—a bath every night, even if I didn't feel like it. I bought a bottle of geranium body wash, two tea-light holders, and a package of vanilla-scented candles. And I promised myself I would make the time.

Now I have a new routine. After everyone is in bed and the house is quiet, I run the water, light the candles, and fill the tub with geranium bubbles. I step in and lie back. I think about the day. I prioritize what needs to happen tomorrow. I replay my favorite moments. I pretend I am my own wise mentor, and give myself advice about things that are bothering me. I pray. I choose to honor one of the lovely habits of my mother, knowing that I've claimed back a little of the space I so desperately need for myself and my thoughts.

It may not quite compare to a spa day, but an evening bath—or some other small way of making yourself a priority—is worth a try. After all, it's a tradition endorsed by two generations of authentic women, learning how to be comfortable in their own skins.

STEPHANIE: In a life crowded with demands and the legitimate needs of other people, time for yourself can seem the most elusive gift possible. But it may also be the most essential.

When I have sat with clients who claim to have "no time," patiently taking apart their schedule with them, time always miraculously appears. It may mean sacrificing some television; getting up twenty minutes earlier; refusing to take work home every night of the week; using "waiting time" productively or turning bath time into a meditation time, as Catherine describes.

People who take time to "be" on a daily basis are measurably more productive, better listeners, less stressed, more alive and more resilient than those who don't.

This is in part because someone who believes that he or she "has no time" is living under the delusion that they are a slave to other people's agenda. This is never true. It is also depressing.

Taking back control of your time even in a small way is a crucial act of positive self-assertion. And it leads to other choices.

Meditation, walking, gardening, inspirational reading, listening to quiet music, or just sitting and taking in the present moment are soul choices that restore us to "ourselves." They put us back in touch with who we really are! They bring our scattered sense of self back to the center where it belongs.

Looked at that way, the time you give to "being" could be the most important investment you make each day.

BODY, INSTINCTS AND EXPECTATIONS

Check your needs simply and regularly.

This sounds so obvious that it is almost embarrassing to write. Yet, the truth is, for weeks, months, years at a time we may hardly know what we need. Or we register only our most excessive and extreme needs.

We don't "notice" when we are hungry, tired, stressed, overwhelmed, frustrated or even outraged until our bodies scream at us or collapse. Even then, we often override those signals with our minds; telling ourselves that we are not feeling what we are feeling, or that it doesn't matter.

Some of us drop dead *before* we connect with how we are living. **A disconnected life is not loving**.

+ *Allow your body to guide you about your emotions and state of mind.* Tune in to your body. Learn to scan internally: "What am I feeling?" Notice your body's signals. Honor them. If something gives you a "pain in the neck," a "weird feeling in your guts," or daily headaches, be confident that there is also an emotional situation that you are not attending to.

+ *Check out what you crave.* If what you "need" is something that compromises your health or behavior, take time to explore what it's standing *in for*. The easiest example is sweets. You want more sweetness in your life, as well as a lift in your blood sugar perhaps because you are not eating enough fresh food and protein. But what else would do it? And why does your life need additional sweeteners? What "sourness" are you trying to balance? Is there another and more loving way? If it's alcohol or drugs that you are craving, also ask "Is there a healthier way to get what I am seeking?" The intensity of the craving tells a powerful story of the intensity of the need. Explore this in your journal or try a seed meditation, using as your "seed" word the name of what you crave most.

+ *Develop your instincts.* It's your instincts that tell you when something "feels wrong"—or "feels right"; when something is dangerous, not as it seems, or worth the risk. Practice "tuning in" around small things. Even tossing a coin can be helpful.

Register your pleasure or disappointment as the coin "decides"; pay attention to those feelings rather than to the coin.

✦ *Find a balance in your expectations (of yourself and others).* This is where the tale of the three bears and their porridge comes in. You need to be Goldilocks—gender non-specific. What you are aiming for are expectations that are neither too high (to guarantee disappointment), too low (to bore and not inspire you) but "just right." When in doubt, aim high.

✦ *Follow through on what your body, instincts and expectations teach you.* They are vital expressions of your unique self. *Value* them.

TRUST YOUR INTUITION

Intuition is key to trusting yourself.

Intuition goes deeper than instincts and it can be a more truthful and valuable way of knowing than learning from "the outside" can ever be.

It's wonderful to read books to discover what and how other people think. (I read copiously, usually with several books on the go at any one time.) It's also wonderful to learn through conversation, newspapers, magazines and formal study what other people's opinions are about the things that interest and engage you.

However—and it is a significant "however"—your own deepest "knowing" also matters.

Discovering what you know takes time. Intuition can appear to come in a flash. But that's only one version of it. Even then it grows in value when it flashes across a mind that's ready.

+ Allow yourself time to drift and think, to contemplate, to explore in your journal or let your mind run free. This is the key to creativity as well as intuitive knowledge. It is never a waste of time, even when it isn't immediately productive.
+ Let yourself return to ideas and thoughts that interest and stimulate you. As your experience grows, you will often see a familiar idea quite differently.
+ Use other people's ideas to trigger your own. Engage with what you are reading or thinking about. Ask yourself what you think—beyond the obvious. Check what's motivating you. Check what fits with your experiences and what you see around you. Keep your vision fresh.
+ Value what you are learning every day from your own unique experiences. Experience and reflection are your most profound and constant teachers.

These are all ways to cultivate and feed your mind and invest in the richness of your inner world. Doing this, your capacity to make good choices—and to know what you want—will grow by leaps and bounds. You will feel less need constantly to ask other people how you should be living your life—or what your decisions ought to be. You will trust yourself. And when you are wrong? You will learn from that too. And move on.

The way you see the world outside yourself will also change. Life itself will become less fraught and far more fascinating.

Listen to Dom Bede Griffiths

My admiration and love for Dom Bede Griffiths is unreserved. An English Benedictine monk who lived in Southern India for almost forty years, Dom Bede not only wrote magnificent books (including *The Marriage of East and West* from which the following quotation comes), but lived a life that inspired countless thousands through its kindness and clarity.

He has this to say about intuition. I think it's well worth repeating.

"Intuition is a knowledge which derives not from observation or experiment or from concepts and reason but from the mind's reflection on itself. What distinguishes the human mind above everything else is . . . its power of self-reflection. The human mind is so structured that it is always present to itself. . . . Before the intellect begins to act, it receives the impressions of the experience of the body, the senses, the feelings, the imagination. This is the source of intuition."

USE FRIENDSHIP AS YOUR GUIDE

Make a decision that, from this moment on, you will *never be less than friendly toward yourself.*

- ✦ No more treating yourself like a slave.
- ✦ No more putting yourself down—ever.
- ✦ No more negative assumptions.
- ✦ No more torment over past events that you can't change.
- ✦ No more "putting up with" other people's abuse or unkindness.
- ✦ No more postponing doing what you love most.

This will radically change the way you feel on the inside. And it will change the way that you think about other people, interpret their behavior, respond to them and act toward them.

It is impossible to see the world as a friendly place (despite the disappointments and hassles) until the world inside your own mind is also friendly.

When the old thoughts or behaviors arise, see them for what they are (tired, useless habits) and move on. They will continue to tug at you, but only as long as you pay attention.

CLOSER THAN YOU KNOW

You are already far closer than you know *to the life that you want to be living, to the happiness that can be yours.*

Only habits of thought stand between you and the person you long to be or the life you long to create.

Any changes you desire are almost certainly a matter of degree only. They might include:

✦ To be kinder to yourself and other people

✦ To "mind" less if others criticize you

✦ To worry less and laugh more

✦ To accept as well as give encouragement and appreciation

✦ To trust your capacity to be creative

✦ To forgive yourself as well as others for past failings and hurts

✦ To be able to enjoy your successes and not talk them down

✦ To feel that you have time in your life

✦ To be able to say what you mean

✦ To stand up for what you care about

✦ To know what matters

✦ To behave in ways that express your highest values

✦ To trust—and love—yourself.

HOW TO TRUST WHO YOU ARE

Essential insights

✦ Inner trust brings peace of mind and happiness—and reflects the strengths, abilities and resources you continue to develop throughout your lifetime.

✦ Your life—with all its complications and joys—is a priceless gift. Appreciating this, "what's wrong" becomes far less pressing.

✦ As you are *right now*, without making any improvements or changes, your life has value. You *matter*.

✦ Often *appreciating your life is the only change needed*. This makes it so much easier to lift your spirits, appreciate other people—and be far less judgmental.

✦ In countless small and large moments, you can choose to focus on what is positive, expansive, uplifting and connecting. Those are the choices that make happiness possible and lift the spirits of everyone around you.

✦ Happiness is found by claiming the best of who you are and recognizing and responding to the best in other people. Putting other people down, or yourself, stifles happiness.

✦ You can develop the strengths you need. This, too, is a choice. You can also "borrow and use" strengths that you see and admire in others.

✦ Be confident that you know yourself (your true character) better than anyone else ever could. Other people's opinions of you are of interest; they *don't determine your self-worth*.

✦ Whatever you give time and attention to will grow stronger in your life. How you think about yourself and what you dwell on inevitably shape who you are becoming.

✦ Trust that you can get over what hurts you (you *can* recover). This makes life less frightening and your own life more of an adventure.

✦ As you learn to trust yourself more, you will demand less reassurance from others. You will be easier to be around.

Essential actions

✦ Use kindness as your benchmark in the way you treat yourself and others. Happiness unfailingly depends on how you treat yourself and other people.

✦ Make conscious choices about how you live and what gets your attention. *Own* your life. This may not save you from mistakes, but it will make daily living more dynamic, truthful and interesting.

✦ Let yourself recognize that you affect other people just as inevitably as they affect you. You grow in self-confidence and maturity as this becomes clear.

✦ Right here, right now, write down three of your own strengths. If you need help, ask a friend. Own those strengths. *I am encouraging. I am loyal. I can find solutions to problems.* Let them work for you. Think of them as the start of a precious collection. Add to it.

✦ Don't ask, "Why did this happen to me?" Ask, "How can I best deal with it?" Switch on "solution" rather than "problem."

✦ Stressed, depressed, unsure? Review the ways to soothe yourself (see page 67). Choose and practice what works for you.

✦ Step back from criticism and attacks from others. Often they say far more about them than you. When you are truly "at fault," learn from the criticism then move on.

✦ When you make a mistake, *forgive yourself*. Learn something. Move on. Trusting yourself doesn't mean doing the "right thing" always; it means learning as you go.

✦ If change is needed, look for patterns. This makes change possible and effective.

✦ When making a change or tackling a problem, draw on the richness of your own experiences. Life is your greatest teacher. Ask, "What have I already learned? What do I already know?"

✦ Be trustworthy. Start small. Make one promise to yourself and keep it. ("I will take responsibility for calling my friends regularly") Then add on. Every promise you keep to yourself builds self-trust—and helps you to trust others.

✦ Take care of your spiritual needs. Make time for what's uplifting, connecting, inspiring. Compassion must translate into action. Don't just wish for love: *be* more loving. Don't just wish for happiness: *live* with greater joy.

Let your values and goals work for you

WALKING THE TALK

The best way to discover what your values are is to look closely at your behavior. Your behavior is the only true measure of your values. Everything else is wishful thinking.

ACTIONS SPEAK

This is one of the hardest lessons that life has taught me. It's also one of the most precious.

Through our behavior, we live out our deepest and most truthful feelings about ourselves.

You might, for example, tell me that you feel terrific about yourself. But if you are putting yourself in danger, going from one unhappy or abusive relationship to the next, staying in a hurtful relationship, allowing other people to take advantage of you, abusing drugs or alcohol, finding it "impossible" to motivate yourself, working or worrying ceaselessly, talking about yourself like a victim, criticizing yourself harshly—or in any other way behaving unlovingly—then I cannot believe you.

I will believe instead that your choices and behavior offer a more truthful description of how you feel about yourself—how you value yourself—than words ever could.

Recklessness speaks volumes about a lack of self-value.

Noticing that—*letting yourself notice that*—already makes a difference. Acting with greater care is the crucial next step.

Is this kind?

If you are behaving in ways that cause you shame, or leave you feeling anxious, disconnected or empty, you need to reconnect with values that can lead you back to a more loving and appreciative experience of yourself.

Is this kind? is an honest and life-saving question.

When the answer is "No," *you must take action on your own behalf.*

Finding that you can act to save yourself, and *allowing kindness to support you,* you will grow powerfully in self-confidence and integrity. You will also become much happier.

WHEN IT'S LOVE YOU ARE SEEKING

We take risks—even put our lives in danger—when we feel split off from ourselves. And especially when we feel split off from our capacity to give and receive love. So, in considering values, we must start with ourselves.

We need to treat ourselves lovingly, or, at the very least, kindly and respectfully, when it's love that we are seeking. And one way or another, *it is always love that we are seeking*—even when we call it "approval," "attention," "affirmation."

Thinking about values, we must also know how to value ourselves.

- ✦ Take good care of your body: choose with care what you eat and drink; how you sleep and exercise; how you "drive" yourself; the care you give to your surroundings. *Value your physical existence.*

- ✦ Take good care of your mind: choose what you pay attention to; what you read, watch on TV and think about; how effectively you stimulate, extend, challenge and inspire yourself. *Value your intellectual existence.*

- ✦ Take good care of your inner world: allow yourself time for the activities (and non-action) that make you feel good about life, that bring you in touch with your senses; that make you feel "in touch" and "alive"; honor what takes you "beyond yourself"; what inspires you and supports you most deeply. *Value your spiritual existence.*

- ✦ Take good care of your emotions: recognize your strengths and talents; know what supports you; spend time with people who uplift and encourage you; be good company for yourself; trust your capacity for resilience. *Value your emotional existence.*

- ✦ Take good care of your part in the social universe: notice how you affect other people; take seriously your power to influence others positively—to lift their mood, support and encourage them; recognize your interdependence with others. *Value your social existence.*

WHAT DO YOU STAND FOR?

There's no knowing *who you are* until you also know *what you stand for.*

Identifying your values is a primary way to claim ownership of your own life—and essential to growing up.

You could, of course, take your values from other people. There will certainly be no shortage of people who would like to create your values for you. And run your life for you. You are exposed constantly to a barrage of opinion. *All of it is values-driven.*

Even the fantasies you have will be values-driven. ("I won't be happy until I have a partner/child/house/prestige job/bigger car/more money." "I'd be more popular if I was better looking." "I'd like to be an important person so that other people take notice of me.")

The question is never whether you are being driven by values. The only question is *what are those values*? Are they life-enhancing? Do they include other people's interests and needs as well as your own? Are they taking you where you most want to go? Are you *choosing for yourself*? Are those values your own?

+ If other people's opinions or values drive your life, *take charge.* Ask yourself whether their ways of seeing the world mesh with your own experiences and insights.
+ Remind yourself: "This is my life. I am choosing how to live it. I am responsible for the values my life reflects."
+ Let yourself know: "What I stand for will create the 'story' of my life. It's what will shape my character, set my horizons, consciously and unconsciously guide me."
+ Notice when you are self-justifying ("Life owes me . . . I deserve . . . I ought to have . . ."). That seriously undermines self-responsibility.
+ Accept that society's values will influence you. This makes conscious "choosing" even more important.

THE CULT OF THE INDIVIDUAL

Individualism rules our age. We are all affected by it: "If I don't look out for myself, who will look out for me?"

The truth is, though, that *we "look out" for ourselves most effectively when we also know how to look out for others.* Our happiness depends upon how we treat other people; it's that simple.

> *Acts of kindness lift our spirits.*
> *Trusting others lifts our spirits.*
> *Thinking about others expands our horizons and lifts our spirits.*

OFF THE PAGE AND INTO YOUR LIFE

Values look great on the page.

It can also feel great to claim certain values as your own. Or to find a workplace where high-minded values are part of the culture. Or to write out a "family mission statement" that glows.

None of that counts for anything if the values are not lived out. And not just on good days either. Every day. Rain or shine.

Values "gain value" only when you *allow them to support you*, when they shift the way you see a situation and respond to it.

We all value or at least give lip service to goodness, kindness, honesty, truth and freedom. We all value *love*.

But what actually grabs your attention—and holds it? What drives your choices when it comes to attention, time, energy and money?

Whatever your answer, that is what you are valuing.

These questions can help.

What do you stand for?
What would other people assume that you stand for, based on your actions, the decisions you make, what you talk about, how you organize your finances—and especially the way you spend your time?
What would you like to stand for?
Are the values you believe you hold the same values you live out in your everyday life?
What does your behavior say about your values?

Crucial meeting—do not disturb

Schedule an urgent meeting with yourself.

Focus on just one of the above questions at a time.

Write out the question, then write without censoring whatever comes to your mind.

When your mind slows or resists, simply write the question again and keep writing your responses (including your emotional responses like "I'm finding this quite irritating as I don't really know what I think. . . .").

When you have finished writing, don't reread. Trust that the question will go on "working" in your unconscious mind.

Return to the same question as often as you need to. Each time, begin as though you had never seen this question before. Allow yourself to be surprised.

Making decisions successfully

It can be exceptionally clarifying to ask yourself, when faced with a confusing or complex situation: "How does this fit with my standards or values? What would promote them and support me right now?"

VALUES ARE FOR EVERYONE

Maybe money drives you? Or the desire to be noticed?

Maybe what matters most is whether your next diet will work? Or whether you will meet someone soon who could change your life forever?

It could be that, as someone said to me recently, "Kindness is my highest value—not easy in a corporate workplace but as essential there as anywhere else when it's expressed as thoughtfulness, encouragement and even patience with *un*kindness."

Whatever is most important to you, whatever is at the forefront of your mind, will inevitably be reflected in every decision you make, and in all your choices, actions and behaviour.

What I am pointing out here is not a moral judgement. It's a psychological reality.

Be real about what matters to you. *Know* what's driving you. *Know* what's "coloring" your life, "flavoring" your thinking. Only then can you discover if this is really what you want.

SPIRITUAL VALUES?

The values that take you beyond selfishness and self-interest *are spiritual values.*

The values that let you connect with and value all living forms *are spiritual values.*

The values that let you glimpse an identity beyond thoughts, feelings, body and desires *are spiritual values.*

The values that teach you kindness *are spiritual values.*

PUT YOUR VALUES TO WORK

Values or qualities come to life *only when you are using and expressing them.*

In the tough moments of our lives, they have extraordinary power to help us.

Here are some practical ways to use them, letting you face *whatever comes* with relative poise, trust and equanimity.

- ✦ Let yourself know what quality or value you need to support you—even on a day-by-day or hour-by-hour basis.
- ✦ When you don't know what value you need, imagine someone you idealize, even a little. What quality would they be calling on in these circumstances? Choose that one. Claim it.
- ✦ Spend some time just "sitting with" and thinking about the quality and what it allows. Giving your attention to that quality, it is already growing in you. Again, you might like to imagine how it would help someone else; then let it help you in that same way.
- ✦ Practice the "seed meditation" using your chosen value as your seed word in the center of the page.
- ✦ Write the name of the quality on a card or even several cards so that you can see it often.
- ✦ Observe other people who practice your quality. Learn from them. And reflect on what you like, and don't. Let that guide you.
- ✦ Let yourself notice the effects of your behavior and attitudes on others. This is your most valuable guide to doing your best by your values.

At the worst of times, your values can be most helpful.

When panic erupts, for example, or great sadness or despair, meet that emotion with your supporting value. In the face of panic you might tell yourself, "I am simply going to hold the word 'trust' in my mind: trust that this moment will pass, trust that I can get through it, trust that it's not all of who I am—trust that I can slow my breathing. I know that this will pass." What matters here is not so much what you say, but what you are paying attention to.

By paying attention to a supportive quality, you are "growing" that, rather than your panic. In the face of sorrow, you might tell yourself, "I am holding compassion in my mind. I am not going to blame myself for sadness—I am going to treat myself kindly and tenderly and with respect." Your sadness won't worsen when you treat it and yourself with kindness; on the contrary it is shame and self-pity that protract it. In the face of shame, you might tell yourself, "The qualities I need are clarity and forgiveness. I want to understand what drove my actions—so maybe I don't need to make exactly the same mistake again! And I want to be able to offer myself forgiveness. And, having learned something, I want to move on."

Write your way out

It can be very helpful to write your way out of "being stuck" or overwhelmed. You can do a simple seed meditation on the quality you are using: writing the name of the quality you want in the center of the page then simply writing down all your associations with it; withdrawing, thinking, then writing again. This will deepen your awareness of the quality and make it more real to you.

Give yourself a chance to dive beneath your most obvious and superficial thoughts. Return to the same seed meditation until a greater sense of ease in your body tells you that you've "got it."

Tuning in to the values in this practical way, you will also become more sensitive to their presence outside yourself. When you see other people practicing the value you are "growing," affirm them, speak up about your appreciation, use your power to encourage. You may see others practicing your quality "better" than you do. Give yourself a treat. Let yourself be inspired rather than envious. Comparisons are potentially harmful; turn that around.

Let yourself know repeatedly: "What I pay attention to is what will become stronger in my life. I *can* support myself. I *can* allow humankind's highest qualities to support me. I am a source of those qualities, for myself and for other people."

Don't ask why

In a stressful moment, or when you feel empty and despairing, do not ask: "Why is this happening to me?" Ask: "What can I learn here? What will support me to get through this? What strengths do I already have from other situations? What's my next step?"

TO THINE OWN SELF BE TRUE, BUT WHAT IF YOU'RE THE PROBLEM?

CATHERINE: My son, Luke, and I went to an old-fashioned birthday party for his swimming buddy, Anna, who, like Luke, had just turned three. Anna and her mom threw the door open to reveal a party in full swing. There were paper streamers everywhere, Anna's homemade puppet theater taped crazily to the front of the television screen, towers of lopsided iced pink cupcakes, chocolate crackles and fairy bread. "I'm a butterfly!" Anna announced, and twirled away into the party. Luke, also a butterfly, with black construction paper and cellophane wings sewn to his T-shirt by his grandmother, was enchanted. So was I.

I watched with admiration as Anna's mom also twirled through her daughter's party. No stranger to a tough corporate career, long hours, and some hard-won lessons about life and love, Anna's mother has an attitude to life that I really admire.

While she passed plates of mini hot dogs and tomato sauce and danced through the spilled punch in high-heeled sandals, the kids ran around the house in bare feet and butterfly wings. Adults chatted; someone dropped a drink; no one seemed to mind. For two hours the kids' bubble-blowing covered most of us in soap, which somehow felt refreshing.

Later that afternoon, driving home while Luke slept in the car, I thought about the ingredients of this not-so-perfect perfect party. The chaos. The dirty faces. The furniture shoved against the walls. Paper streamers. Tomato sauce. Not a pretension in sight.

I thought about the values I express—all the usuals for "Type A" people—like honesty, industriousness, and perfectionism. I thought about the parties I have given my son so far, with a small guest list, carefully made invitations and decorations, fresh vegetables, democratic party games and baby wipes for faces and hands. I thought about the joy and freedom I rarely let myself express, even when it is simply a gift, there for the taking.

Many of us live overextended, uptight lives! How can we be true to our values but relax enough to let in some air?

STEPHANIE: I would question Catherine's view of "perfectionism" as a value (or as a valuable value). I'd prefer to call it a habit—driven by *a lack of valuing of who and what Catherine really is.*

This is a habit that reflects fear and anxiety rather than loving self-acceptance and encouragement. In fact, it expresses this thought: "I'd better be perfect or I won't be good enough."

Perfectionism is a true spoiler. As Catherine points out, it disrupts our capacity to feel joy and freedom. It certainly ruins spontaneity. It drags our attention away from what's actually happening, and what we could actually be enjoying, to focus on what isn't yet (and will never be) *perfect.* It takes us out of the present moment, into a future that may never come.

When Catherine comes up against this old habit, she can simply notice it for what it is. ("That's my perfectionism revving up again.") Observing it, rather than falling for it, is already helpful.

But in addition to that I would suggest that Catherine meet the energy of her perfectionism with the energy of a value she believes is more life-enhancing. Catherine speaks longingly of "joy and freedom." Those values are hers to choose and use.

Choosing them will be far less automatic for her than "choosing" perfectionism. Because perfectionism is so familiar, she may feel quite shaky trying to give it up. She might even tell herself that if she isn't being perfectionist then she won't be "trying hard enough."

This won't be true.

It is possible to maintain very high standards while *valuing process more than outcome.* And without confusing "who you are" with "what you are producing." What's more, as Catherine consciously allows herself greater ease and freedom, the self-doubt that drives her habit of perfectionism will lose much of its power.

It's a double win.

Catherine will feel more pleasure moment by moment. And judging herself less harshly (and not comparing herself to other idealized mothers!), she will feel much greater ease with herself.

YOUR VALUES ARE CHANGING THE WORLD

Whatever you wish there was more of, *be that.*

Whatever you want your relationships and friendships to be, *be that.*

Whatever you want the world to be, *be that.*

If you want there to be less fear and more love in the world, *start with yourself.*

If you want there to be less stress, anxiety, depression and tension in the world, *start with yourself.*

If you want the world to be a more peaceful place, fairer, more generous and compassionate, *start with yourself.*

Listen to Anthony Robbins

Mega-motivator Anthony Robbins usefully challenges us all when he suggests:

"Any time you sincerely want to make a change, the first thing you must do is raise your standards. When people ask me what really changed my life . . . I tell them that absolutely the most important thing was changing what I demanded of myself. I wrote down all the things I would no longer accept in my life, all the things I would no longer tolerate, and all the things I aspired to becoming."

THE LIBRARY OF STRENGTHS

Imagine that these values or strengths live in a library that's always open to you. *Everything is yours for the taking.*

Best of all, whatever you take need not be returned. It's yours to have and to keep forever. You can try it on, use it for a while, replace it with another value, add to it with more values: the choices are entirely yours. These strengths are your human inheritance.

love	*peace-making*
inclusiveness	**peace of mind**
good will	*empathy*
simplicity	**restraint**
appreciation	*tolerance*
clarity	**friendship**
joy	*good humor*
kindness	**flexibility**
wisdom	*resilience*
hope	**cooperation**
care for the physical world	*harmony*
humility	**curiosity**
generosity	*creativity*
courage	**honesty**
freedom	*integrity*
abundance	**patience**
playfulness	*self-acceptance*
forgiveness	**self-knowledge**
awe	*trust*
encouragement	**trustworthiness**
happiness	*fairness*
service	**fidelity**
compassion	*respect*
constancy	**responsibility**
self-control	*loyalty*

Let the values work for you

Focus on just one value at a time.

✦ Choose instinctively from the previous list.

✦ Start by putting the word somewhere you can easily see it—perhaps written out on a card propped up next to your computer screen or by your bed.

✦ Let the word resonate with you. Let it work on you.

✦ Next time you are making a decision, *use that value as a guide.* Let it support you. Let it help bring clarity, especially in a complex situation. ("If I value service it may make it easier to decide between two job opportunities." "If creativity is my highest value I might refuse a promotion to gain more time for myself." "Because cooperation is what I value I am willing to work on my issues of irritation and frustration with my family.")

✦ Visualize yourself using the value, growing more familiar with it, feeling supported by it. *Use it.*

✦ Let yourself know how you will be positively affected as that value becomes stronger in your life. Claim that in the present tense. ("I am more playful at work as well as at home." "I am more accepting, especially with my family." "I am tolerant of myself as well as others." "I am appreciative now rather than critical." "I am getting so much from being encouraging.")

✦ Be supportive and appreciative every time you see others expressing "your" value.

THIS TIME, THIS PLACE

You may believe that you are choosing your values freely. You may even believe that you are living them out consciously. Nevertheless, you are profoundly affected by the values of the society you live in.

Your values powerfully and inevitably reflect the time and place of your existence. They are a crucial part of your social conditioning. And your values, in turn, influence the society we are collectively creating.

This essential relationship between your private values and society's values makes it still more urgent to choose values consciously, to allow your values to support you, and to ensure that your vision of what you can afford to value extends beyond your own garden gate.

CRAZY CONTRADICTIONS

We live in a society that gives lip service to some excellent values while actually living by quite different values.

Here are some obvious examples. You will think of many more.

We praise peace but prepare for war.

We debate abortion, but not death from global poverty and starvation.

We promote cooperation as a value but live competitively.

We give lip service to racial and gender equality but tolerate gross inequality.

We value short-term profits over long-term care of planet Earth.

We value the "Golden Rule" ("Do unto others as you would have them do unto you"). But not when it clashes with our own interests.

These disparities should not discourage you from naming your values and trying to live by them. In fact, the opposite is true. Those inconsistencies speak volumes about the gap that so frequently exists between good intentions and self-focused actions. The challenge then is to look more honestly at your own values—and the actions that express them.

WHOLEHEARTED LIVING

We all have our preferences. We want life to go the way we want. Yet to live life fully we have to be able to accept and deal with some aspects of life that are distinctly unwelcome.

To live wholeheartedly is a value. And it takes genuine, minute-by-minute courage. The great thing to know is that **courage is always learned on the run** and never a moment before it's needed.

Calling on the values that you need to get through a demanding situation can make a profound difference. Even as you face those difficulties, your trust and self-respect will increase and your anxieties and fears will recede.

Pay attention to what will support you rather than to what's defeating you. You may discover some of the highest qualities *only* in tough times and darker moments. In your easier, sunnier moments, you may not need them.

Discover what supports you

Forgiveness and Other Acts of Love is a book that I wrote at an extremely difficult time in my life. Nothing I had learned seemed of much help to me. On top of that, I blamed myself bitterly for not coping better.

To break this terrible impasse, I undertook to do a series of interviews on ABC Radio National on the great humane virtues: courage, fidelity, restraint, generosity, tolerance and forgiveness. I decided that as these qualities had stood humankind in good stead throughout human history, paying close attention to them might mean that they could also do something for me.

In fact, they turned out literally to be my "saving graces." Absorbing each one as I prepared and did the interviews, then as I wrote the book that followed, I learned exactly how much stronger and more resilient I felt when I paid close, thoughtful attention to what could support me, rather than to what was causing me anguish.

My outer circumstances did not change for some time. But my life most certainly changed.

My sense of possibility changed. My trust in myself changed. The way I viewed the outer world—and my place in it—also changed.

This doesn't mean that I felt inspired or sublime at every moment. I had to keep consciously returning my attention to those eternal qualities. (I still do.) But learning patience and tenacity was essential to the experience.

ONE VALUE AT A TIME

CATHERINE: I start the day with the best of intentions. My plan is to wake up and before I even get out of bed, decide on three values that I am going to practice that day. But sometimes by evening all I can think of is that I've forgotten them all—especially patience. How can I hold on to these values through the pressures of the day? And what can I do about feeling bad when I fall short of the mark?

STEPHANIE: Focusing on the value Catherine needs as she wakes is terrific: mini-meditation and goal-setting all in one. But one value is better than three!

Keep things as simple as possible. That's always most supportive. And when it comes to values, be as practical as possible.

Catherine is already actively reflecting on the qualities she needs. She is certainly open to inspiration. But I suspect that she needs to be much less tough on herself and much more realistic about how to let that quality support her.

Values are there to support us. They only come to life through us. They should not be yet another measure for failure!

Let's look at patience, the quality that Catherine wants most. Surely patience deeply challenges every mother who is home with tiny children, up with a new baby through the night, and trying to keep her work life alive in a corner of her sitting room. That was absolutely my experience too, with two children born just over a year apart, and constant writing to pay our way. So I really do know that a living saint is needed and not an ordinary human woman who wants nothing more than four or five hours of unbroken sleep!

This *is* Catherine's wonderful, complex, challenging life. What would support her to be more patient in *this* moment, in *these* circumstances?

She is already wonderfully patient for much of the day (and night). She needs to give herself positive acknowledgment for that. She *is* a devoted mother. She can help herself to see that (not least by ceasing to compare herself to her internal image of an idealized mother).

Letting herself off the hook of her own self-criticism will already help. (Meeting her self-criticism with patience: "Boring old self-criticism again. I can let it pass.")

What else would make it easier for her to be patient all day, which is what she wants?

Recognizing the moments when patience is most likely to go underground is tremendously helpful. Leaving her home and going to the park *before she loses patience* will make a difference. Knowing that her time alone with the children is going to end with her husband Luther coming home just half an hour earlier will make a difference. Making sure that she has the company of other mothers some days, and that more generally some of her non-Mommy needs are met, will make a difference. Taking catnaps and letting her standards of housekeeping and cooking *plummet* will make a difference. Knowing where her limits of interest are with her four-year-old's favorite games will make a difference. *And being patient with herself will certainly make a difference.*

There is no tougher and more constant job than mothering, nor one that leaves you more emotionally vulnerable and physically exhausted even in the face of amazing delight and joy. But even when the circumstances are less extreme, we need to check that *we too are benefiting from the quality we want to express.*

In Catherine's case, she can be *more patient* with herself. Be *more practical* about what will allow her to be patient. And if she wakes up and wants the same quality for several years, with the occasional dash of self-forgiveness along with oodles of self-encouragement, so be it. It's already a triumph to be willing to ask ourselves what we need, and to go about receiving and giving it.

(Rereading this, I am reminded of the day, almost twenty years ago, when my dear kind friend Wiebke said to me, as I struggled to produce perfect food for my perfect, precious children, "What's wrong with frozen vegetables, Stephanie?" Way beyond the rights or wrongs of vegetables, I felt as though I had been given sacred permission to do things a little more easily. The relief was indescribable.)

THE "GREATEST" VALUES ARE THERE FOR YOU

Some of us don't draw on or connect with the most inspirational values because that feels too hard or unfamiliar. Or we feel unworthy ("I'm not up to that"). Or there seems to be an atmosphere of moralism around those values that quite understandably turns us off.

Yet the highest values, the values that are guaranteed to make you feel genuinely connected to other people and the best in yourself, are not just universal, they are also *universally available*.

You don't have to be "special" or "worthy" or "spiritual" to call on the most inspiring values, make them your own and *let them work for you*. The highest values are for everyone.

Listen to Saint Paul

"Whatever is true, whatever is noble, whatever is right, whatever is pure, whatever is lovely, whatever is admirable—if anything is excellent or praiseworthy—think about such things."

Activating the highest values, you also activate your highest potential.

A BETRAYAL OF VALUES

It's tough to be the victim of someone else's inconsistencies when it comes to values.

I experienced this when I was warmly interviewed a few years ago by someone I had met a number of times. On this occasion the woman was again highly enthusiastic about my work, personal in her responses to it, and in every possible way courteous and appreciative. Imagine my surprise then to open a major newspaper a few days later and find that she had written a trivializing and dismissive review of the book she had discussed with such warmth.

I can only assume that she was quite unable to recognize the gulf between her two distinct sets of behaviors.

And in response?

I can't pretend that I wasn't hurt. It's because I was hurt that this incident stayed with me. But I highly value giving the benefit of the doubt—and felt that for my own sake I needed to extend that to her, despite my own hurt. I had to assume that, like most of us, she is blind to her inconsistencies. It was my choice to be reserved, certainly somewhat wary, but not condemning.

I also had to tell myself that even though this happened around my work—which I care about intensely—in the greater scheme of things it wasn't that important.

When you have assumed that you shared values with someone close to you, maybe someone who shared your life in an intimate way, and those values are betrayed, this causes suffering of quite a different order.

In those circumstances (and I have been there too), it is certainly necessary to call on the very highest values for support: love, self-regard, equanimity and—eventually—forgiveness.

CONSIDERING FORGIVENESS

Issues of forgiveness become highly charged when there has been a betrayal of shared values.

It can help to remember that:

✦ Forgiveness is not condoning. You are not pretending that a "wrong" was "right."

✦ Forgiveness (even partial forgiveness) benefits you more than the person who has hurt you.

✦ It is extremely difficult to "forget" and look ahead until the seeds of forgiveness are "watered" by your desire to move on.

✦ Forgiveness allows you to see the big picture (including the things that are "right" as well as those that are "wrong").

✦ Forgiveness releases you to move into the present moment; to learn from the past even as you leave it behind.

It can also help to remember that human beings (including us) frequently act unconsciously.

If you are quite certain that it was a conscious betrayal of shared values, you will have to accept that the other person's priorities had changed. What you shared was no longer as important to them; certainly it was not what mattered most. This doesn't make the hurt go away, but sometimes you can gain invaluable distance by facing the facts, and knowing that "the facts" are never about you only. They may, indeed, be only peripherally "about you" (that is, the other person has their own continuing internal drama driving them).

Our development, including the development of our highest values, entirely depends on how we deal with the hardest, toughest and least welcome situations in our lives; not the easiest. In stretching ourselves to forgive others, we may also learn something vital about forgiving ourselves.

HARMONY AT HOME

We generally feel most "at home" with people who more or less share our most treasured values.

Often this is quite unconscious. You may not ever have discussed values or alluded to them. Nevertheless, what you share is deeply reassuring.

Alternatively, you might admire someone very much, but getting to know that person, you begin to feel uneasy. Why? Often it's because you do not share values. Or their way of living is at odds with what you believe is important. This doesn't mean you won't have friends, colleagues and family members with whom you might have real differences when it comes to values. But in your most important relationships, some continuity or at least respect for the highest values that you hold, supports and maintains the relationship—even when there are "personality" differences.

For example, you might find your partner's father extremely irritating. He constantly frets about money and feels he has the right to comment on your life far more often than you regard as appropriate. What gets you through? Like you, he is passionate about social justice issues. Or he is unfailingly thoughtful when it comes to your kids. Those values connect you—and increasingly carry greater weight than your irritations.

RESOLVE CONFLICT

Shared values have the power to heal emotional wounds and reduce conflict. Explicitly acknowledging what you mutually value—your love for one another, your shared history, a commitment to the other's emotional and spiritual well-being—you are allowing that to support you. This gives you a basis for looking *together* at what's causing you problems, rather than looking at the issues in an adversarial way.

+ Use friendly, cooperative language.
+ *Listen more, talk less.* Open up to the other person's reality.
+ Talk about *mutual gains.*
+ Let generosity be an explicit value.

Working through difficulties using values to support you can deepen the relationship in a way that good times alone cannot.

Many hurts are not deliberate

We all act unconsciously. There are often yawning gaps between what we say and how we behave. Or between how we think we have behaved and how the other person experiences our behavior.

When you are resolving conflict or just "clearing the air," make listening a higher priority than talking. Often, as the other person speaks, they themselves will come to recognize those gaps. This is most likely to happen when they feel least defensive and attacked.

These are useful prompts:

+ "Tell me how you see the situation." (*Listen*, without interrupting!)
+ "What were your expectations? What did you have in mind?"
+ "Can you see where some confusion crept in?"
+ "May I explain it from my point of view?"
+ "Is there something else that I haven't seen or understood?"
+ "What would help us both to avoid repeating this?"

WORKPLACE VALUES

How have you chosen to earn your living?

Do you feel that you did "choose"—or that other people or life chose for you?

How do you behave toward colleagues, bosses, clients and customers?

How do you view your paid work in relation to all other areas of your life?

Is "work" your primary identification? ("I'm a teacher, dentist, graphic designer, professional sports player …")

Do you give your best self to work, and bring home what's left over?

These are uncomfortable questions for many of us. But worth addressing. Yet issues of work and values don't stop there. Even when we are lucky enough to have some choice about where and how we will work, we may still face some painful situations where we feel torn between self-interest and integrity. Or when our personal values clash with the values of our workplace.

- ✦ "I want this job but hate it that we're not always straight with clients."
- ✦ "There's bullying at work. But I'm scared to speak up."
- ✦ "I have to flatter clients even if their demands are totally unreasonable."
- ✦ "The way colleagues talk about one another makes us all feel unsafe."
- ✦ "My firm gives lip service to family-friendly policies yet the partners only really care about how many hours you can bill."
- ✦ "It's hard to compete with my own colleagues when what I value is teamwork."

Behaving in ways that feel compliant rather than authentic in order to keep a job or gain a promotion can add huge stress to your life.

It also creates an uncomfortable and potentially harmful split between your so-called private and public lives. You want the job *and* you want to be "yourself." You want to feel valued. Yet you don't want to have to surrender self-worth in order to achieve that.

To maintain a genuine sense of self, you need to be able to stay in harmony with your deepest values and cultivate and express the same values in whichever situation you find yourself. This can require you to be subtle, diplomatic and discerning—and sometimes courageous.

In extreme cases, it may require you to consider what you value more: approval from others or self-respect; approval or integrity; freedom or security; competitiveness or cooperation; honesty or expediency.

PAID TO GROW

You may regard "personal development" as something that happens outside work hours. This isn't so. *The complexity of the contemporary workplace offers outstanding opportunities for personal and social growth.*

For most of your adult lifetime, you will be giving more hours to your paid work than to virtually any other single activity:

✦ You may well spend more waking hours with colleagues than with friends, family or your partner.

✦ You will make more decisions in your workplace than you are likely ever to make at home.

✦ You will probably have more opportunities to consider moral, psychological and spiritual questions in the workplace than at home; and they are no less relevant there.

How you spend those working hours, how you make those decisions, how you allow yourself to be shaped by work and how you in turn shape the work you do, will profoundly affect your overall sense of well-being. *Your workplace offers unique opportunities to identify and refine your values:*

✦ You have to learn to get along with a wide range of people, some of whom you may not especially like.

✦ You have to learn to compromise, postpone gratification, resolve conflicts, take criticism and cope with disappointments and injustices.

✦ You have to get on with your work whether or not you "feel like it."

✦ You have to be able to support other people and meet a variety of expectations.

✦ You have to test your creativity, flexibility, resilience and persistence.

Being equally alert, alive and "true to yourself" at home and work is an increasing challenge, but few contemporary challenges deserve more attention or are more worthwhile.

WORKPLACE VALUES IN PRACTICE

Value people:

+ See other people as people, not as "opportunities," "competitors" or "nuisances."
+ Look people in the eye. Let them see you.
+ Offer respect unconditionally. (You are not free until you behave the same way whatever the external circumstances.)
+ Practice the Golden Rule ("Behave toward other people as you want them to behave toward you").
+ Never get other people to do your "dirty work."
+ Be a constant source of support and encouragement for others.

Value constructive behavior:

+ Recognize the emotional trail you are leaving behind.
+ Talk less, listen more.
+ Listen to your own language and voice. What effect will they have?
+ Walk "the second mile." Do more than is absolutely required.
+ Never miss an opportunity to be generous.
+ Value work as a place to give service while earning a living.
+ Be solution- not problem-focused.
+ Know that "objectivity" is a highly subjective experience.
+ Accept that when someone disagrees with you, they may not be wrong.
+ Test your assumptions. Ask yourself, "Have I understood correctly that . . . ?"
+ Hear all sides before judging.
+ When you observe problems, speak up constructively rather than destructively.
+ Don't moralize or make other people "wrong."

Value consistency:

+ Be consistent with your values across all areas of your life.
+ Focus on who you are; let "what you do" reflect that.
+ Let values guide your feelings; not the other way around.

✦ Let values guide your behavior.

✦ Be true to your own definitions of success. They don't all have to be defined by the workplace.

✦ Be honest with yourself. Then trust that you can be honest with others.

✦ Your character is what shapes your encounters with others; take that seriously.

✦ Know what matters. And what doesn't.

✦ Recognize and value what you have learned from your experiences.

✦ Monitor your self-talk. How you talk to yourself about work will affect your efficiency and attitude; it will increase or decrease stress; it will guide others in their responses to you.

Value these values

In your work and in your life, value courtesy, cooperation, dignity, simplicity and creativity.

Value "flow" and process—not just results.

Value your continuing education.

Value honesty and integrity.

Know that a peaceful mind can be highly alert.

TAKE YOUR BODY TO WORK

Many of us take our mind to work. And we dress our bodies nicely. But then, if we are not in a physically demanding profession, we behave as though one was detached from the other.

In every situation where: your mind is racing; you believe there's lots at stake; you are second-guessing others; you are tense, fraught, anxious, vulnerable; you are turning your nervousness into body symptoms via a headache, churning stomach, clammy palms; *use this fail-safe method:*

+ Focus on reducing your own physical tension.
+ You can continue to listen as you do this but a few moments of split attention as you *calm your mind by calming your body* will be more than justified.
+ Imagine pulling into your center all your scattered "bits" (literally, your energy) that disperse the more anxious you get.
+ Feel yourself *from within* becoming more solid.
+ Feel yourself *from within* letting tension go.
+ Let yourself consciously feel the ground beneath your feet. If you are seated, put your feet flat on the floor.
+ Sit or stand "solidly"—this is especially useful for women who might feel awkward about enjoying their "bigness." It can also be very useful for both women and men who are more cerebral than physical.
+ Breathe very slowly and into your center; imagine that you are oxygenating your spine and "core."
+ Switch on the "soothe" function in your brain: "I can deal with this one moment at a time."
+ Focus on what's happening *moment by moment*. Stop second-guessing about what may never happen.
+ Any time that your symptoms of tension return, simply refocus on the inside of your body and reduce the tension from inside out.

Detaching from your barrage of thoughts is already helpful. What's more, it leads rapidly to clearer thinking.

QUANTITY TIME

CATHERINE: Every person I know is tired and time-poor. Babies and children are often away from home for the equivalent of a ten-hour workday at child care, school or after-school care. Teenagers look particularly tired, especially when homework demands more hours a night than hours available after sports, lessons, and dinner. Most parents race from child care centers to school to work to the shops and home, only to start a second workday. Career people are also frantic, commuting and traveling, processing hundreds of e-mails each day, attending meetings, trying to find time to produce actual work both in the office and at home, while also getting at least some of their social needs met.

With our families and the people we love, we've swallowed the myth of quality time because *quantity time just isn't available.* Often when we leave the house my four-year-old son says wistfully, "We're not in a hurry today, are we, Mom?"

Maybe we're simply addicted to being busy. After all, we compare the number of e-mails that arrive while we are out of the office in the same way that teenage girls used to compare phone calls from boys on a Saturday night. The mania makes us feel important. But it also makes us feel overstretched, desperate, superficial and angry.

I don't know how much faster we can live, but technology is inviting us to do just that. Somewhere along the line we have confused overwork with self-worth. And I wonder what we're gaining.

How did this happen?

STEPHANIE: The e-mail craziness happened one e-mail at a time! In other words, like so many profound changes happening "out there" that affect us "in here," this revolution happened incrementally. And because it happened in that way, we barely noticed. Or we simply accepted that it was inevitable and buckled down.

It's "not noticing" that makes us vulnerable.

"Not noticing" what is driving our lives—way beyond the

e-mail drama—leads to a situation where we live *as though we had no real choices*.

Is this true?

You say that every person you know is "tired and time-poor," yet the people you (and I) know, are among the most privileged in the world. Without getting too heavy here, there are millions, possibly billions of people in our shared world who truly do not have choices: carrying water, grinding maize, tending crops, eating their one meal a day. For them, "choice" has a very different meaning.

Our lives are filled with choices. Yet, in describing them, we often use the language of slaves. Time is our master and we scuttle to obey.

Being busy *is* a kind of addiction. It reassures us that we are "someone." It lets us know that we are alive—even when we feel half-dead. It gives us the best possible excuse not to look a little more deeply into our lives. It may be saving us from loneliness.

But being constantly busy estranges us from ourselves.

Our tiredness is not simply physical. We exhaust our spirits when we drive ourselves like slaves and talk to ourselves as though we had no choices. We (and our children) need time to relax, drift, recover and renew. We need time to live through our senses, as well as our minds. We need time to connect: with ourselves, with other people and with life's meaning beyond our next appointment.

Catherine's question really pushes us to consider one of the few questions that really matters: *How are you choosing to live your life?*

My hunch is that many of us—and especially those of us who are highly work-focused—are out of touch with our power to choose. Or we see choice in "all or nothing" terms. We make no time *to look deeply into the situation* and see it with new eyes.

We save no energy to think about what we want, beyond the immediate.

Valuing our own lives differently is the place to start. We won't have to give up on what society values most. But we can choose to follow that path far less slavishly.

REVIEWING AMBITION

Ambition—especially around work, status and money—occupies a highly emotive place in our society.

On the one hand, it is clearly wonderful to feel inspired to reach your highest potential and to make a significant social contribution through your paid work. At the same time, it's almost impossible to avoid getting swept up in a mind-set that *confuses your value as a human being with your value in the marketplace.*

Fear and anxiety drive this phenomenon: fear that there are not enough of the good things to go around; anxiety that you will "miss out" not just on the good things but on the love, approval and applause that seem to go with them. So enslaved are many of us by these fears of insufficiency that they drive our behavior even toward our youngest children.

We want our children to be "ahead" before they are even standing. *We compare our children's progress using measures more suitable for the workplace than the classroom.*

We require our children to sacrifice pleasure, creativity, spontaneity and even cooperation and social rewards because of our concerns about their eventual status and income. (And concerns about how their choices reflect on us.)

We validate study and career choices applauded by our brash, competitive society without quietly considering whether this will best support the development of our children as well-rounded, fully alive human beings—or best reflect their own desires and choices. And we make those same decisions about ourselves, often without considering whether this is how we most want to expend our brief, precious lives.

+ It takes courage to disentangle ourselves from the hold ambition has over us.
+ It takes courage to see how much we gain when we stop looking at other people as "competitors."
+ It takes courage to know that "work" is not all of who we are; cannot meet all our needs; isn't the only place where we can make our mark. But it can be done.

FRESH AMBITIONS

Intensifying your awareness of choice around this complex issue of ambition, ask yourself:

- ✦ Who am I trying to please/impress/persuade through my ambitions?
- ✦ Do my ambitions express and support the best of who I am?
- ✦ What (and who) do I need to sacrifice to achieve this ambition? Am I happy with that?
- ✦ Am I choosing my ambitions or are they choosing me?
- ✦ What emotions drive my ambitions?
- ✦ If I achieve what I set out to do, will this change my life for the better?
- ✦ Could I achieve my ambitions less painfully—driven by *delight in the process* rather than anxiety about outcome?
- ✦ Who are my role models?

And then ask:

- ✦ While remaining sensitive to what others think, how could I free myself from any residual belief that my value as a person depends on my professional success?
- ✦ Am I also ambitious about enjoying my life, encouraging others, deepening my relationships, taking on activities I am not especially good at, chilling and hanging out?
- ✦ Am I ambitious about living as well as doing?

Awareness ahead

Much of what drives our ambitions, or holds us back, is unconscious (but very powerful). It can be exceptionally helpful to explore this issue slowly and in some detail to increase self-awareness and choice. Writing a response to each question in your journal, brainstorming with a good friend, or just alerting yourself to the complexity of this issue, are all effective ways to gain invaluable and perhaps unexpected information.

WORKPLACE INSIGHTS

Ambition drives the hidden (and sometimes not so hidden) agenda in many workplaces. It prevents people from being open with one another. It can certainly prevent them from feeling supported and safe.

This adds to workplace stress. It can also threaten the quality of our work as well as the quality of our lives. Competitiveness and ambition can be inspirational, but not when they drive your life, limit your choices, or you experience them on a continuous basis. Then your attention is divided and distracted ("How well am I doing?"), rather than focused and clear.

It is worth considering what role ambition plays in your own life. (Your journal can be a real help here: treat it like a whiteboard.) But it can also be a fruitful topic for shared discussion in a workplace.

For this to be effective, it would need to be done within a context that is safe and structured. "Ambition" would then be looked at alongside the espoused values and goals of the individuals and the company or corporation.

We take so much for granted when we use emotive terms like "ambition." We assume that other people attribute to them the same meaning that we do. This is not always the case.

It may even be that people are afraid to explore this topic in case their own private feelings don't match the public ethos. Where that is the case, there would be more reasons, not fewer, for having this kind of discussion. But it would need to be skillfully guided.

The goal in seeking such discussion is not to establish "right" and "wrong" ways to think about ambition (and what you are willing to sacrifice for it). It would be to establish a greater sense of openness, clarity and trust. Those are qualities that benefit communities and organizations of any size, just as much as they benefit individuals.

NOT AMBITIOUS ENOUGH?

It's easy to argue that many of us are too ambitious. Could it be that some of us are not ambitious enough?

Your life is your ultimate creation.

What kind of life are you creating?

How ambitious are you to create a *whole* life that nourishes and expresses the very best of who you are?

This may help.

Let yourself fully imagine the life you want to be living. Until you can imagine it, you will never achieve it.

- ✦ Monitor the "trail" you are leaving behind you. You will be influencing and affecting other people for better or worse. How you do it is up to you.
- ✦ Be clear about what you would most like to be remembered for—especially by the people who love you most.
- ✦ Praise and support the people who are already living the values you rate most highly.
- ✦ Identify some role models. Allow yourself to be inspired.
- ✦ Value your own mistakes—however appalling. There's golden knowledge in every one.
- ✦ Give priority to whatever increases your sense of being fully alive.

Know that across time and cultures, one fact stands out. *The happiest people are also the most altruistic.*

FIRST BE WHO YOU REALLY ARE

My first "career" was in the widely admired field of law. In those far-off days relatively few women studied law and the atmosphere in the law faculty made it clear that women were there under sufferance. For a girl to do well you had to be brilliant or mature. I was neither. I was also working full-time as a law clerk to pay my way, living in a house with other wild girls, and was—when I started—sixteen years old.

I chose law because I thought that choice made me look good in other people's eyes. (Looking good in my own eyes was a concept way out of reach for me then.) Fortunately my lack of talent and real interest eventually overruled "looking good." After three years in legal offices I went to work for a year in the university library, saved every cent that I could and, aged twenty, left my home country, New Zealand, to see the world from the other side.

What followed were two more years of doing work in London and Berlin that I found alienating and depressing. Then, at the age of twenty-two, after six years in the workforce, I landed a modest job in publishing and my whole life changed. In terms of work, I was home.

Publishing, like writing, is not something you would do for the money. In my first years in publishing I did additional work constantly, including writing, to subsidize my starvation wages. And in all my years even as a best-selling writer I have always additionally taught, reviewed, practiced psychotherapy—which I loved—given workshops and talks, written articles, also to support my life as a writer.

A writer's life is a quirky one. It's much less glamorous or even inspired than it appears. It's extremely demanding, physically and mentally. Few sane people would want to spend countless hours alone hunched over the technological equivalent of a blank page. But those six years of being in various versions of the "wrong job" gave me invaluable insights.

It is a privilege to have work that supports your growth as a human being.
It's a privilege to have work that lets you make a social contribution.
It's a privilege to have work that challenges and extends you.
Most of all, it is a privilege to have work that reflects your values and develops them.

MORE THAN YOUR BUSINESS CARD

CATHERINE: To finance my graduate studies after I finished my undergraduate degree, I landed a job as a technical writer for a telecommunications company. I can still see myself in my first (royal blue!) business suit, proudly marching to my tiny office cubicle with my name and credentials embossed in bold type on a box of business cards.

After graduate school, several jobs followed that first one. Each time I gained a new sense of identity from what was printed on my business card. Then I emigrated from Canada to Australia. For many months I gave up both my job and along with it, the self I had carefully constructed.

At parties people would ask, "What do you do for a living?" *I'm in between jobs*, I'd say. *I just moved here*, I'd say. *I'm considering a career change*, I'd say. I didn't care what they thought, but I did care about how lost I felt—adrift without my name and job title printed on a card, summarizing for the world and myself who and what I was.

I think about the number of people I know in their forties and fifties and older who have been retrenched and can't find meaningful work. I think about the immigrant taxi drivers I've chatted with who have a Ph.D. in chemistry or physics but will never get work in their field. I think about my mother who raised six children but still laments that she "never worked." I think about a married couple I know who after three years of trying haven't found the work they are trained to do. I think about the fathers in my mothers' group who have chosen to stay home and raise their children while their wives pursue their careers. I think about men who have "retired" a decade too early.

Some of these people have business cards. Many don't.

When the world asks for your business card, it's reassuring to be able to hand over something solid and embossed. But life is changeable and careers today can be all too fleeting. How can we retain a strong sense of self whether we have a business card or not?

STEPHANIE: The irony is that if you have a tremendously impressive business card (and what goes with it) you may be worse and not better off in finding and establishing a sense of self that does not depend on other people's values or judgments.

It is so easy to slip into a role that goes with a particular career or lifestyle—and let the role do the living for you. Sometimes—as with Catherine's royal blue suit—you literally put on clothes that tell other people who you are (and how important you are). But is "the suit" more real than you are?

Catherine describes how she missed that shorthand version of herself when she came to Australia. I can understand that. When I myself came to Australia twenty-one years ago I was pregnant with my first child, embarking on a new career as a writer, and leaving behind a publishing career that sustained me and gave me a highly visible identity. I missed that. What was worse, I was also leaving behind loved friends who knew me well. Although it had been my wish to come to live in Australia (at least for a couple of years!), I felt agonizingly adrift without those anchors of work and close friendships. But it was precisely the loss of that role, and those anchors, that forced me to accelerate the fundamental work of discovering what "self" means.

This is the work of recognizing that you are "someone"—a unique someone with her own values, gifts and talents—even when others might think you are a "no one."

This is the work of valuing your life from the inside; for who you are and not for your job description or for what you produce. In a society like ours which worships money, fame and success, such inner work requires genuine trust, courage and persistence. But it's worth it.

For the truth is, a business card—even the most illustrious—cannot give you an authentic sense of self; it can only wrap you in what the pioneering writer and psychologist Carl Jung called a *persona*. This basically means a role that you play. You might identify with that persona; you may love and cultivate it; you may welcome other people responding to it; *but it is not who you are.*

The imprint you will leave behind on this universe will

have nothing to do with your business card; it will have everything to do with your values.

Discovering who you are, and what your values are, is a lifelong task that is frequently accelerated in the face of loss: loss of job, country, marriage, health, loved ones, or friendship. When the familiar props fall, you are left with "nothing," nothing but your own self and values. And these most crucial questions:

What gives your life meaning?
What meaning are you bringing to life?

As I write this I am thinking that many of us move through an entire lifetime defined as someone's son or daughter, spouse, employee, parent, grandparent ... and so on. These are all invaluable roles; but if we are fortunate we are pushed to ask, who is the person "occupying" them?

It's through our values that we create our sense of self; interpret and respond to the world; judge others; exercise choice and responsibility. This is what we can and eventually must do for ourselves. This is what no one else can do for us. *This is what no one else can take from us.* It's certainly a process that's impossible to encapsulate on a business card! But it goes to the heart of engaged and committed living.

Looking to work to save you?

Many of us look to career to tell us who we are. When that career has prestige and status, we expect to be rewarded emotionally as well as financially. That doesn't always happen. If the career is right for us, then emotional rewards will flow. If the career is wrong, then financial rewards rarely compensate for increasing feelings of alienation. No career or work choice is globally "right." Work is an area where we need to test our strengths, find our own measure of success, and express our own truth—and we may need to repeat this many times through a working lifetime.

WHO NEEDS GOALS?

The world cannot be neatly divided between those who set goals and use them, and those who don't.

Despite the highly paid efforts of armies of motivators, *fewer than 5 percent of people regularly set goals* and use their goal-setting with any genuinely effective sense of purpose.

I suspect that passivity plays its part. (It can feel easier to let other people direct your life for you.) But also goal-setting for many people reveals a quite painful gap between head and heart.

There are the things we "ought to do"; there are the things we want to do. The lines between can feel distinctly fuzzy.

Goal-setting is supposed to help us to set priorities, plan, focus and complete. It should activate our will as well as our imagination and experience. It should tell us what is important and what is not. It should certainly serve as a beacon to let us know where we are heading.

But goal-setting sometimes fails us.

It can feel like an activity that other people want for us more than we want it for ourselves. It can suggest a kind of tidying-up of ambivalence that may feel false. It can also seem like an obstacle in the way of spontaneity.

For goal-setting to be effective, it needs to be:

Authentic—you identify goals for your own sake, not to please or impress someone else.

Inspirational—setting the goal activates your sense of potential.

Realistic—a stretch, but not entirely out of reach.

Clarifying—it lets you sort your priorities and act decisively.

Integrating—it aligns you with your purpose and values.

Awareness of our power to choose is at the heart of successfully setting goals and achieving them.

CHOOSE GOALS—AND ACHIEVE THEM

Start here:

+ Define what you want to achieve. (Even when the goal is part of someone else's agenda, as it often is at work, *own* it.)
+ Don't wait to be motivated. **Getting going is the finest motivator.**
+ *Trust that tenacity and the ability to learn from others count for more than raw talent.*
+ Your mind thinks in pictures. Visualize the outcomes you want. Engage your right as well as left brain (creative and analytic strengths respectively) in establishing goals and purpose.
+ Having visualized the outcomes, how will you achieve them? List the steps.
+ Break the goal into mini-goals. Encourage yourself with plenty of "achievement" before the entire goal is completed.
+ Where you anticipate problems, let yourself know in advance who and what will support you.
+ Make time for what you want to achieve. *Own your time.* No goal is ever achieved successfully without prioritizing time intelligently.
+ Monitor the way you talk to yourself. Choose to make your internal commentary thoughtful and encouraging.
+ Don't allow your achievements to be your sole measure of self-worth. Be involved. Allow yourself to flow with your actions. But don't kid yourself that your entire self is on the line. (That level of anxiety decreases efficiency; it doesn't increase it.)
+ If you go in a "wrong" direction or make a mistake, learn from it and regroup. Research proves that this often leads to a better outcome.
+ Value process—especially what you are doing moment by moment. The more absorbed you are by process, the more that "goal" can take care of itself.
+ Value what you are learning as you go. This makes tough moments far more palatable.
+ Bring something of yourself to everything you do. Regard even mundane tasks as a platform for creativity.

✦ When something matters to you, *commit yourself to excellence*. It is far more inspiring than mediocrity and far more achievable than "perfection."

✦ There may also be tasks or behaviors you want to limit in order to be kinder to yourself. That can be a legitimate goal.

When you feel stuck?

✦ Take a walk, move your body. A "stuck" body houses a "stuck" mind.

✦ Listen to music—this can switch on the right (more intuitive and creative) hemisphere of the brain.

✦ Draw or doodle—experiment with using your non-dominant hand.

✦ Complete another task that's easy and manageable.

✦ Eat some protein to stabilize your blood sugars. Drink lots of water.

✦ Formulate a question or statement: "What I am not yet clear about is . . ."; or "How can I best move from A to B?"; or "The primary issue at stake here is . . ." Write that question or statement down. Then sleep on it. Let your subconscious creative mind go to work. Trust that.

✦ Ask yourself what your mentor or hero would do when stuck, or about this particular situation.

✦ Read something inspiring—even when it's not immediately relevant it may jump-start new thoughts.

Form a clear picture in your mind of what you want to achieve.

Keep your vision of what you want to achieve bright and constant. (Envisage it in detail; how you will feel; what satisfaction you will experience.)

Sustain your intention through visualizing its completion.

PLANNING DAY

CATHERINE: Every January my husband and I have a planning day to identify our goals for the upcoming year. And I love this day! We splurge on a babysitter for six hours on a Saturday and head off to Luther's empty office. On the way in, we pick up a new spiral notebook and coffee. Then we sit down and talk.

We divide our year's goals into eight areas: spiritual, marriage, family, health, learning, career, friends and service. We spend several hours talking over what we want to accomplish and by the end of the day we have a list. Not a list of jobs—a list of goals.

We also try to capture the spirit of the year ahead in a single sentence. For example, when we faced a demanding year that would stretch the limits of our time, patience and finances, our statement was "This will be one of the most stimulating, challenging, and rewarding years of our life together!" (We thought that sounded more positive and inspiring than "This year will be completely exhausting and way too hard.")

Though we only review our goals periodically, we post our statement where we can see it daily. It reminds us of the challenge ahead and the *attitude* we want to bring to the year as a whole.

This year we fell short of our plan in two essential areas: devoting time to our spiritual growth and to our health. We got caught in the trap of focusing on what's urgent (family, work, friends) and neglecting what's truly important (our bodies and our spirits). But without having our plan to nudge us, we may not have even noticed.

For us, whether we meet each goal fully—or even adequately—is not really the point. The point is that *we've chosen where we want to go.* Our imperfect plan still guides our lives, clarifies our direction, and certainly supports our desire to pull together as a couple and a family.

ENJOY THE REWARDS

A goal looks very different when you recognize *the rewards that are inherent in the process.*

Perhaps you are studying at nights after long days at work. It's hard to do this. And all the reasons why it's hard are well known to you. You rehearse those reasons in your mind. You talk about them. Other people agree how hard it is.

But other than "hard," what else is going on here?

Maybe it is also stimulating, companionable and intellectually challenging? Maybe it's great to be part of a class and not running it? Maybe there's some relief in having your sense of direction so clearly defined for a set period of time?

The more consciously you enjoy the process—and are willing to identify and focus on what you enjoy—the less necessary it will be that the goal itself has somehow to compensate you. ("I'm only doing this slog to get my credentials.")

In fact, the more positive you feel about the process, the more likely you are also to relish the goal. And to experience genuine satisfaction when you achieve it.

You are also in a better position to *redefine your goals appropriately* when a single outcome doesn't hang on them.

When you have denigrated the process or fought against it, your goal will be soured, no matter how brilliantly you achieve it.

MISTAKES ARE NOT DEADLY

Setting the wrong goals, "wasting time," following false trails, falling flat on your face repeatedly, making a total fool of yourself: this rarely matters.

In the course of a lifetime, we can never know in advance which events are going to support or teach us most. Some of the worst events in our lives, some of our most idiotic and even most shameful moments, may be exactly what will teach us something invaluable. (That has certainly been my own experience.)

Winning and losing, succeeding and failing, are relative terms only.

Winning and succeeding certainly feel good. But our pain at losing or failing becomes far more manageable when we stubbornly ask, "What can I learn here?" Or when we see a setback as only part of the big picture.

What matters most is that you are:

+ Identifying your own sense of purpose
+ Making your own decisions
+ Taking risks intelligently
+ Mopping up after yourself when that's needed
+ Observing and learning
+ Living relatively fearlessly.

Fearing your own mistakes diminishes you. Remind yourself, "My mistakes don't define me. Getting over them is far more significant."

THERE ARE NO PROBLEMS

Can you imagine a life without problems?

I can't either! What I can recognize, however, is that the vast majority of our problems are self-made. This doesn't mean that they don't hurt us; they do. Nevertheless much of that pain is also self-made and therefore unnecessary.

You can choose to eliminate all the problems that may never happen. This would already radically free you.

You can learn to be ruthlessly discerning. "Is this something that I can do something about—or not?"

+ If you can do nothing about it, why are you holding on to it?
+ When you can do something about it, the problem becomes a "situation" that you can meet using your experience, insights and values.
+ The useful questions are: "What's needed here?" or "How would a wise and experienced person deal with this situation?" (If the "situation" is complex or tough, write down the questions and spend time writing out the answers. Let the dross emerge; then the gold.)

You can make a decision that you won't add pain to the problem by beating yourself up.

+ Hovering over the problem and rehearsing your total hopelessness, incompetence, stupidity, etc., etc., guarantees misery.
+ Paying attention to what's needed, and taking appropriate action, right now, guarantees a burst of energy and lifting of spirits as your creativity ignites.

You can give up identifying with your problems. This means giving up describing yourself using "problem" terms; talking incessantly about your problems; "watering them" with your attention, "growing them" in your mind.

✦ See yourself as someone who can meet complex situations as they arise.

✦ Strengthen your identification as someone who is unafraid to meet life.

✦ Focus on what's needed in the present moment, not two days or two years from now.

✦ Know that when your mind is less cluttered by fear and second-guessing, you can deal with real situations far more effectively.

✦ Know that all the strengths, values and insights you need already live in you. You have only to activate them.

THE POWER OF "AS IF"

Acting or behaving "as if" you were the wise, calm, confident or creative person you want to be is magically effective. It's highly motivating and energizing; it also sends powerful signals to you as well as others about the direction in which you are heading.

Acting "as if" is not fake, false or "pretending." It's a very real way to access genuine potentials that may otherwise remain dormant.

YOUR LIFE, YOUR TIME

Time is your greatest resource. This doesn't mean that you should "use" every moment. On the contrary, neither you nor time exists simply to be devoured. However, comprehending how brief your life is, and how precious time is, the way you use time will begin to look very different to you.

Some of what you are "putting off" may come closer.
Some of what seems to matter will no longer matter.

Your sense of purpose may also look different to you.
Your goals may change.

Let time serve you

Dare to ask: "If I had a year to live, six months, one month—would I now do anything differently?"

DANGER! LEISURE AHEAD

Have you had the experience of getting up after a long evening "relaxing" in front of the television or your computer screen and finding that you are feeling low in mood or irritable and dissatisfied?

Have you sometimes spent a longed-for morning with the newspapers, only to feel empty rather than energized and renewed?

Living breathlessly, many of us ache for "free" time and the chance to be spontaneous. But the truth is, as delicious as such time can be, without a sense of purpose and goals, with nothing to motivate us, harness our feelings, and stimulate and shape our thoughts, most of us do pretty badly.

Rather quickly, we feel bored. Then depressed. And when shapeless days loom ahead into an indeterminate future, we may despair.

Sigmund Freud, father of psychoanalysis, was adamant that human beings need work as well as love. Work—by which he meant paid or unpaid work that has structure and purpose—gives our days a shape. It provides social contact and a sense of usefulness. More crucially, work *organizes us internally*. Without stimulation and social anchors, we can feel dangerously adrift.

We may protest about how much work preoccupies us. We may complain about the meaninglessness of some of what we do. We often complain about our boss, employees or colleagues. Yet our gratitude for having work usually extends beyond our paycheck.

However—and it's a big proviso—one of the happiest groups in all Western societies are active retirees. These are people who are no longer in full-time paid employment but still feel useful, engaged, motivated and alive.

This group proves three things:

+ We need purpose and structure to feel fully alive.
+ Our minds need stimulation to keep our spirits up and our feelings positive.
+ Goals don't have to be (paid) work-driven to be of value.

THINK HARDER AND DEEPER

Whatever your age, you will feel best when you are doing one or all of the following (few of which resemble most of our holiday activities!):

+ Solving a problem
+ Meeting a challenge
+ Finding out or experiencing something new.

Worthwhile shared pursuits also lift our spirits. And psychological research has shown that the more worthwhile it is, the more alive we feel, whether it's fighting bushfires, helping out bereaved neighbors, working to raise money for the local preschool or joining an environmental renewal program.

This doesn't mean that chilling out, reading a trashy novel, watching some mindless television, or "doing nothing" is bad. In small doses, it may be fine. But our hungry minds need more.

"Activity" can include times of stillness and silence, reading, thinking, meditating, daydreaming: all of these can be uplifting and highly constructive. It's the *content that counts*. And the variety.

Let your body guide you

Your body is a highly reliable guide to what's serving your mind and feelings. When the way you are spending your time leaves you feeling flat, heavy, empty, weary, irritable or depressed, *take notice*.

Then take action.

UNWRAP YOUR MOTIVES

The way in which you approach and engage with a task, a situation or a person will differ greatly depending on what your motivation is. Yet we easily overlook this. All too often, we take motivation for granted. Or we hold on to the usual socialized reasons for doing things ("Everyone wants to have a baby by the time they are thirty") without perhaps going a little deeper and asking, "What's driving *me* in this situation?"

You might, for example, want to get work that pays well. Your father employs you. He does pay you well. But what he wants is for you to love his business as much as he does. He wants you to identify with it—as he has. (Doing that, you will not just be working for the business he cares about. You will be modeling your life on his; mirroring back to him the values he has lived throughout his adult lifetime.) You, meantime, are thinking that if you can save enough in a couple of years you can leave to study in France. That's what you most want. Neither of you tells the other what your agenda is. Smiles turn to disappointment, frustration and anger.

Without awareness of what's driving us (and without some awareness of what is driving or motivating the people closely engaged with us), we can far more easily be disappointed or even hurt. We may also disappoint or hurt other people.

Even when we try to be conscious of what's driving our choices, or motivating us to make particular decisions, there will be much that we overlook.

Our unconscious drives and our biological drives remain strong throughout our lifetime, often pushing us into situations that—if we saw them consciously and clearly—we would do almost anything to avoid. (Sometimes our unconscious also pushes us into situations that benefit us greatly! Those are the situations where we might say, "If I'd known how hard this was I would never have done it. But I am so glad that I did.")

In learning to understand your motives, trust your choices, and to make choices and decisions with greater engagement and awareness, these questions can be unexpectedly useful:

- What do I want from this person or situation? What am I hoping my connection (or involvement with the situation) will bring to me and to them?
- What am I willing to give? What am I *not* willing to give?
- What am I "acting out" through my choices and behavior?
- What part do responsibility and commitment have here—if any?
- What's the underlying basis of this situation or relationship? Do we both (all) understand that? Have I ever inquired what the other person's expectations or hopes are?
- Is this the best way that I can get what I believe I am needing or wanting?
- What are the needs that I hope to meet? Beyond the most obvious, what could be driving this choice?
- Is this kind of choice familiar? Does it mark (or promise?) a new chapter? If it promises something different, what is that promise?
- Where there are problems, is this because of differences in motivation and understanding? If so, how could we come to a greater mutual understanding?

Of course, some situations are straightforward. You need a job. The local video store needs an employee. You do your work cheerfully. You get paid adequately. End of story. But many situations are much less clear-cut than that.

Where you are making a major decision, or find yourself caught in a situation that feels uncomfortable—especially when there is something of a pattern developing—it can be immensely useful to explore these questions in your journal.

Come back to the same questions as often as you need to. You may discover that your motivation was crass! Or that it was very different from what you were telling yourself. This can happen to any of us. Discovering this doesn't make it more difficult to deal with the situation honestly and straightforwardly; it can make it clearer. ("I want this job to provide me with an income. I will get my needs met elsewhere for making friends and being creative.")

An exploration like this one clarifies your motives. Even more crucially, it increases your power to choose.

THE POWER OF PURPOSE

You can only become what you dare to imagine.

Purpose goes way beyond intention. It embraces the inner picture you have of yourself and your sense of what's possible.

Purpose gives your life continuity, while supporting you to be alive in the present moment.

No one else can "give" you purpose; only you can discover and live it.

Purpose lets you know:

✦ What kind of person you are and want to be
✦ What kind of life you want to live
✦ What "trace" you want to leave behind.

Discovering your purpose is your journey.
Discovering your purpose is central to the great adventure of living.
Discovering purpose is also about discovering love: what you love to do; what makes you feel most alive; what brings you most easily into connection with others; what brings and gives happiness.

A brand-new day

Focusing on your intention each morning is a powerful way to begin your day. Even when your intention is familiar, experience it as though the thought itself was newly born *this* morning.

YOU DON'T HAVE TO BE A STAR!

Finding and using your gifts, and allowing your gifts to help you find and deepen your sense of purpose, releases you from the mad notion that we should all be trying to be "stars."

The greatest souls are rarely "stars"—or need to be.

Finding and using your gifts means something far simpler and more liberating:

+ Bringing yourself to whatever you do; making it your own in the way you do it
+ Allowing yourself to be absorbed by what you do; surrendering to it
+ Letting yourself be a complete beginner—repeatedly
+ Trying things that interest you whether or not you are "good at them"
+ Celebrating the positive emotions.

VALUE OTHERS' GIFTS

Most of us can rise to an occasion. However, in valuing life, and living purposefully and well, it really is the little things that count.

The people who bring a note of grace and beauty, kindness and friendliness, good humor and patience to the smallest moments of connection, *truly transform all of our lives.*

I am thinking of hospital cleaners and porters who may attend to the spirits of patients in ways doctors rarely do.

I am thinking of the bank clerks, supermarket checkout workers and school secretaries who give that precious moment of time to make eye contact as they wish you well.

I am thinking of the teachers who greet each child each morning with fresh enthusiasm and delight.

I am thinking of the children who make other children laugh, feel welcome, and include everyone in play.

I am thinking of council workers and gardeners who often go way beyond making our public spaces clean; they also make them beautiful.

I am thinking of the countless carers of the very young and old, the very sick, the very needy and demanding, who give something newly generous, day after day.

I am thinking of the women in refugee camps who keep their children and tiny shelters clean, and grow a tiny patch of vegetables or flowers, in the most arduous and demeaning conditions.

I am thinking of those who pray unconditionally and universally, making no one more important than another and leaving no one out.

HOW TO LET YOUR VALUES
AND GOALS WORK FOR YOU

Essential insights

✦ Value your entire existence: strengths, experiences, challenges, failures. In the course of a lifetime, you can't know which events will have the greatest impact.

✦ Valuing your own life, you will take fewer harmful risks. You will treat yourself with compassion and love. (And give happiness a chance.)

✦ Value your time (and yourself!)—more than your hourly rate.

✦ The value of your life extends way beyond what you "do."

✦ Valuing the gift of your own life, you will recognize and value all of life. And *life itself*.

✦ Your values operate in every aspect of your life, including your work. The workplace provides repeated opportunities to practice living out your highest values.

✦ Values are not something merely to "live up to." Values "gain value" only when you allow them to support you.

✦ You can choose to hold even the highest values. You may not always live them out, but they can continue to inspire and support you.

✦ Your values give you a stable basis for principle-centered living. This frees you from entering unforeseen situations (conflict, loss, disappointment) "helpless" and unprepared.

✦ Your behavior and choices are a true expression of your values. Actions really do speak louder than words.

✦ You are inevitably affected by society's values. This makes it more important to know what yours are.

✦ The majority of people do not set goals. Most successful and creative people do.

✦ Choosing and meeting your goals, you give your life shape as well as direction.

Essential actions

✦ Choose your own values. Make them "real" by writing them down. They may change over your lifetime but choosing is an essential act of maturity and self-assertion.

✦ Behave in the same way across all areas of your life. Practice the same values at work as you do at home. This makes you more straightforward; it also enhances your stability and well-being.

✦ Use your values in complex situations. Ask: "Which choice supports and reflects my values?"

✦ Don't impose your values—live them out instead. If you influence others positively, that's a bonus. But it's secondary to honoring your own life by living it the best way you can.

✦ When you want to make a change, raise your standards.

✦ Align your goals with your values.

✦ Value other people's gifts and strengths. This becomes much easier once you value your own. It also saves you from wishing you were living someone else's life—rather than yours.

✦ Set small goals as well as big. Small goals help you practice keeping promises to yourself. They are also clarifying. Write them down. This is far more effective than just thinking about them.

✦ Value tenacity. Often you achieve greater results after false starts than if the path is smooth and easy.

✦ Recognize the difference between problems and inconveniences. Use your creative mind to problem-solve. Frame and ask questions; write them in your journal; let them "rest": put your unconscious mind to work.

✦ Value process as well as goals. Allow yourself to be fully present; it transforms everything.

✦ Celebrate achievement. It's easy to pay attention to what didn't happen, what went wrong, what should have happened. Rejoice in what is right.

✦ Never wait to "feel like it" before doing something that needs doing. Get started; it's the finest motivator. And it lifts your spirits.

✦ Set goals for all areas of your life, including your social and spiritual development. Choose what connects you to others; what expresses love, interest, forgiveness, tolerance. Greater happiness will inevitably follow.

Choose your attitudes and responses

It's not your money that counts
Basic attitudes, profound effects
The greatest attitude of all is love
Your attitudes are contagious
Peace on earth?
Striving and straining
Too fat? Too thin? Not rich enough?
Follow the clues to find your attitudes
Eavesdrop on your self-talk
Think of life as a series of imperfect facts
Thoughts can be changed
How thoughts work
You are not at the mercy of your own thinking
Positive thoughts are not enough
Drop those limiting perceptions
"I don't feel like it"
Choose like an adult
Facts are not fate
The invaluable moment of choice
Other people, your guilt
"I can't stop. My habits are stronger than I am"
Live encouragingly
Value what you can give
You are bigger than your dress size
Saying no as well as yes
A declaration of personal choice
Focus on process not applause
Practice gratitude

IT'S NOT YOUR MONEY THAT COUNTS

It's not your wealth, success, beauty or social standing that determines the quality of your life. It's your attitude—to life itself.

Even better, attitude, beyond anything else, can change. From one moment to the next, your life can look, feel and *be* quite different.

We don't see things as they are, said writer Anaïs Nin. *We see things as we are.*

BASIC ATTITUDES, PROFOUND EFFECTS

Conscious of it or not, *you have a basic attitude toward life and living.*

This gets expressed and lived out through countless thoughts, beliefs and assumptions that profoundly affect not only the way you see things, but also how you unconsciously invite other people to "see" and respond to you.

You can't really make any kind of claim to self-knowledge without knowing what your basic attitudes are.

Here is a list of positive attitudes. Take time to see if your attitudes are reflected here—or if these attitudes prompt you to see your own attitudes more clearly.

◆ Life is a gift.
◆ No one is condemned by their past.
◆ I can survive and learn from setbacks.
◆ Change is possible.
◆ Other people's lives matter.
◆ We all have something of value to contribute.
◆ I can afford to be generous.
◆ I can survive things not always going my way.
◆ My life is part of something awesome.
◆ I believe in something greater than myself.

Your attitudes drive all kinds of unconscious choices as well as conscious ones. *Know what they are.*

THE GREATEST ATTITUDE OF ALL IS LOVE

Love can be your context, inspiration, consolation and joy. What's more, it doesn't have to be romantic love, or love for one special person. It can be a love for life, for the goodness and kindness that is in the world, despite the misery. It can be love for nature. It can be love for friendliness as well as for friendship. It can be love for the opportunities that present themselves on a daily basis to be more open, alive and involved. It can be love for what is touching and healing and beautiful and true.

YOUR ATTITUDES ARE CONTAGIOUS

Your attitudes shape your inner world. They also profoundly affect other people. *Attitude is expressed through presence*—before a single word is spoken.

Just think about the difference in atmosphere created by someone who is good-humored and relaxed—and a tense, uptight person. Both may be on their "best behavior," but you can literally feel the shifts in energy each of those people creates.

What they are expressing is not simply a "good" or "bad" mood, but attitude. And you, in turn, experience an immediate physical response to that attitude.

Be aware that these effects do not run in one direction only. *Your* presence, *your* attitudes, also affect every person and situation, no matter how powerless you may be feeling.

You are affecting other people constantly.

You are experienced by others in all kinds of subliminal as well as more conscious ways. When your attitude is at odds with your overt behavior, it's *your attitude that will leave the strongest and most lasting impression.*

Cultivate attitudes that support your finest vision of living. Then let yourself live them out.

PEACE ON EARTH?

Peacemaking is a shared responsibility. Each of us contributes, moment by moment, to more peace in the world—or less.

If we want to live in greater peace (and who doesn't?), we have to come to a state of peace within ourselves.

There is nothing that speaks more clearly about the relationship between our inner worlds and the world around us than the presence or absence of peace. Step into a peaceful atmosphere and your whole being surrenders in relief.

We need to create that atmosphere, commit to it, live in it—and know that is what we are also giving to other people.

It must start with ending the violence of self-criticism and self-hatred, and be sustained by thinking more peacefully and with much more gratitude about our own beautiful selves. Self-acceptance is a peaceful action. It leads inevitably to greater acceptance of other people—and respect for all.

Listen to Judith Pemell

The author of *The Soul Illuminated*, Judith Pemell has practiced Raja Yoga meditation and taught peaceful living for many years.

"When anger, fear, resentment, hatred, jealousy or bitterness exist in our community, even at the level of thought, there cannot be peace. Peace is not an absence of violence, but is present where there is non-violence at the level of thought. Attacking the self with criticism and negativity is one of the most common forms of violence … Peace begins with me. When I take responsibility for changing my consciousness, another giant step towards world peace is taken."

As a peacemaker

Peacemaking supports happiness. But it's no easy option! It calls upon high levels of self-awareness and self-control yet is a wonderful example of how values and inner strength can develop together.

As a peacemaker I will:

- ✦ See the good in other people
- ✦ Give the benefit of the doubt
- ✦ Treat myself and others respectfully
- ✦ Remove myself from harm
- ✦ Shield the vulnerable
- ✦ Reduce violence—including talking to or about myself angrily
- ✦ Refuse violence as a "solution"
- ✦ Listen with an open mind
- ✦ Cooperate with others
- ✦ Value community
- ✦ Practice forgiveness
- ✦ Offer encouragement and kindness
- ✦ Practice tolerance
- ✦ Notice my effect on other people
- ✦ Protect the environment
- ✦ See the unity in all of life.

STRIVING AND STRAINING

CATHERINE: While I do my work for this book, I am also growing a son. As I write this page, I have twenty-six days and counting until delivery. It's an amazing miracle to feel a baby move while also working creatively. Like some kind of inevitable ticking time bomb, my body, filled with kicks and tumbles, constantly reminds me of the person inside who is striving to be born.

It seems like the striving never stops.

Throughout my life, I have set goals and worked endless hours to achieve them. And hard work is good. But at times I can get so focused on the goal I want that I don't leave much space at all for life to unfold, or for destiny to intervene.

Every athlete, actor and musician whose work is based on high performance knows that when you tense up, strive and strain, you lose flow.

But this is something I forget.

I'm learning slowly that there are seasons in our lives when striving and straining *doesn't* lead to growth, or to success. When I'm heading in the wrong direction, when I ignore my inherent talents in favor of what makes money or holds prestige, when I conveniently forget or set aside my values and stride ahead anyway . . . at these times, striving and straining will not necessarily bring the rewards I wish for most.

Maybe it's right, sometimes, simply to be present to the moment and let life happen. To trust that life will progress as it should, and that we can handle it.

At 3 A.M. last night, when I was anxious about delivering this baby, my husband whispered, "Cat? It's going to be okay. You just need to show up, and this little life will unfold."

I love Luther's attitude. And I'll remember what he said.

TOO FAT? TOO THIN? NOT RICH ENOUGH?

Almost all of us spend significant chunks of our lives worrying that others will find us "too" something: too old, too young, too rich, too poor, too fat, too thin, too eager or too withdrawn. (Whatever it is, we are painfully far from perfect.)

Or maybe we worry that others might see us as "not enough": not smart enough, not young enough, not original enough, not pretty enough, not successful enough, not sexy enough, not important enough.

We credit those judgments to other people. Just as likely though, those are the harsh thoughts and judgments growing like weeds in our own minds.

And *those thoughts are not loving.* (They are not helpful either.)

You give enormous power away when this kind of too much/too little attitude has you in its grip. And you seriously undermine your relationships with other people.

It's hard to feel good about someone when you are telling yourself that they are judging you—and maybe condemning you. And maybe if they do try to reassure you, you push them away or disbelieve them. This, too, injures your relationships.

In this kind of situation you are giving power not to what other people actually think about you. (Often you don't know what that is.) Instead *you are giving power to the thoughts you assume they are having about you!* ("I know he thinks I will never get a good job." "Her father hates me. I can tell." "My boss never smiles at me when she comes into the office. She wants me out of here.")

Those assumptions are convincing because they coincide with your own worst fears. In fact, they *are* your own worst fears! You are attributing those views to someone else—but it's you who is driving them.

When judgmental thoughts persist, take a reality check.

- ✦ Give others—and yourself—the benefit of the doubt.
- ✦ Recognize that the judgments originate in your mind—and that you are attributing them to other people.

+ Know that you will read "clues" negatively when you in any case feel anxious or self-doubting. (Perhaps your boss isn't smiling because she has a toothache . . .)
+ Accept that you are not always uppermost in other people's thoughts. Most people are thinking about themselves, rather than you. (And perhaps fearing *your* judgments.)
+ Ask yourself whether there's a pattern to this kind of thinking: both a pattern in the judgments themselves and when they occur.

You might even want to check with someone close to you, "Am I often talking about how misjudged I feel?"

Most of us are highly sensitive about particular issues and this may even get worse at particular times. Once you get a handle on that, it's much easier to see how your own attitudes (and fears) drive your interpretations of other people's behavior.

Check if your "worst fears" arise from a guilty conscience. Is there something that really does need changing, doing or addressing? If so, take the assumed judgment as a useful prompt. Perhaps you are assuming people are judging you as "lazy" because you are in fact unmotivated, or as "obsessive" because in fact you are bogged down in detail, or as "secretive" because you are finding cooperative work difficult. Let the judgment (if it carries an emotional resonance) work as a useful if tough catalyst to moving forward.

Accept that you will be "too-something" for some people at least some of the time. This may say more about them than you. You will deal with it most easily when your opinion of yourself doesn't rest on *what you assume other people are thinking.*

Assumptions are not facts

It's worth writing on a small card: *Assumptions are not facts.*

Remind yourself that the worst judgments you will ever experience originate in your own mind. It's up to you whether you pay them attention.

FOLLOW THE CLUES TO FIND YOUR ATTITUDES

You can check out your attitudes *even when some of them are barely conscious.* This is because your attitudes are being lived out—perhaps especially when you are oblivious to them. **The more conscious you are of the attitudes that drive you, the greater your experience of choice.**

◆ *Watch your behavior—especially how you routinely respond to situations.* Do you expect other people to like you? Do you expect things to go well? Are you willing to give other people the benefit of the doubt? Are you honest when no one (but yourself) is watching? Is your stance basically generous—or not? Is it kind—or not?

◆ *Listen in on your self-talk.* Discover what you routinely tell yourself. Are you preparing yourself for the best or worst? Are you generally working yourself up or soothing yourself down? Are you recovering fast from difficult situations? Are you dwelling on small failures while ignoring large successes? Are you mostly thinking about yourself—or the world beyond yourself?

◆ *Monitor your body.* Our bodies are "speaking" to us constantly. Most of the time, however, we aren't listening. Tune in to your body and you will find out what uplifts, comforts or frightens you.

◆ *Monitor your emotions.* Know what jump-starts your emotions; when and where you feel "flooded" with feelings or highly reactive. Recognizing those situations and what triggers them makes you less vulnerable when the emotions are difficult.

◆ *"I didn't mean to . . ."* The things we "don't mean to do" are often powerfully self-revealing. They express our deepest attitudes toward ourselves as well as other people. Make use of those lapses, not to blame yourself but to learn what's driving you.

◆ *Observe what gets your time and attention.* More than anything, this reveals what you fundamentally believe is most important. Sometimes this is totally at odds with what you tell yourself. ("I love my family—but it's true that I'm hardly ever home." "I value my friends—yet rarely call them.")

EAVESDROP ON YOUR SELF-TALK

The way you experience your everyday life depends almost entirely on the commentary that's running through your mind.

Whatever you're doing, *if you view it resentfully you will feel resentful.*

Whatever you're doing, *if you describe it to yourself positively you will feel uplifted.*

Support that change physically. When you relax your body, and the muscles in your face, when you smile or sing or hum, your spirits also inevitably lift.

Here is an old story that describes the power of attitude. I learned of it during my psychosynthesis training. It is also told in Roberto Assagioli's *The Act of Will.* I read and tell it often.

Once there were three stonecutters engaged in the building of a cathedral in medieval times. A man came up to the first stonecutter, in the exhausting midday heat of a dying Italian summer, and asked him what he was doing. The stonecutter barely looked up. "As you can see," he said, bitterly, "I am cutting stones." The man waited a while. Then he went up to the second stonecutter and asked him the same question. This stonecutter didn't hesitate. "I'm providing a living for my family," he replied. Some time later, the man went up to the third stonecutter. Again he asked the question, "What are you doing?" This stonecutter put down his tools, looked up at the man asking him the question, wiped his brow and smiled. "I am building a great cathedral."

THINK OF LIFE AS A SERIES OF IMPERFECT FACTS

Like so many helpful insights that circulate today, "Think of life as a series of imperfect facts" sprang from a Zen mind.

I have used this reminder in countless ways for my own personal development and in my psychotherapy practice and spiritual teaching.

It takes a phrase like this one to remind us that very often our reactions and outrage reflect an unconscious belief that life *ought to be* perfect. Or that *our* life ought to be perfect.

Of course, if I were to ask you, "Do you expect your life to be perfect?" you would almost certainly say no. So it is worth checking how often you become angry or frustrated when something relatively minor goes wrong, or when events don't turn out in the way you most wanted. You may even feel insulted as well as outraged when life refuses to follow your commands!

Turn such moments into Zen moments: *think of life as a series of imperfect facts*. And know, too, that sometimes those apparent turns for "the worse" are favors in disguise.

Accept yourself and other people as "imperfect" also

In the same way that we can be outraged when life "goes wrong," we can sometimes react very harshly when people let us down, or when our internal image of who they are (or should be) is shattered by some very human behavior on their part.

Our relationships do best when we can accept that sometimes people will behave badly, inconsistently or thoughtlessly. Sometimes they will let us down. As long as this doesn't happen constantly, and is not causing us real problems or putting us in danger, it helps us as well as them to see these behaviors as part of the big picture and to get over relatively small disappointments.

Focusing on those disappointments, our relationships will weaken and may disintegrate. Seeing those people as flawed as we are, but generally doing their best, our relationships become easier, more relaxed and far more generous and rewarding.

THOUGHTS CAN BE CHANGED

No one is born with a bad attitude although it's possible that rather too many people die with one.

Why?

Because they routinely think negatively. Analyze a bunch of attitudes and you will see that they are driven by thoughts or beliefs that have for a whole variety of reasons taken root in your mind and flourished there.

However, *thoughts can be changed*. It is possible—even easy—to stand back from your thoughts and observe them. Observing your thoughts, you can experience, *"I have thoughts. I am not my thoughts."*

The capacity to observe not only what's going on outside your mind but also inside it is the sublime gift of human consciousness. This is the foundation of your capacity to exercise choice and free will—and to create change.

HOW THOUGHTS WORK

You can't change unhelpful attitudes unless you understand how thoughts work.

This is something to experience—not just read about.

When you catch yourself thinking the same thought or small collection of thoughts repeatedly, especially when they are affecting your mood or outlook negatively, sit back and watch them.

"Watching your thoughts," you will become aware of several things:

+ Your thoughts are running on a loop. When you are anxious or preoccupied the same "thought" tends to appear with monotonous regularity.
+ You can observe your thoughts; they are not who you are! (As the observer, you can "direct" them differently.)
+ Thoughts drive emotions: *as you think, so you will feel*.

Even when your repetitive thoughts seem to be the product of your anxiety, know that it is the *thoughts that are feeding the anxiety* rather than the other way around.

If you want to think and feel differently, it is immensely freeing to experience that:

+ Your thoughts are not inevitable.
+ Your thoughts are self-made.
+ Thoughts affect mood—not the other way around.

YOU ARE NOT AT THE MERCY OF YOUR OWN THINKING

You can lift your mood and shift your attitude in a number of ways:

Thinking about something else entirely—switching your attention to something that engages and stimulates you.

Doing demanding physical work, dancing, walking, listening to music, playing, engaging in anything that minimizes wasted thought.

Challenging unhelpful thoughts: "Are these the 'facts' or my dreary interpretations and assumptions? Even if they are facts, how am I going to deal with them?"

Writing your concern down and then taking decisive action. ("I feel like such a fool after going to that meeting unprepared. What was stopping me from getting ready in time? How can I minimize the chances of this happening again?")

Taking positive action changes your internal energy: thoughts, attitudes, mood.

You can also radically change your mood and even your mind by changing your behavior:

+ Pushing yourself to act even when you don't "feel like it"
+ Acting "as if" you were already feeling energized and active
+ Choosing to be with people or in places that are stimulating and uplifting, or restful and beautiful.

The outer environments in which we place ourselves—and which we ourselves create—are also critical. They have a direct effect on the inner environment of our minds, on the ways we think, feel and perceive. Changing the outer environment could be as simple as taking a long walk; rearranging a room in your house; gardening; visiting a friend, a park, an art gallery—or any place that is stimulating or peaceful, depending on your mood.

You can also use music or books to take a stimulating and refreshing "journey," giving your mind and emotions a break and changing and lifting your mood. It works best to choose something with which you need to engage actively—not just stare at (like a television screen).

Choose happiness

Recognize what lifts your mood or lowers it.

Make this assessment when you are feeling good.

It may help to jot down a few strategies or ideas. Then, when your mood is low or your thoughts are dark or overwhelming, *do what you know will lift your spirits*.

Don't ask yourself if you "feel like it." You probably won't. However, as you give your mind something more positive on which to focus, and as you engage your body more actively, your thoughts and especially your feelings will change for the better.

Two reasons for this. First: you are doing what lifts your spirits. Second: you are taking charge. That always helps.

POSITIVE THOUGHTS ARE NOT ENOUGH

Positive thinking can powerfully support you. There are countless examples in this book and many others about how thinking more positively can and will support you.

But many people have tried "positive thinking" and given up in disgust. This may be because in lifting your attitude—and with that your mood, outlook and health—positive thinking is not enough. (Good intentions are also not enough.)

If your underlying attitude to life is one of suspicion or fear, if you see yourself as isolated from everyone around you or regard your life as ultimately meaningless, then all the positive thoughts and all the best intentions in the world won't help you in difficult or dark moments.

Those moments will simply "prove" to you that your positive thinking is like a layer of rose petals spread across arid ground. As soon as the rose petals fade or blow away, the starved ground is again exposed.

Positive thinking can flourish only when it emerges from a positive attitude toward life itself—and gets lived out through positive actions.

DROP THOSE LIMITING PERCEPTIONS

We are all limited by some of our attitudes. Often these are hangovers from the past, held in place by nothing more substantial than habit.

The trick is to recognize that *they are not needed in the present moment*. In fact, they are hindering the present moment.

Looking out for *patterns of response* is tremendously useful.

+ "I panic if I am asked to do something when I'm already busy."
+ "I get belligerent and defensive when I've been drinking."
+ "It's when I am feeling unsure about myself that I'm most critical of other people."
+ "My feelings of loneliness are far worse at the weekend."
+ "I've never dared to apply for a job that I really want."
+ "I look for what's wrong—and then what's right."
+ "Teasing feels more 'natural' than praising."

Recognizing a pattern, you can more easily see what attitudes are driving it—and what changes need to be made.

It's acting differently that energizes and empowers you.

+ "If I'm already busy I now tend to ask my boss which job he wants finished first—rather than sweating about my own inadequacies."
+ "I can't afford to drink excessively. I told myself my drunken behavior didn't matter. It does."
+ "I use my negative thoughts about other people like a barometer: 'Hey, what's going on with *me*?'"
+ "I was sitting around thinking life had to come to me. It's really difficult to make efforts every weekend, but it's better than fantasizing about other people's marvelous lives."
+ "The thought of getting something that I want *is* terrifying, but not going for it was simply reinforcing a negative attitude about myself. I'm ready to be terrified!"

179

"I DON'T FEEL LIKE IT"

"Feeling like doing something" is not always the best reason for doing it. "Not feeling like doing something" may be just as limiting. It's immensely liberating to know that you can do what needs to be done *whether or not you feel like it*. And, as you do what needs to be done, your feelings, motivation and energy will anyway change.

Feelings are not always your best guide

Negative feelings can be highly seductive, keeping us stuck in patterns of apathy, depression, hopelessness or despair. Stepping over those feelings to engage more constructively with our outer environment can be tremendously helpful. As our environment and level of activity changes, those limiting patterns of feeling will also change.

CHOOSE LIKE AN ADULT

Your attitudes, and the choices and responses that express them, may be much younger than you are.

This is especially true if you are stuck in any kind of addictive patterns.

An addiction reflects a fundamental attitude that whatever you are addicted to is more powerful than you are, and that your fears, anxieties or limitations could not be eased or supported in any other way.

Challenge this attitude and the beliefs that arise from it, and you may find the addiction itself begins to look different.

Even in less severely limiting situations, you may "believe" that you are much less capable of change and choice than you actually are. Often it's simply habit that's holding you back. You have "always" thought, acted, responded in particular ways—even when it didn't get you what you want. (Isn't that a strange thing about human nature— that *we keep doing what doesn't work?*)

Forget the way you have "always" done things, especially when it's not working. Ask, *What's the best I can do in this situation, right now?*

FACTS ARE NOT FATE

Viktor Frankl, author of *Man's Search for Meaning*, was a holocaust survivor, brilliant philosopher and psychotherapist, and hero to millions—including me. He reminds us, eloquently, how attitude changes everything.

"Facts are not fate," he wrote. "What matters is the stand we take towards them."

THE INVALUABLE MOMENT OF CHOICE

CATHERINE: It seems to me that before we behave badly, there is a hidden moment of choice—where we actually *give ourselves permission* to behave this way. What practical technique could we use to signal to ourselves that this is happening? How can we stop giving ourselves permission?

STEPHANIE: I'd love to know what kind of situation Catherine is thinking about! For most of us, there will probably be a certain routine to those moments when we "give ourselves permission" to respond or behave badly. For some people, it will be yelling at their children or their beloved. For some, it might be drinking far too much. For others it may be a withholding of generosity or even fairness—not sharing information that would help a colleague; not taking your turn with household tasks; not "lifting the load," even when you perceive it. For some it will be saying that unnecessary mean or bitchy thing. For others it will be looking down and realizing that the entire package of chocolate cookies has mysteriously disappeared. And for many it will be imposing grim, angry or resentful moods on everyone around them.

Of course there will also be moments when we spontaneously let ourselves down. We say the worst thing; we let ourselves get exhausted and start to whine; we are enraged by an aggressive driver and start yelling; we put someone "right" when they are perfectly capable of getting on with things in their own way.

The most successful technique that I know is to STOP—the moment you recognize that what you are doing is not what you should be doing—even when it's what you desperately want to be doing.

STOP—in mid-flow, mid-mood, mid-word. However revved up you are, however driven you feel to complete your compelling drama, *you stop*.

Whatever you tell yourself, no one can force you to behave badly. You may have developed some habits of reacting that feel completely out of your control. And certainly you will have unconscious as well as conscious drives that can feel extremely powerful. But not even your habits or drives can make you replay behaviors that no longer fit with your values or benefit you and other people.

The moment you recognize that your behavior is hurting yourself or someone else—you can stop. **Awareness of consequences is key to conscious living**. It is so empowering to know this.

As you get worked up, you may feel as though you are power-less to stop. And if you are drunk or taking drugs you will certainly have radically diminished your power to choose. But you are not powerless. As you begin to write that hurtful e-mail, you can stop. As you open your mouth to say something unkind, you can close it. As you begin to collapse into your preferred pose of self-pity, you can straighten up.

Your power to choose grows with practice.

Before action

In the moment before taking action resides our power to do good, as well as to prevent harm. In less than the time it takes to think a thought, we are directing ourselves—and choosing.

Small moments count

Let yourself see that rising to the big occasions is not enough. Our lives are lived moment by moment, through countless small events. Let those small moments count.

OTHER PEOPLE, YOUR GUILT

I have observed with sadness countless times in my life how plain nasty people can be when *they themselves feel uncomfortable or guilty.*

Rather than acknowledging their own guilt (perhaps they let that person down, spoke unfairly about them, even betrayed them), they try to make the other person "bad." In psychological terms, they are projecting their own inner bad feelings onto the other person in an attempt to protect their own internal self-image.

If you are tempted to disparage another person, trivialize them or hurt them, ask yourself a few tough questions. "What's my motive here?" "What's my history with this person—or with this kind of situation?" "Is there some unfinished business I should be looking at?"

Making other people "wrong," "small," "bad" always says far more about us than it does about whomever we are attacking.

The same pattern can apply when someone feels consciously or unconsciously envious.

Cynicism or disparagement may seem to be convenient masks. In fact, the opposite is true. Cynical or disparaging remarks reveal a great deal more about us than the person we are attempting to belittle.

"I CAN'T STOP.
MY HABITS ARE STRONGER THAN I AM"

When "choice" seems like a mirage, use the power of your mind as well as honest information from your own body to create significant changes in action and behavior.

First:

> Know what your weak spots are. (I once had a client who told me her entire life felt like a weak spot . . . other than her sense of humor.)
>
> Accept that you do, in virtually every situation, have a moment of choice.
>
> Recognize that *your self-mastery and inner stability depend on that moment of choice*: recognizing you have it and getting better acquainted with it.

Then:

> Use your power to visualize (remembering that your mind thinks in pictures). Run a few "typical" situations across the big screen of your mind. *Pinpoint the moment when you chose badly.*
>
> Recognize the emotions, needs and desires that led up to that moment.
>
> Listen in to what you are telling yourself and watch out especially for any self-justifying ("I couldn't help it . . . if he hadn't, I wouldn't have . . .").
>
> Decide whether your needs or emotions, or your wishes, could be met in other ways.
>
> Rerun the same scene choosing differently.

You are now entering the same territory as elite athletes.

You can begin to change a habit and "lift your game" purely through your power to visualize positively. I love this!

Here's how:

> You rehearse a different response that reflects your motives, desires and values more closely.
>
> You rehearse it in detail, running it moment by moment until it's

"yours." Your body-mind does not distinguish between imagining a situation fully and completely twenty times, and actually experiencing that same situation twenty times. You can "get it" totally, using the power of your imagination.

Pay attention to the feelings; engage the "feeling" brain where real change is made. Relish the experience of self-mastery and choice.

When a similar moment arises, your feeling of choice will be magnificently increased. *Your "natural" response will be the one you have rehearsed.* You can and will act and behave differently. As you continue to act more positively, your experience of choice will grow.

Your body is also an ally

Often when you are about to make a poor choice, or react badly, you will have a physical response as well as an emotional one. Know what *that is.* You may feel tense, excited or sweaty. Maybe you are breathing fast or very shallowly. Recognize what your pattern is. Know what the warning signals are. Heed them.

Let your body support you as much as your mind.

Too nervous to do your best?

The power of visualization can also be used to overcome fear and nervousness especially in situations where there's an element of "performance" and you may be judged.

Use your powers of visualization to play the scene in detail repeatedly. See yourself moment by moment doing as well as you want. Refine the details until you are completely happy with them. Focus on feeling alert, calm, positive and excited.

Trust that you can coach yourself to act differently. "See" what you want to achieve; then make it real.

LIVE ENCOURAGINGLY

Nothing builds and conveys a positive attitude more effectively than encouragement.

If you developed no psychological skill but encouragement, your sense of yourself would already be stronger. Some people have this naturally; the rest of us are learning.

Encourage yourself:

+ Believe in your own strengths and qualities. Behave in ways that express them.
+ Trust your intuition.
+ Let yourself be inspired.
+ Tolerate setbacks. (They sometimes take you in a better direction.)
+ Learn from your mistakes.
+ Simplify your life.
+ Appreciate what you already have.
+ Silence your criticisms and complaints.
+ Talk about what others have done for you.
+ Explore your spirituality.
+ Cultivate your passions.

Encourage other people:

+ Comment positively ("I love the way you . . .," "Thank you so much for . . .," "Congratulations on . . .," "I have been so helped by . . .," "It was such fun when . . .").
+ Be aware of that person's strengths; focus on them.
+ Let small upsets and petty disappointments go.
+ Support their interests. Take a genuine interest in their interests.
+ Appreciate the ways in which they are different from you.
+ Take time to listen with good-humored attention.
+ Talk to them about what matters most to you. Share what's positive.

Check that your encouragement and "approval" are not conditional upon other people doing what *you* want. Then it becomes "controlling"!

VALUE WHAT YOU CAN GIVE

Each time you meet someone, give that person something that you also value—even if it's only your undivided attention for a few seconds.

Private feelings

There is no such thing as a private feeling. All your feelings get lived out through your attitudes.

Be pleased for other people.

Even when you feel disgruntled or sour, *don't spoil other people's pleasures*. There is so much honor in limiting impulses that are negative and substituting behaviors that are positive.

YOU ARE BIGGER THAN YOUR DRESS SIZE

It is a big call to recognize that it's *your own responses to circumstances that hurt you most.* So it's wonderful to know that your own responses to circumstances also have the power to heal and save you.

Let me share a really familiar example.

A friend of mine in her early twenties broke up recently with her boyfriend. Throughout their three-year relationship, her ex-boyfriend had nagged her about her looks and weight, despite the fact that he knew this deeply disturbed and upset her. (In fact, it's tempting to assume that he was passing along the "hot potato" of his own lack of self-worth.)

A month after their break-up, she was speaking to him on the phone and he began lavishly praising some other girl he had begun to see, emphasizing how skinny she was, how small, how good-looking.

From the outside, it's easy to see how his need to hurt her stems again from his lack of self-worth. But my friend found that hard to accept. Because his unkind words reflected the unkind words that hover in her own mind, she allowed them to become "true." *She responded to them as though they were true: as though her "worth" as a human being was tied up with her dress size.*

It took her several days to see that her emotional state was in part self-induced. Her ex-boyfriend had certainly triggered it. (And perhaps he inadvertently made her happier that she'd had the courage to end the relationship.) But his words gained their power to hurt her *because she allowed that.*

Here's what can help in those painful situations:

+ Freshly value who you are (a human being, not a dress size).
+ Recognize that other people's criticism and meanness say more about their state of mind than it ever could about you or your objective reality.
+ Choose to pay attention to what's encouraging; minimize the attention you pay to what's harmful. (Don't keep turning the same thought or mean statement over and over in your mind.)
+ Recognize your freedom to choose your attitude.

✦ Recognize how attitude colors everything that "happens to you." ("My feelings are hurt—but I am ready to move on: from that old relationship and also from the mean-spirited attitudes of that ex-boyfriend.")

✦ Consciously choose to look at the big picture rather than focusing on the detail, however compelling that detail feels.

Remember: that wounding, unkind, unfair remark always says more about the person expressing it than it does about you.

SAYING NO AS WELL AS YES

CATHERINE: For the first half of my life or longer, I truly didn't understand that I had the *authority* to choose what I would or wouldn't allow to happen to me. And at the same time, I didn't know that I had the *responsibility* to choose my actions and responses to people and events, rather than simply reacting based on my feelings of the moment.

Here's a hard question—why do so few of us know that we can choose? And if you wrote a Declaration of Personal Choice, what would that list include?

STEPHANIE: These are a tough couple of questions, but the reality Catherine describes, "I truly didn't understand that I had the *authority* to choose what I would or wouldn't allow to happen to me," is painfully familiar to me also. And although I want to cry as I read this, I am so glad that she has raised it.

That inner authority that lets us refuse to be treated badly or to treat ourselves badly arises from self-acceptance and self-love. **Without recognizing the value of our own lives, we cannot know how to take good care of ourselves.**

We might be able to take good care of other people. We may even be immensely caring of others. (It's not true that we can only give what we already have.) However, if we don't have that precious sense of our own value, we will find it extremely hard to judge what's appropriate in our relationships. We might become a compulsive rescuer who "needs to be needed." Or we might let other people make unhealthy demands on us because we have no idea how to set limits or that *we are entitled to set limits.*

We are likely to be confused about other people's demands, overvaluing their needs and undervaluing our own.

Self-respect, based on self-love and self-acceptance, changes the picture dramatically. "I am a person of value, irrespective of what I have done or not done. My life has value. I can treat myself with kindness, dignity and respect. And expect nothing less from other people."

This switch in attitude—which truly is possible—lets us choose to act in ways that do no harm to others but, most crucially, *do no harm to ourselves.*

What's more, our self-respect and confidence in ourselves can only grow as we consciously refuse to do what hurts, belittles or shames us, or what causes us to "split off" from ourselves ("I can't remember a thing about last night I was so wasted").

Catherine feels deeply the pain that so many people "don't know that they can choose." She's empathizing with their helplessness, their sense that "Life is happening *to* me."

This is not a black-and-white situation. Many people will make effective choices in some areas of their lives, even while they feel helpless in others. For example, you might function very well professionally while going from one abusive sexual relationship to the next.

This can make it more difficult to recognize your basic attitude toward yourself. Your accolades at work, or the admiration of friends, might mask a painful hollowness or sense of unreality that is only revealed by a crisis.

Looking into the heart of your life, you will discover that it is always your most personal, intimate "choices" which reveal most about your attitude toward yourself. Those relationships should never be less than the best you would want for someone you love. *Let that first person you love be your own self.* Then you can safely choose to love others and truly enjoy them.

As to the Declaration of Personal Choice, I am turning that back to Catherine, fascinated to see what she will choose!

A DECLARATION OF PERSONAL CHOICE

CATHERINE:

I can choose my thoughts.

I can choose to be optimistic.

I can choose to be daring, innovative and high-spirited.

I can choose to change my mind.

I can choose to act differently than my past may dictate.

I can choose to acknowledge my mistakes—and move on.

I can choose to stop replaying my past.

I can choose to forgive myself.

I can choose whose love I will return.

I can choose who has access to my body.

I can choose to say no without giving an explanation.

I can choose to remember that nothing lasts forever—"this too shall pass."

I can choose not to be defined by my external successes or failures.

I can choose to be different from my family without disrespecting them.

I can choose to focus on my strengths, and stop obsessing about my weaknesses.

I can choose to reinvent myself, or parts of myself that are no longer working for me.

I can choose to start over, every day, every hour, or even every minute.

I can choose to be happy.

Your choices?

I would suggest that before making a list of your personal choices, you explore the theme laterally.

Perhaps you could put the word "choice" in the center of a blank page and jot down your responses to it as you would in a seed meditation.

You may also want to consider other people's choices that you have admired, and draw inspiration from them. Or you might reflect on what you would wish and choose for your loved ones, if you had the chance. That may also broaden your perspective on "choice."

FOCUS ON PROCESS NOT APPLAUSE

Our culture is highly critical as well as competitive.

This inevitably influences your attitudes and judgments so it's marvelous to know that you can do extremely well—even excel—without judging yourself through other people's eyes or constantly setting yourself up against them.

In fact, many years of psychological research have shown that resisting the tyranny of competitiveness, *you will do better at whatever you tackle and not worse.*

This is because you are *free to focus on the process rather than on your fears.* You can afford to be fully engaged. Rather than constantly assessing your performance, and worrying about it, you are absorbed by what you are doing and giving it your complete attention.

You might now get to be "the best" more easily and often. However, this is secondary.

Your primary reward is already in place: *feeling better about yourself and better about whatever you are doing.*

When you no longer have to be "the best," or feel devastated because you are not "the best," and when you no longer live in fear of others' judgments, you will also see other people (and their needs, talents and strengths), quite differently.

◆ You can *afford* to be encouraging rather than critical—of yourself as well as others.

◆ You can afford to be generous rather than cynical or envious.

◆ Your vision of "success" can broaden. (Getting pleasure out of what you do can be your new hallmark of success.)

◆ You can see other people as friends, family, colleagues or neighbors—not as competitors.

◆ You don't need to live in fear of failure.

◆ Envy and bitterness can take a back seat.

◆ Your aptitudes and strengths can flourish. (Hurrah!)

PRACTICE GRATITUDE

Nothing changes attitude faster than practicing gratitude.

Thank people for everything they do for you.

Look for opportunities to express pleasure in what comes your way.

Focus on what's uplifting.

See more and more to be pleased about. Comment on that.

Monitor what you talk about. Complain less. Or not at all!

Treat strangers with real courtesy.

Treat family with real courtesy.

Practice kindness on the roads.

Wake up to all your senses: how they allow you to engage with and appreciate other people and the world around you.

Have something beautiful in every room.

Let yourself notice how much goodness is in the world.

Give thanks

Set some time aside to write down the names of the people who have helped you—and what you gained. You might be surprised how long the list is and how invaluable those gains are.

Don't limit yourself to those who have given to you consciously and wisely. Sometimes we are helped by people who seem to be blocking our interests—or by strangers.

Once you become skilled at noticing what you gain from other people, be upfront about thanking them and letting them know what's helpful. Be part of an unbroken chain of appreciation.

A CHANGE IN ATTITUDE
CAN CHANGE A RELATIONSHIP

Attitude rules your inner world. And because attitude drives behavior, it also rules your relationships. **"Attitude" can heal relationships—or bring them to a painful end.**

Two (or more) people may feel blocked and unhappy. They may even be reinforcing in one another a "stuck" attitude that means both feel resentful and neither feels heard. Nevertheless, a highly positive shift in attitude remains possible.

Looking at the problem together already moves people into more hopeful territory.

- ✦ Resist the urge to see a situation from a narrow win/lose, right/wrong perspective. Look for the big picture.
- ✦ Take time to listen. Sometimes your attitude will change totally once you get to hear what someone else's reality is. *Your assumptions could be entirely wrong.*
- ✦ Make a conscious decision to look at a problem or challenge cooperatively.
- ✦ Use cooperative language: "This is a shared problem. What can we jointly do about it?"
- ✦ Speak up honestly about what you need. Don't rely on someone else reading your mind.
- ✦ Listen with interest to what the other person needs.
- ✦ Take time to respond.
- ✦ Focus on supporting rather than undermining.

Bring your attention back consistently to *how to support one another effectively.* This works like magic.

PAINFUL FEELINGS, PAINFUL ATTITUDES

Jealousy, envy, bitterness, resentment, hatred, cynicism are all feelings driven by attitude. Often that underlying attitude is one of fear:

✦ Good things happen to other people—but not to me.

✦ If I hold on to my pain, the other person will eventually suffer.

✦ My pain is real and familiar. Where would I be without it?

✦ Your gain is my loss.

✦ There are not enough of the "good things" to go around.

✦ Life (God, the universe) is short-changing or cheating me.

✦ I deserve more than I've got.

✦ It's not worth making an effort. I will only stuff things up.

✦ You have ruined my life and ought to suffer.

✦ As long as I'm hating you, we are still connected.

✦ Love gives me "rights."

✦ No one is worthy of my trust.

There is tremendous pain in all these attitudes; the suffering they cause can be intense. But sometimes the suffering that damages us most comes *on top of the pain of the original situation*. And that can be eased with a change in attitude. Here's an example.

Perhaps your partner left you for a good friend. You are doubly betrayed. The grief and anger you feel will take time to dissipate. They may never entirely disappear. They could become, over time, much less acute and much less "present." *But this won't happen as long as you are replaying and rehearsing an attitude that both expresses and reinforces negative emotions.* ("I was an idiot to trust him; people are not trustworthy; anyway, I am a loser.")

We do this not because we are bad or stupid, but because we are turning that pain in upon ourselves—even when we seem to be directing our rage or grief or outrage outward.

Beating yourself up, reminding yourself repeatedly how dreadful and unfair life is, denigrating a relationship that once mattered to you, making yourself small or helpless in relationship to other people: this does nothing but add suffering to your pain. It does not relieve your pain. It doesn't release you from it.

A change in attitude is needed.

HOW TO DEAL WITH A PAINFUL SITUATION

Often people don't recognize that there could be kinder ways to take care of a painful situation and themselves. They regard their thoughts as "inevitable," "natural." They don't know how to change them. In fact, it has never occurred to them that they could change them.

This can help.

Face the truth head-on. If your way of dealing with a painful situation is making it worse rather than better, only you can change that. You have to "take it on."

Take a few moments to write down what the original painful situation was. Describe it as though to a wise and accepting friend. Keep it brief. Writing it down is far more clarifying than chewing it over in your mind.

Now write down what your attitudes are about this situation. This may include some feelings as well. ("I feel so hurt and betrayed—and I have a right to that.") Don't judge. Just get it down.

Now write down what your beliefs are about how this situation has impacted on you; where it will take you; how your life is now going to be because of it. ("I will clearly never trust anyone again so that rules out ever having another relationship. I will be on my own forever and will be old and lonely.") Again, be as tough and as truthful as possible.

Rest.

When you return to these thoughts a few days later, make two lists. Head one of them up "Helpful attitudes" and the other one "Hurtful attitudes." You will see very clearly which of your attitudes go into which list.

If you have no helpful attitudes, "borrow" some. Imagine what someone else might do in this situation who has more resilience than you have right now. How would they be talking to themselves? What help would they be asking for? How would they be moving themselves through this?

Know that making someone else "bad," "wicked," "wrong" never helps you; it keeps you attached; it also discounts the good things you did share. This is also true when your *hatred or jealousy is directed toward someone who has what you want.* Those negative emotions also keep you connected; and they keep you small and powerless.

Once you recognize that you have two potential "sets" of attitudes, *pay close attention only to what supports you.* When the other attitudes flood you, step back from them mentally. Remind yourself of what you know; don't give them "house space" in your mind. Distract yourself by doing something that fully absorbs you. You will gain immense self-mastery through doing this; *it is possible.*

You will still be left with your feelings of pain. This exercise doesn't deny those feelings or trivialize them, but you will be able to endure them without adding to them through the agony of self-blame, blame of others and fear. Your feelings will have their season; and the seasons will change.

Remind yourself: "I'm taking positive action on my own behalf." "I'm getting through this." Or—my favorite: "Whatever's happening now will pass."

UNEXPECTED STRENGTHS

Doing research for this book, Catherine occasionally came across a survey or psychological test available online that she was so excited by that she persuaded me to do it too. One of these tests was the "VIA Signature Strengths Survey" <www.authentichappiness.org>.

To my total surprise, my top strength was "bravery and valor." (Catherine's was "spirituality.") Having struggled with self-doubt all of my life, and never more so than when I wrote about courage in my book, *Forgiveness and Other Acts of Love*, this was not a strength I would have identified for myself. The times when I have had to be "brave" or courageous have almost all been times of great sorrow, grief, illness or emotional hardship.

They were times and situations that I would have done anything to avoid. In the face of them, I felt at best inadequate and at worst, desperate and angry. I never once felt remotely "brave." Yet, somehow, I had to rise to those situations and meet whatever it was that was being asked of me (because the alternative was unspeakable). And, being somewhat driven, and psychologically tenacious, I did indeed learn something from them. In fact, as reluctant as I am to tempt fate, I have to say that those difficult times taught me invaluable lessons, and certainly brought a depth to my work and spiritual development that I cannot imagine acquiring otherwise.

This doesn't mean that I want more opportunities to be brave or to gain insight! On the contrary, I'd be happy to have the chance just to develop some of my cozier strengths, like "curiosity" or "love of learning." Nevertheless, I also have to face the facts.

The choice about what events arise in my life won't always be mine. There will be times when, against my desires and wishes, I will have to find the strength to move through a difficult situation, doing the best I can, however ill-equipped I feel. That's what "bravery" is: it's keeping going when we don't want to. And what has that taught me? That I cannot control what happens but I can summon up an attitude that supports me to survive—and allows me to gain meaning.

LISTENING IS AN ATTITUDE

Listening carefully reflects a powerful attitude: **other people's lives matter**.

It's only through listening carefully that you can leave yourself behind and enter another person's world. When you listen, you are giving your time—but even more crucially, you are giving your attention. You are saying to the other person, "I want to know more. I want to know more about you. You are valuable to me and my life." *This is crucial for intimacy.*

Nothing resolves conflict or hurt faster than careful listening. In fact, successful conflict resolution depends entirely on the capacity of each person to set aside their assumptions and their agenda—to listen.

Careful listening eases and often restores relationships. It validates the speaker's issue or complaint. It eases tension for the listener as well as the speaker.

Workplaces also depend for their emotional health and even for their creativity and problem-solving on how carefully people can listen.

People who "have a voice" at work, and can trust that they will be respected, listened to and heard, invariably report high levels of self-confidence and loyalty and much less tension. They are, in turn, better able and more prepared to listen to other people also. They solve problems faster, treat others more routinely with respect and have a greater sense of continuity between their home and work lives.

Not listening is a way of exerting control, but it is never healthy.

Listening is crucial for self-respect as well as for respect for others. It is the key skill of emotional intelligence; it literally has the power to transform attitudes and even lives.

Listen carefully to *how* you speak

People listen selectively and subjectively. Much of what they "hear" is unsaid. Some of that is colored by their own expectations and assumptions. Much of it is driven by your *tone of voice*, your body language and by what you are thinking but not saying. *Notice!*

CAREFUL LISTENING SUPPORTS YOU

It's fairly obvious that the capacity to listen carefully will benefit other people and markedly improve all your relationships. What is perhaps less obvious is that the self-control and focus that careful listening demands and develops also supports *your inner development and sense of self.*

The people who talk over the top of you, who never "shut up," who assume they already know what you have to say, who interrupt, top your story, put you right and control the agenda by returning conversation constantly back to themselves are demonstrating a lack of self, a lack of inner security. And certainly a lack of awareness!

It is only when you can trust yourself enough to leave yourself behind that taking in someone else's story and experiences becomes possible.

Practicing careful listening, and especially *giving yourself permission to listen carefully*, you are making your sense of self more real and certainly more stable.

YOUR LISTENING HISTORY

Your attitude toward listening was formed in your original family. Those crucial years of early experience will not only have shaped your attitudes about listening; they will have shaped your attitudes and beliefs about yourself.

+ I can afford to be myself.
+ My views have value.
+ I can afford to be wrong/honest/straightforward.
+ Who I am is acceptable.
+ People close to me will believe what I have to say.
+ My inner world is of interest.
+ No one cares about me.
+ No one could ever understand me.
+ I have never felt "heard."
+ Better not to get into the big emotions. Trivia is safer.

When uncovering your current attitudes to listening (both listening to others and being listened to), it can be extremely helpful to think back to your family's patterns of talking and listening.

Let yourself recall who listened to you in your childhood (or didn't) and whether listening was part of the family culture. Perhaps people "joked," rather than listened. Perhaps there were unspoken (but "heard") taboos on "suitable" subjects. Perhaps talking (and not listening) was a way of taking or keeping control. Perhaps you were told that you were "too curious."

Perhaps you heard the criticisms and not the praise?

Childhood patterns need not rule your adult experience.

As an adult, you can choose to transform your attitude to listening—and your experience of it.

As an adult, you can afford to let someone else have time to talk—or to talk about "difficult" or "painful" topics.

As an adult, you can discover how careful listening heals and supports your relationships.

As an adult, you can choose to be curious and to listen deeply; to talk about what really matters and listen to others' deepest experiences.

As an adult, you can set aside your own concerns.

As an adult, you can say no to listening when that seems appropriate.

HOW TO LISTEN CAREFULLY

Careful listening does not come naturally to everyone.

Interrupting, correcting, criticizing, complaining, offering well-meaning but unsought advice, launching into your own self-focused anecdotes, trivializing what you are hearing, dishing out banalities, ignoring the emotions that lie behind the speaker's words—all that is far more "natural" to many of us than careful listening is.

The encouraging thing to remember is that *all of us can learn to listen more carefully.* And this will dramatically benefit every aspect of your life.

It is also encouraging to know that careful listening is not needed in every situation.

On the contrary. The trick is to be able to do it when it's needed, and to do it well. Here's how.

- ✦ Clear space in your mind. Set aside your preconceptions.
- ✦ Relax your body. Pay attention to inner tension. *Focus on letting that tension go.* The less tense you are, the more comfortable the speaker can be.
- ✦ Give yourself permission to do nothing but listen: no preparing the brilliant thing you are about to say.
- ✦ Activate all your senses as you listen. Watch the other person's face, breathing, body and gestures. Listen to what lies behind the words.
- ✦ Be respectful of the emotions that are being expressed. Make an inner decision to accept them.
- ✦ Do not interrupt. Even when there's a pause, let the speaker have time to think.
- ✦ Strictly censor your questions—especially nervous or intrusive ones. They are a way of taking control.
- ✦ Value silence. Your listening, attention, facial expressions and body language are all "speaking." If the person is very upset, let them know you care: "I'm sorry. It must be so hard." Keep the focus on them, not you.
- ✦ *Accept the other person's experience.* Their experience belongs to them. It doesn't need "tidying up" or interpreting by you.

✦ Let yourself be surprised. Keep checking that you are listening to what the person is saying and not to the assumptions in your own mind.

✦ Do not top their story with your own ("I understand completely . . . in fact, I used to . . ."). If it seems appropriate to say something, keep focused on the speaker and their story.

✦ Do not give advice unless it's asked for. Even then, *hesitate long and hard.* ("I'm not sure yet . . . why don't you brainstorm aloud?") Giving advice can be nothing more than a way to deal with your own tension. If you must give advice, do so in the first person. And do it undogmatically. ("I might . . ."; "What's sometimes worked for me is . . .")

✦ At the end of the conversation, acknowledge what has been shared. ("I am really touched by what you've told me." "You've given me so much to think about.") Let the speaker know explicitly that you care.

✦ When you agree to listen, you also commit yourself to listening in confidence. *Never gossip about what you have heard.* If what the person is telling you is frightening or disturbing, let them know that they should call a professional helpline. If they are suicidal, get professional help *immediately.*

✦ When you don't have time to listen, let the speaker know that now is not a good time to talk. Make time as soon as possible.

✦ Use your listening skills to listen to yourself. Find out what you habitually talk about; know how your voice sounds; recognize the emotions that drive the way you speak; what version of your "self" you are most often presenting.

✦ Remember that careful listening is not only for difficult topics. Make it a habit to share what delights you.

If you are having a mutual deep talk, when you are both sharing and listening, ensure that you are giving more time to listening than to talking; that you are hesitating to give "advice"; that you are acknowledging the speaker's reality rather than rushing in with your own.

Be a person you would like to listen to: encouraging, tolerant, curious, warm, interesting, positive. It is possible.

Parents and older children

Between parents and older children (and even adult children), "conversation" can frequently deteriorate into giving and refusing advice. *Deep, appreciative listening is the only remedy.*

It cultivates acceptance and love. And it demonstrates it.

CURE FOR ALL CRITICS

Criticism can be helpful, even inspiring, but never when it descends into a chronic whine or becomes a way of life. If there is someone in your life that you feel especially free (or, worse, "obliged") to criticize, try this:

- ✦ *Every day* for an entire month, find at least one specific thing that you will speak about positively and directly to that person.
- ✦ Explicitly encourage, express gratitude or praise them.
- ✦ Take an interest in their interests. You don't need to take on their interests or share them; but offer your curiosity and willingness to listen as a mark of respect for who they are and what concerns them.
- ✦ Keep finding fresh, new things to comment upon positively— as well as what you praised yesterday or the day before.
- ✦ If you hear yourself begin to criticize, STOP. Leave the room.
- ✦ Only by behaving less critically will your habits of criticism begin to change.

If you feel silly or self-conscious, regard this as a tiny, private act of reparation.

You are doing this primarily to express your respect and affection for that other person and, only incidentally, to grow in self-respect.

You are not doing it for praise! And you won't stop doing it if you don't get enough praise.

Enjoy the benefits as the people around you respond, relax, rejoice.

Pressure points

Notice when you feel most critical.

Ask yourself, *what's going on with me right now?*

Why is it today that my partner's habits seem especially disgusting or my children seem "impossible"?

Once you recognize how directly your own moods affect your perceptions, it will seem far less urgent to lash out at others or "put them right."

HOW TO CRITICIZE—IF YOU ABSOLUTELY MUST

Criticism as a way of life is always lethal. And being around chronic critics is always depressing.

However, there are times when "things need to be said" and issues need to be aired. Catherine and I, in working on this book, have had to be very direct when something one of us had written or suggested wasn't working. We actually saved time by being direct, but I believe we saved each other's feelings also and I certainly did not ever experience feeling personally attacked. In fact, I felt encouraged by that directness and comfortable that I, too, could be just as direct with Catherine. Nevertheless I was aware that *this kind of communication has to occur within a general context of support and encouragement.*

Here's another example. Just a couple of days ago my daughter told me that I often frown when I am dealing with something that makes me uncomfortable—and that it makes me look "cross" even when that's far from what I am feeling. I was grateful for that feedback and immediately knew that she was right, even though my "frowning" had been out of my awareness. I felt supported rather than attacked.

It is possible to criticize constructively—but this should be done only when it is genuinely helpful; only when there is no malice or bad temper driving it; only when it occurs within the context of a generally supportive and uplifting relationship.

The Golden Rules for criticism:

- ✦ Keep criticism to an absolute minimum. Certainly check that it is only a very small part of your interactions with that person.
- ✦ Never criticize the person, the people closest to them, or their beliefs. Limit your comments to behavior and actions.
- ✦ Offer criticism only when neither you nor the other person is tired, tense, angry, sad or depressed. "Bad-mood thinking" muddies criticism.
- ✦ Be ready to offer something constructive alongside the criticism.
- ✦ Speak in the first person. ("I feel," not, "You always.")

Here's how to criticize (if you must):

+ Let the person know what it is you want to talk about. Don't make a big deal of it but check whether this is a good time. (Maybe they have just had bad news, have a headache or are racing to get away for a rendezvous with their lover.)
+ Make sure that you don't feel wound up or insistent that you are "right." Calm yourself and approach the whole interaction lightly. Ideally, you will both be learning something.
+ State the problem—briefly. Stick to this problem only. Do not take the opportunity to give them the benefit of your memory of the last five years' worth of errors.
+ State how you feel about the problem—not about the person. (When it's a work matter this is often unnecessary. Simply saying, "This isn't working for me. I think the point isn't clear enough yet . . ." is often enough.)
+ Make a positive suggestion if that seems appropriate and welcome.
+ Ask for feedback but don't insist that it's immediate. ("Do you want to get back to me on this or talk about it now? Either way would work for me.")
+ Be aware that often people will respond *not* to what you are saying but to their own painful feelings of insufficiency or uncertainty. ("Nothing I do is good enough.")
+ If their response is aggressive or defensive, drop the matter. More often than not, they will raise it again at a time that's better for them.

In both workplace and personal situations, where genuinely constructive, respectful criticism is consistently rejected or is taken up as a personal attack, you have a communication issue that needs attention. Asking everyone involved to brainstorm about how to give and receive information of all kinds, including constructive criticism, is a good place to start.

Any problem that is approached creatively and with respect and goodwill loses much of its sting.

LISTENING TO COMPLAINTS
(AND CRITICISMS)

Complaints and criticisms may be the very last thing you want to listen to. (And the last thing you want to offer.) You will have a much more relaxed attitude toward them if you know that you can take what's useful and deflect the rest.

- ✦ Pay attention to your body; relax yourself from the inside out.
- ✦ Accept that sometimes the other person is projecting their own dissatisfactions onto you.
- ✦ If there's anything in the complaint that's even remotely useful, acknowledge that. ("It's true. The rest of the team have been held up.")
- ✦ If there's nothing useful, simply acknowledge the complaint. ("Okay, I'll certainly think about that.") Don't get into defending yourself while the other person is wound up.
- ✦ When the person has voiced their complaint, they will often let it go—especially when you have clearly heard it. Very often they are wound up by their need to speak. Your challenge is to defuse the situation by hearing what they are saying while keeping calm.

Sometimes you defuse most effectively by saying you want them to get *everything* off their chest, rather than trying to cut them short. (Paradoxical responses like this one effectively break habitual reactions.) If it's a serious matter, acknowledge that and say you need time to think about it.

When you make that time, speak collaboratively, rather than defensively. ("I'm keen to get this worked out . . . as I'm sure you are.")

If the person consistently criticizes or complains, let them know that you want to talk about this. Use "I" statements: "I notice that I'm bracing myself for these complaints . . . maybe we should make a time to talk about the bigger picture?" Sometimes people are completely unaware that their own bad moods are spilling over into chronic complaints about everyone else.

IS EMPATHY YOUR ENEMY?

Empathy is a wonderful quality. Without it, the world would be incredibly unsafe. However, empathy can tip into a kind of anxiety that speaks more about our need to be needed or liked, or our lack of knowing how to care for ourselves, than it does about concern for and interest in other people.

I know that some of the worst judgments I have ever made have come about because I was afraid to hurt someone else, or of being seen to be unkind or selfish. In my confusion about how to take good care of myself emotionally, it often seemed much easier to take care of someone else. This was especially true if they were much better at stating their needs than I was.

Now I know that empathy and love are not well served if, in the process, we abandon ourselves.

It's good to be able to pause and ask what's best for the other person. *It's also necessary to be able to pause and ask what's healthy and supportive for us.*

And when there's a clash of interests?

That needs to be thought about with some subtlety. All I can say, from my own quite hard-won experiences, and from listening to many people in my years of work as a psychotherapist, is that we don't do another adult any real favor when we continue to rescue them emotionally at our own expense. If we feel emotionally exhausted, unappreciated, exploited or abused—and are tolerating this or even making excuses for the person who is acting like this—we do that person no favors. And we do ourselves no favors either.

"Is this kind?" is a powerful question. In the context of relationships, *it must run two ways.*

CATALYSTS FOR CHANGE

Change itself depends on attitude.

Here's a list of potential catalysts for change that includes some common arguments *against* change! Pick just one or two that speak to you. Ignore the rest—at least for this moment.

"I have a day left to live." This could be true. What would you do differently? How would you make it count?

"I am tired of being rescued." As long as you see yourself as some kind of victim, rescuers will continue to play their part in your human drama. What would allow you to see yourself as a survivor with resources, as someone who has learned something as she's gone around the block many times? List your worst situations. List what you learned from them. Know that what you learned is your greatest resource. Recognize your own resources and strengths. Become your own rescuer.

"I never ask for help." Why not? Some of us are too eager to be rescued. Some of us are too afraid to reach out for help in case it's refused, or it comes in the wrong package, or it makes us "weak" or it shows us up as needy. Experiment with the idea that the help you get is "perfect" even in its imperfection. As for being needy, this is part of being human. We all have needs, some of which we can meet ourselves, some of which are met through our interconnectedness. Receiving gracefully is as much part of maturity as giving generously.

"Nothing ever works for me." Effective change needs to be self-generated (not forced upon you) and incremental. The subtle stages required to effect positive change are easily smothered by global pessimism: "I never"; "Nothing ever"; "It always." Challenge your global thinking with a touch of reality. Let yourself remember what has worked, what has gone well, what has been uplifting. *Analyze those situations.* What did you learn from them? When you hear yourself going into global mode, stop. "There I go again. How can I think about this situation more realistically and productively?"

"I have no role models." Find some. Borrow their qualities. Make them your own. No one has an exclusive right to the great human qualities. They belong to all of us.

"I'm depressed." Here you have a chicken and egg situation. You can't think about making effective change because you are depressed and being unable to make change effectively is itself depressing. Catch the chicken first. What change would you be making if you were not depressed? What would you be doing differently if you were not depressed? What do you currently envy others for; what are they free to do that you are not? Do those things. *Behave as though you were not depressed.* I do not mean change your feelings or thoughts. I mean, change your behavior. Act "not-depressed." Shift your body, get going with whatever needs your attention; focus on and meet a demand outside yourself. Even if you achieve this for one hour each day you will lift your feelings and change your thinking. When this seems impossible, seek professional help. Remind yourself: "No mood, good or bad, lasts forever. This will change."

"I want other people to like me." This is a powerful catalyst for change and a healthy one. Almost all of us want this; when we no longer want it, we are in trouble. Be a good friend to others, and friendly in *all* your encounters. But also learn how to be a good friend to yourself. Until you like yourself, it's a tough ask to want others to like you. Behaving encouragingly and with good humor is the place to start. Also check how you are interpreting other people's behavior. What you may see as carelessness or thoughtlessness may come about because the person is stressed or overcommitted. Or they may be self-absorbed in ways that limit their capacity for genuine friendship.

"My life has no value." I believe that your life has intrinsic value. Sometimes we discover this when we allow ourselves to value other people's lives more actively; to throw ourselves into life more consciously; to take bigger risks with what we engage with. For example, most of us feel most alive when we are contributing something of value—then we don't even need to think about whether we value ourselves. Volunteering, getting involved, reaching out: these are difficult things to do when we feel low. But the rewards are exceptional.

"Life isn't fair." Probably true. Currently, 1.2 billion people live on less than a dollar per day. Each day 40,000 children under the age of five die

of preventable illnesses. Each hour 1,200 people die of preventable malnutrition. "Fairness" is not a determinant of whether or not people appreciate life and see themselves as capable of making personal change *and* as a catalyst for positive social change.

"I can't go on like this." Despair can be the beginning of a profound change for the better. When we genuinely run out of energy for continuing with the life we have been living, we have no choice but to create something better. None of us would wish to hit rock bottom, yet sometimes this is exactly the place from which the most significant and positive changes are made.

"I *CAN* HELP IT"

Many people go through their entire lives enslaved to their emotions. When they feel angry, they yell. When they feel hurt, they sulk. When they feel confused, they rant. When they feel injured, they blame. When they feel injured or confused, they attack.

They genuinely believe their emotions are more powerful than they are.

Emotions *are* extraordinarily powerful. You need to take them very seriously indeed. You certainly need to respect them. What you don't need is to be ruled by them.

You will be far freer to feel a whole range of emotions, and not just those closest to hand, when you are confident that you don't always have to react in the face of them.

Sometimes all you need do is be aware of them, even while they are disappearing and making way for something else.

CHOOSE TO RESPOND RATHER THAN REACT

It's tremendously empowering to recognize that you have the power to choose new responses over habitual reactions.

When your mother starts talking to you as though you were still nine years old, *you don't have to react as though you were nine years old.*

When someone criticizes you, *you don't have to leap to your own defense.* You can assess the situation to see whether the criticism is valid, or if it reflects that person's prejudices and mood.

When you come up against a problem at work, or your contribution is overlooked in a meeting, or your closest friend says something that's unfair as well as unkind, *you can remind yourself this may be less "about" you than it is "about" them.* Then, if asserting yourself is appropriate, you are more likely to do it creatively and constructively than automatically.

Our habitual reactions are generally defensive. (That's why we often attack or sulk when we feel "injured" or under threat.)

Our considered responses are far more relaxed.

+ *They take in the complexity of a situation.* ("Mom talks to me like a nine-year-old when she's worried about me. I can tune in to her concern rather than how damned irritating she is.")
+ *They reflect the present rather than the past.* ("I can let her know I appreciate her input rather than feeling hysterical.")
+ *They reflect our capacity to choose,* and perhaps to change the mood and agenda.

Remember: you don't have to *react.* You can choose your *response.*

SET YOUR INNER COMPASS

When you wake, and your mind flies forward to the day ahead, take a few moments that can powerfully influence your day.

Set your inner compass.

+ Remind yourself that no matter how crowded the day is with other people's needs and demands, you still have crucial choices about how your day will unfold.
+ Consider what strengths you will need. *Trust that you have them.*
+ Consider what values you may want to call on. *Trust that they'll be there.*
+ Remind yourself: "Even in the midst of the busiest day, I can inspire myself and meet the day with confidence."
+ You may want to write down that quality that you will need on a Post-it note—or on several where you will see them throughout the day.

Catherine often reminds me that this is one of the earliest and most powerful "lessons" she took from my work. She says, "This works for me at the beginning of the day. And as a refresher throughout the day. When my anxious temperament prompts me to react rather than act, speak before I think, or jump before I plan, I've learned to pause. Those simple words, 'Set your inner compass,' remind me that I have the power to choose my direction day by day and *minute by minute.*

"Now when I am faced with a difficult client or a challenging situation in a meeting, or in a tough moment at home with my two little boys, I give myself permission to stop for a moment and think. *I reset my compass.* And I remind myself that I have the freedom to choose my response."

THE POWER OF PAUSING

Pausing—before choosing—is powerfully healthy.

Pausing and choosing, you hesitate to judge someone else too quickly.

Pausing and choosing, you say what's encouraging—or you keep quiet.

Pausing and choosing, you listen carefully and allow yourself to be surprised.

Pausing and choosing, you remember your highest values and are guided by them.

Pausing and choosing, you remember that other people feel as vulnerable as you do.

Pausing and choosing, you know and express the very best of who you are.

RESPOND IN SLOW MOTION

Reactions are usually fast, automatic and driven by feelings, not thought.

A response can also be driven by feelings, but not necessarily those closest to hand.

Choosing to respond rather than to react, *take your time.*

Slow down.

Breathe.

Think.

Act.

HOW ARE YOU AFFECTING OTHERS?

Most of us are full of opinions about how other people affect us. And there's no doubt that how others treat us does have a dramatic and lasting effect on our lives. But how we choose to treat other people—and whether we acknowledge our power to choose—is just as crucial in creating the person we are becoming.

You affect everyone with whom you come in contact, no matter how powerless or insignificant you may feel on a particular day.

The choice is yours as to whether you will affect others (and yourself) positively or negatively. Those "choices" don't affect other people only. They create the relationships on which you depend. They also determine how other people will experience and judge you.

KNOW WHAT YOUR PREJUDICES ARE

Responding is never a neutral activity. It is always driven by emotions, assumptions, preconceptions and prejudices. In fact, not only is responding driven by prejudices, it also reveals them.

> *You see a photo of an attractive young woman.* Then you discover that she is the person who broke your brother's heart. In an instant, she looks very different to you.
>
> *You hear someone laughing "too loudly."* You bristle. Then you get to know this person, and to enjoy their company and love for life. Suddenly "too loud" becomes delightful.
>
> *You read someone's résumé.* They are of a race or culture of which you know little, but about which you have strong views. You meet with that individual reluctantly; they break all your preconceptions.
>
> *You were raised to believe that people with different beliefs from your own were not to be trusted.* As you move through your own adult life, you discover how untrue this is.

Your responses are highly subjective. *And so are other people's.* Sometimes people are responding to you, too, not as an individual but as a "type" or even as a stereotype. This never feels good.

Gay people and racial, cultural and religious minorities in all cultures including our own suffer greatly from this kind of stereotyping. *It never feels good.*

We do this individually; we also do it collectively (the nation that was our "enemy" in one period becomes our "ally" or "friend" a decade later—and we respond even to the individuals differently). As prejudices change, so do behaviors.

You can certainly guide other people to respond to you positively through your own behavior and your inner attitudes. But you cannot control this. (They will also be responding to *their* own prejudices, assumptions and projections.) All that you can control are your own efforts. What remains most important is that *you* focus on people rather than stereotypes or preconceptions—and that *you* allow yourself to be moved and touched by the complex reality outside yourself.

YOUR POWER TO CHOOSE

Whenever I talk about the power that we have to choose at least some of our responses, I am asked two questions.

◆ "Won't this make me self-conscious and false?"
◆ "How can I choose my responses on the run?"

I love those questions.

To the first, I would say that in many situations we have no need to do anything different at all. No one wants to be monitoring their actions and reactions unceasingly. That would be exhausting. And I am not sure that it would be possible.

However, we do all have our "hot spots," situations that habitually trip us up and cause us to react to others in ways that may cause harm.

Recognizing those hot spots, in part through the highly defensive emotions they arouse, already gives you a head start in self-awareness. But self-awareness is not enough. *You also want to be able to respond and act differently.* To achieve this, it helps to recognize how frequently you are already exercising that power to choose.

Even the most "hot-tempered" person usually controls herself when she's in a meeting with a client or applying to the bank for a house loan. How can she do it everywhere else?

Even the "meanest" person may be generous when he's newly in love. How could he learn to extend this?

The challenge is to exercise your "best behaviors" always. And to recognize how thoroughly this benefits you. Saving other people from your negative reactions, you develop some invaluable qualities: equanimity, self-control, peace of mind.

We associate these qualities with the finest people in our society. But how did they get to be that way? *By practicing their power to choose.* That's all.

*

CHECK YOUR RESULTS

It's an odd thing that intelligent human beings can do the same thing repeatedly—even when it doesn't bring us the results we want!

You might, for example, always leave your report writing to the last minute—*even though you know that you will then suffer torments of panic and frustration.*

Or you might hear yourself criticizing a friend, or letting her know something "for her own good"—*even though you know that this undermines your friendship.*

Or you might constantly harass your partner, son or boyfriend to get something done that you believe is important—*even though you know you are making it less and not more likely that they will do what you are asking.*

Or you might regularly allow your children to stay up too late, eat too many sweet things and watch too much television—*even when you know this will make them irritable and you cranky.*

Free up habitual actions and responses. Here's how:

+ *Start with the results you want.* Think about how to achieve them. You don't have to do things the way you've always done them.
+ *Wake up to the incredible range of choices you have.* Look hard at the situations you do handle well. What qualities or insights can you borrow from those situations?
+ *Look at other people who handle similar situations well.* What can you borrow and learn from them?
+ *"Dialogue" with the wisest person you can imagine.* Write a very brief note to that person stating what the issue is ("Dear Dalai Lama . . ."), then write out your own imagined version of his or her response. You may be quite surprised and delighted to discover how close to home that "wise person" really is.

CHOOSE WHAT GOES INTO YOUR MIND

Feed your mind at least as well as you feed your body. Censor what is negative, dispiriting or disturbing. Those choices matter.

If you have young children, see it as an act of love also to limit their exposure to what will harm rather than nourish their minds. It's not healthy to watch constant images of violence or to listen to news bulletins that reflect our society's obsession with conflict. Little children can never benefit from this.

> *Choose to feed your mind* through thinking and acting creatively. Value your own creativity. Make time to develop it.
>
> *Choose to feed your mind* through opening your eyes to the beauty and wonder of the natural world.
>
> *Choose to feed your mind* by sleeping soundly, resting when you need to, listening to music that's uplifting, or absorbing with pleasure the healing sounds of silence.

It's as important to choose what goes into your mind as it is to choose what comes out of it in the way of attitudes, speech and response.

KNOW WHAT YOU CAN CONTROL—AND WHAT YOU CAN'T

As wonderful as it is to be sensitive to other people, this need not involve giving away your power.

How you do something, you can control.

How others react is beyond your control.

Their reactions may say far more about them than you.

Even their praise may say more about them than it does about you.

Your integrity deepens when you can say to yourself, "I have done my best. I am happy with that."

WHAT ABOUT ANGER?

CATHERINE: In high school and university, one of my closest friends was Lauren, a true free spirit. I loved Lauren's sense of humor and her relaxed attitude; it was diametrically opposed to my seriousness and anxiety. With Lauren as instigator, we cut our hair into outrageous styles, tried on micro-miniskirts, and learned to play women's rugby. I loved being her friend.

But there was one part of Lauren that made me extremely uncomfortable. She routinely admitted to being angry or jealous. And then just as routinely, she seemed to forget about it.

Unlike Lauren, I have spent a good chunk of my life denying my anger, wasting too much energy thinking in circles and not confronting people when sometimes I should have. Other times, especially as a parent, I get angry far too quickly and am ashamed.

I'm well aware that the world is already too angry a place. And I'm not so sure I want to add to that. My question is this: What am I supposed to do with anger when I feel it? Where can I put it? Where does it belong?

STEPHANIE: Anger can be a quick flare, easily forgotten. It can be an outbreak of irritation. It can be a slow, sour eroding of goodwill and kindness. It can be self-focused, self-righteous aggression. It can be rage. It can be a sadistic attacking of someone's most basic sense of self. It can be a mean spoiling of other people's pleasure.

My sense is that Catherine's friend was practicing anger "lite" without much substance. Does this matter?

Sometimes it doesn't matter. There are times when a quick flare of anger is appropriate and ensures your own safety or that of someone else. Anger can be a way of setting limits as well as expressing that you have reached your limits. Anger can also be a catalyst for action.

But, like Catherine, I am quite sure that the world is already "too angry a place," and possibly getting angrier. Countless people apparently have no inhibitions about their anger. They feel entitled to be angry. And, because they habitually allow themselves to become angry, they find more and more to be angry about.

I believe that aggression is the enemy not just of peace but also of love and trust. **Habitual anger as well as habitual passive aggression (sulking, stonewalling, "storing up" injustices) kills relationships**. It makes it really difficult to be around that person. It also makes it hard to *be* that person.

It is possible to use "anger" as a signal that something is wrong—and needs to be put right. Catherine regrets the occasions she has not confronted people, and she regrets the times that she flares too easily. "Confronting people" is often fueled by anger, but is *best done when you are not angry*. Anger drives self-righteousness and arouses defensiveness. It escalates problems; it doesn't solve them. Whenever possible, "confronting" should be done only when the heat of anger has subsided. As for flaring too easily, this, too, is an issue of timing. Here the regret is about not recognizing limits sooner; it's about wishing things were other than they are; it's about demanding too much of yourself and then spitting out your disappointment and irritation onto someone else. It's about *not noticing*; the cure is noticing. At the first burst of irritation and anger ask: "What am *I* needing?"

Take care of yourself. Then you can take care of the situation.

ANGER NEED NOT DRIVE YOU

The world we are collectively creating is our shared responsibility. Some of us certainly do have more power than others—but we all play our part.

When it comes to anger, we can add to the world's sum total of anger, rage, frustration and aggression—or we can reduce it. This is one of our most serious social responsibilities and how we think about it has profound effects on our moral and psychological development.

These insights and strategies can help—if you will let them.

Pay attention to yourself:

+ Know that whatever the provocation, the anger is in you.
+ The thoughts that drive your anger will almost always be distorted. *Anger prevents clear thinking.*
+ Sometimes depression or hopelessness emerges as anger—especially in young people. Take this seriously. If "everything" makes you angry, get professional help.
+ Monitor your self-talk, especially the justifications for your own behavior.
+ If you love the rush anger gives you, find another source (do something physical that is genuinely demanding: surfing, running, singing, deep-sea diving).
+ Don't use "angry" language—even when you are not angry. By this I mean, language that is outraged, insulting, violent.
+ If you feel chronically self-pitying, switch to solution-focused mode. "What does this situation need? What can I do to help the situation and myself?"
+ Know that anger rarely helps you. On the contrary, it almost certainly harms you and anyone who cares about you.
+ Surrender your childish beliefs that everything should go your way, or that life "ought" to be fair. They won't. And it isn't.

Pay attention to what goes into your mind and body:

+ Monitor what you eat, drink, ingest; how tired you get. If you are chronically angry, avoid all sugary foods, alcohol and recreational drugs. Get enough rest and sleep.

- ✦ Exercise every day without fail. Put this at the top of your priorities. It won't be the only "cure," but it will certainly help.
- ✦ Limit your exposure to violent media—or cut it out altogether.
- ✦ Passive entertainment like hours of TV can leave you feeling depressed, irritable and sometimes quick to anger. Use your recreation time more actively and diversely.
- ✦ Do much more of whatever brings you joy, happiness, delight, pleasure.
- ✦ Reduce stress by learning to think and react more positively and by making clear priorities about how you allocate your time. Anger can be a signal that your entire life feels out of control.

Pay attention to the situations you may experience as especially difficult:

- ✦ We often get angry when we are out of our depth. Focus on problem-solving in small stages. Be unafraid to ask for help.
- ✦ Avoid people who "drive you crazy." If it's someone you have to work with or see regularly, protect yourself by identifying which of the behaviors get to you most, and mentally practicing detaching from them. "There goes Ed again, asking me for twenty different things at the same time."
- ✦ Let people know if something really bothers you. "I hate being told what to do when I am already doing it."
- ✦ Know your own temperament. If you have a "short fuse" or a volatile nature you may be easily aroused. Tell yourself, "I can stand back. I don't have to let this get to me."
- ✦ Never, ever blame someone else for your anger. That increases your sense of helplessness—and it's always untrue. *You are responsible for your own reactions.*

Pay attention to what will help:

- ✦ Blows to self-esteem (fears of rejection, of being "wrong" or helpless) make us angry, but nothing increases self-respect as effectively as learning that you are not at the mercy of anger.
- ✦ Use the entries in this book that help you to switch on "soothe." Practice doing this on a daily basis if anger is an issue for you—or for the people around you.

- ✦ Walk away from any situation where you feel yourself losing control. Anger magnetizes you; pull yourself away from those situations.
- ✦ When you feel resentful, *deal with the problem by focusing on the solution*, not on how outraged you are.
- ✦ Train yourself ruthlessly in the practices of empathy; recognize that you are a unique soul, but sharing the planet with 6 billion others.
- ✦ In situations where you routinely get irritable, practice other reactions. (In stalled traffic, creatively review your plans for the day. When someone is late, consciously instruct your mind to *rest*.) Turn frustrations into opportunities; this will dramatically change your habitual responses.
- ✦ Slow your breathing. *Practice this constantly*. Breathe deeply as well as slowly. Angry people breathe shallowly and fast. Be inspired by the knowledge that the species that breathe most slowly live longest.
- ✦ When you are in the heat of anger, watch it rise *and fall*. Do not react unless you are in a genuine crisis moment and swift positive action is needed.
- ✦ Attend to what you believe is the trigger *when you are not angry*.
- ✦ Review your strategies to maintain inner stability, equilibrium and good humor. Focus on building strengths. Support yourself from the inside out.

Anger by any other name

Irritable, fractious, argumentative, sulky, withdrawn, edgy: these are other ways of being angry that may seem less dramatic than yelling or shouting but they can make it just as difficult to *be* you, and just as difficult to be around you.

Find the strategies in the above list—or from any other source—that make most sense to you. Get into "good humor training" fast.

GOOD HUMOR: THE ESSENTIALS

Good humor is the essential foundation of loving and respectful relationships. I value it almost beyond any other psychological strength, so powerfully does it support a stable experience of happiness.

Let me describe the good-humored person! You probably know someone like this. I know I do. And she has changed my perception powerfully of what kindness-in-action and happiness-in-action really mean.

Perhaps you are such a person already? If not, know that these are *accessible* qualities that will make a profound difference as to whether or not life feels good. For you, and for everyone around you.

- ✦ Reliable in mood—not hot one day and cold the next
- ✦ Cheerful
- ✦ Interprets events positively
- ✦ Honest and straightforward
- ✦ Gets over things; does not hold a grudge; does not sulk or "punish"
- ✦ Focuses on the present and the future
- ✦ Gives the benefit of the doubt
- ✦ Does not seek to make others "wrong," "small," "insufficient"
- ✦ Never says or does a mean thing "by accident"
- ✦ Does not assume that when things go wrong it must be your fault
- ✦ Has excellent self-esteem and self-respect
- ✦ Expects to be liked (and is)
- ✦ Is adventurous and willing to try new things
- ✦ Can tolerate things not going their way
- ✦ Sees the good in others
- ✦ Seeks out the good in others
- ✦ Is overtly positive, warm and encouraging
- ✦ Enjoys life.

HOW TO CHOOSE YOUR
ATTITUDES AND RESPONSES

Essential insights

✦ Your attitude to life is far more important in determining your happiness than your money, appearance, social status or talent.

✦ You see and respond to the world through the filter of your own attitudes.

✦ Happiness—like love—is itself an attitude.

✦ A loving, positive attitude to yourself, others *and life itself* brings your greatest chance for happiness. This can survive difficult and even tragic times.

✦ Our minds need positive stimulation. Most of us are happiest (and least self-conscious) when we are fully engaged with something worth our attention.

✦ Attitude can be changed in an instant. Feelings, behavior and responses will follow.

✦ You are affected by the circumstances of your birth and socialization. Within those boundaries, however, you have the power to choose your attitude and many of your responses. *Your power to choose is the key to happiness.*

✦ Your attitudes—both conscious and unconscious—will affect everyone with whom you come in contact, no matter how powerless you may feel.

✦ Your attitude toward yourself and other people determines the quality of *all* your relationships.

✦ A happier and more peaceful world starts with the changes we make in our own minds.

✦ The difference between reacting and responding lies in the moment of choice. *Choosing*, you are responding. This makes you feel safer; it also leaves you with less to regret.

✦ Your thoughts are powerful and determine your feelings. The good news is that you are not at the mercy of your own thinking. You can learn to observe and direct your thoughts.

✦ The way you describe events to yourself matters more than the events themselves. "Facts are not fate."

✦ We often respond to what we assume others are thinking or feeling. Know that *assumptions are not facts*.

✦ Careful listening expresses a crucial attitude: other lives matter.

✦ Understanding your power to choose, you grow not just in happiness but in inner stability, trust and confidence.

Essential actions

✦ Get to know which of your attitudes support you. Listen in to what you are telling yourself, how you are routinely interpreting situations and whether you are giving yourself your best chance to engage with life and live it fully.

✦ Make choices like an adult, not like a child. This gives you more freedom, not less. (Choosing like an adult means always taking into account the effect of your choices on other people.)

✦ Be honest about what gets your time, attention and money. Are these choices supporting the life you want to create?

✦ When you are spinning down emotionally, step back from your thoughts. Choose where your thinking is taking you. When your thoughts take you back into negativity, redirect them as often as you need to.

✦ *Pausing and responding*, relax your body first. This will positively affect your mind also.

✦ Peace of mind and happiness go hand in hand. "Peaceful" does not mean "passive"; it involves highly conscious choices that help you grow in self-confidence and maturity. Make three choices that will support a more peaceful way of living. Write them down. Talk about them. Live them.

✦ Know what is worth a fuss. And what is not. Monitor it in your journal until you are clear.

✦ If anger or any other powerful emotion is causing problems for you or others, review the ways to deal with it (page 231). Choose what will support effective change. Experiencing that you *can* change lifts your self-respect immeasurably.

✦ Listen with interest and respect: to how you speak to yourself in your own mind; to how you speak to others; and to others when they are speaking to you.

✦ Keep criticism to a minimum. Make encouragement (of yourself and others) a top priority. When you feel the need to criticize, *stop*. Ask yourself, "What's going on with me right now?"

✦ Practice gratitude. Start by thanking people for everything that they do for you. Train yourself to *notice*.

✦ Choose what feeds your mind, heart and soul. What goes in will closely reflect what comes out.

Build
self-respect

Self-love and self-respect
Other people's opinions matter. But less than you think
Give yourself good advice
Entitled to be yourself
Tidying up the people around you
No beating up on yourself
Small steps are perfect
Speak respectfully
Transform defensiveness
Detox negative assumptions
Solutions, not problems
When others treat you disrespectfully
"My life, your fault"
The power of forgiveness
Shame can be healthy
Guilt
How to apologize
Stop, in the name of love!
"I have to put up with this. I'm in love"
You can act differently
Coping with setbacks and mistakes
Think, plan ... and play

IN YOUR OWN HANDS

No one else can give you self-respect. After a while, no one can take it away either. No one can buy it for you. No one can pass it on.

Self-respect does not depend on age, wealth, good looks, status, race, religion or culture. In fact, some of the people who are most inwardly comfortable, and whose dignity, integrity and self-respect make them wonderful company and utterly inspiring to be with, have none of what "the world" values most.

Self-respect comes from within. It reflects and develops your inner life, your view of yourself and the depth of your appreciation for life itself. It also shapes utterly the way you see and interact with the world beyond yourself.

THE POWER OF CHOOSING

How other people see you and behave toward you inevitably affects you. But this is not what determines whether or not you have self-respect.

Your self-respect depends on how you perceive yourself and what choices you make.

Your life is made up of millions of choices. They don't all need to be made wisely. In fact, they won't be. But they do need to be made consciously, whenever possible.

You need to be conscious that this is *you* who is choosing, *you* who is acting, *you* who is reacting, *you* who is responding.

Your choices—especially your choices of values, attitudes and behavior—will shape your life more powerfully than your genes, social conditioning, upbringing or opportunities. They gradually form you into the individual you are becoming.

The power to make positive choices is arguably the greatest gift that we human beings have. It is the gift of conscience and of consciousness. Treasure it.

Listen to C. S. Lewis

"Every time you make a choice you are turning the central part of you, the part of you that chooses, into something a little different from what it was before. And taking your life as a whole, with all your innumerable choices, all your life you are slowly turning this central thing into either a heavenly creature or into a hellish creature."

NOT CHOOSING IS ALSO A CHOICE

Passivity is a quite understandable reaction to our overscheduled, overdriven, relentlessly superficial culture. But it is not a healthy one.

Not choosing is also a choice that will shape your character as inevitably as any other.

Letting yourself know that you are choosing, making your large and small choices consciously, and taking responsibility for them, are the basics for living well.

Self-respect and integrity depend on conscious choosing.

Who you are, and who you are becoming, depends on what and how you choose.

THE "TOO BUSY" EXCUSE

Being busy can be our greatest excuse for *not* taking charge of our lives, not taking responsibility for how we are affecting other people, *not* acknowledging or expressing our values—*not* being real.

"I don't have time," is a statement that is never more than half true.

When it becomes, "I don't have time to think about my life, what I am making of myself and how I am affecting other people," it is never true.

What's lacking is not time, but self-value.

TREAT OTHER PEOPLE WELL
— AND YOURSELF

Self-respect, like happiness, lives or dies on how you treat other people—as well as yourself.

If you behave reasonably well most of the time, if you are able to apologize when you have hurt someone and genuinely make amends, if you value "giving" more than "getting," if you are able to learn from your mistakes and move on—then self-respect is certainly within your grasp.

OLD FEARS, NEW FEELINGS

CATHERINE: Over a decade ago, I faced a thoroughly terrifying scandal and relationship breakdown. Both were caused by my own lack of responsibility and a series of small wrong choices, each leading surreptitiously to what became a grand public failure.

As a result, there have been times when I was afraid to open my mail because of what I might find there. There were days when pressing "play" on my answering machine took incredible courage. There was a whole year when walking into work made my stomach churn. Even now I remember and feel those fears.

Their relentlessness reminds me of the nesting blackbirds that would dive at me when I ran down the laneway toward home after school. Shrill. Dangerous. And always ready to attack anyone in their territory.

Whenever they surface now, my old fears feel the same. I look back on my life and wish I had done more to confront them: to talk back to the bully at school who teased me mercilessly, to put a stop to other people's intimidation, to find the courage to speak up for myself. I know now that I didn't have the tools I needed. And I'm not sure I have them yet.

Sometimes when I'm afraid and want to move forward, I ask myself the useful question, *What would I do if I weren't afraid?* And I try to take my own advice.

Still, I wonder—do our fears ever really leave us, or do we have to live around them forever? And how can we move through our fears from the past into a more courageous, open approach to life?

STEPHANIE: In the context of self-respect, and in the light of her own values, I would like to see Catherine experiment with looking at fear itself more compassionately.

The fears that she felt during that tough time in her life were a legitimate response to a very difficult situation. What else should she have been feeling?

She was making, at that time, a significant break not only with a relationship that wasn't working for her but also with an image that she had of herself that was pretty dear to her. Knowing

Catherine now, I suspect that she entered the relationship with the best intentions in the world, including the intention to "make it work."

But life is not always available to be managed (or ordered around) in the ways that we most want! We make all kinds of decisions and choices. We make them to the best of our ability. And some of them then turn out to be disastrous. Or are they?

One of the exercises I sometimes use in my spiritual development workshops invites people to reflect on seven key situations that have supported their spiritual growth. Participants take a long time to draw and write on separate sheets about these situations. Then I invite them to reflect on seven situations that were unwelcome, tough or even shaming, and to write and draw about each of those. Each person ends up with fourteen sheets of paper on which there are clear images of those two sets of events. And that's when notions of "good" and "bad" begin to break open. "Welcome" and "unwelcome" may still be reasonable distinctions, but there has never been a person in any workshop who did not express deep gratitude for what the *accumulation of experiences* has given them. Many say how much they have gained from the second group of experiences also—and that one set of experiences could not exist without the other.

When we are deep inside a difficult situation, it's quite natural that we would wish it away. And after it's over, we probably still wish that it had never happened. But our mistakes are also part of who we are; they are also our teachers—if we let them.

The person who has not been humbled and bewildered cannot know compassion.

The person who has not been afraid has had no reason to seek and find courage.

Catherine asks: "Do our fears ever really leave us, or do we have to live around them forever?"

And I would answer: We can learn to be less afraid of fear— especially by meeting it with love.

Sometimes fear is an ally, warning us off dangerous situations. Even when that's not the case, and what we are fearing lies more within us than outside us, we can learn to ask: "What is fear teaching me here? Where is it taking me? If I look deeply into the heart of fear—if I look at fear fearlessly—what will it become?"

I like Catherine's question, "What would I do if I weren't afraid?" Yet I would like to add another: "What does this situation need, *whether or not I am afraid*?"

DO YOU REALLY WANT TO BE WELL?

Years ago, when I was managing director at the Women's Press in London, we published a book called *The Salt Eaters* by African-American writer Toni Cade Bambara. I have never forgotten the first line of this novel (although I have read literally thousands of novels since and forgotten most of them).

In that scene-setting moment, one of the characters—who as it turns out has been having a rough time and believes she wants to change that—is asked a key question: "Are you sure, sweetheart, that you want to be well?"

It's an incredibly challenging question. And it remains highly relevant.

Being as "well" as our circumstances allow is a decision. Some of the habits that keep us back from being "well" (positive, enthusiastic, open, confident, hopeful) are very dear to us! It may even be hard to imagine life without them. They can feel as much like a supportive corset as like a straitjacket.

No one but you can change those habits.

You probably made them unconsciously; you can change them consciously.

I was reminded of this very powerfully a few months ago. The son of a close friend and someone I have known since he was an enchanting, constantly smiling baby, was admitted for the fourth time in three years to a psychiatric hospital in a state of acute despair and depression.

He is twenty-one, talented, lovely looking, highly likable. He has "everything," including loving parents, but his inner feelings were of devastating worthlessness and emptiness. He has struggled for years with an anxiety disorder, debilitating panic attacks, social anxiety and bouts of crippling depression.

Despite this, he did well at school. But since school came to an end, he has felt increasingly socially isolated and dangerously emotionally adrift.

Going to the hospital was a relief, he said. But after a week or so it began to be less of a relief and more of a confrontation. Despite earnest discussions with the staff and other patients, he realized that they could do almost nothing for him. They could adjust his medication; they could listen to him; they could challenge some of his thinking. But if there was to be a change fundamental enough to make the choice to live seem like a real possibility, then that change had to come from within his own mind and heart.

He had to activate his will to live, his determination to live. What's more, he had to activate his determination to live well—whether or not his panic attacks and social anxiety continue. *He had to accept himself.*

This was, for him, literally a life and death choice. And, ironically, it arose from a moment of utter desolation and loneliness when he realized how limited the help was that he could get from outside himself. His devoted parents and long-term psychiatrist could not save him, much as they longed to. Hospital could not save him. A change in his circumstances would not save him.

The meaningful "saving" had to come from *switching on his own will to live.* He essentially had to save himself.

So do we.

TO THINK WELL OF YOURSELF, CHECK YOUR BEHAVIOR

You need to behave well to think well of yourself. Or you need to be able to learn something of value, make amends and get over it when you haven't behaved well.

Good intentions are, alas, not enough. In one of the countless sweet ironies of human behavior, we tend to judge ourselves by our good intentions ("I didn't mean to . . .") and others by their actions.

To grow in self-respect, we must reverse this. (What a shame!)

We must scrutinize our own actions to see whether they are helping or harming other people. And we have to give to other people the benefit of the doubt that we have been liberally giving to ourselves. *This means assuming that their intentions were good, at least when it is halfway reasonable to do so.*

Of course you (and I) know people who appear to have plenty of self-respect despite behaving hideously. I would suggest that it's less self-respect that they have than self-importance. And I can see my old spiritual teacher saying, "And what person could possibly need our compassion *more?*"

Concern for others

Self-importance, self-aggrandizing, self-promotion are not signs of a healthy sense of self, or genuine self-respect. Self-respect *always* coexists with genuine interest in and concern for others—and a dose of good-natured reality about your place in the universe.

ARE YOU SUPPORTING OR UNDERMINING YOUR SELF-RESPECT?

Be your own careful and compassionate observer.

It may be helpful to jot down some notes over several weeks observing which of your behaviors and choices support your self-respect (and integrity), and which undermine it. ("I felt great when I made some coherent suggestions in that difficult meeting." "I wish I'd told Karen how I honestly felt about her being late again." "I managed not to speak to Teddy while I was still fuming." "I fell into the trap of getting too tired and then burst into tears when my boss criticized me.")

Note your excuses or self-blame, but *as if you were hearing them from someone else.* Don't judge yourself for them. Just note what's occurring to make it more conscious.

You are looking for patterns *in order to support yourself better.* Very quickly you will see what needs transforming.

It will also help to ask yourself in moments of stress or confusion, "What's the best I can do right now?" Let your mind go there—and *then* act.

BEHAVING WELL FOR A PAT AND A BISCUIT

Self-respect arises quite naturally when you recognize that you are responsible for the quality of your own life—*and for your impact on other people.*

Of course there are always factors over which you have no control. These will include social, racial, cultural and genetic influences. These factors may also include some things that you might call "luck" or destiny.

Whatever life has brought you, however, you can choose to cultivate your strengths, look for inspiration and learn to recover from mistakes. And you can make a profoundly crucial decision that you will treat yourself and other people with respect, friendliness and goodwill, whether or not those people "deserve" it.

Many of us "give" our respect (kindness, interest, courtesy) only when we think the person is "good" or "important" enough, or when we hope to receive the emotional equivalent of a pat and a biscuit.

But your behavior doesn't need to be determined by people or rewards outside yourself; *behaving well is intrinsically worthwhile.*

Recognizing this gives you the freedom to determine and choose your own behavior.

This doesn't mean treating everyone equally. Some people are negative or cruel. Other people will generously encourage and support you on your journey. Clearly you can choose to spend far less time with the former than the latter. Yet whomever you are with, you are free to behave well and to be guided by your values. This profoundly supports your inner stability and self-respect.

LEAN ON LOVE

Self-respect doesn't depend on moral righteousness; it depends on love. Loving your life; valuing others' lives; loving life itself: these are the ingredients for a self-respect that brings you to life, rather than dampening or squashing the life that is in you.

Making changes because of love, and with love, bestows a lightness and an honesty that the "shoulds" and "oughts" never can.

GROWING IN INTEGRITY

This entire book is integrity-focused. It is an explicit, continuing invitation to wholeness. Here are some specific ways to develop integrity further. (Read the list fast. Return to it slowly. When something captures your attention, focus and develop that idea only.)

+ Seize the courage to be yourself, considerate of others—but *creator of your own life.*
+ Know what's happening right here, right now. *Now* is the only moment when you can bring integrity to life.
+ Listen to the small, still voice of your conscience—it's the lifeline to your integrity.
+ Value consistency (rather than being the "life of the party" at the office and a "sad sack" at home).
+ Understand that your "true feelings" will always emerge through your behavior.
+ Know that your deep-seated beliefs will always write themselves across your face and shape your existence.
+ Be your best self with those who love you most; and with those who don't.
+ Say "No" to what is wrong for you.
+ Let yourself learn from all your experiences. Value it ALL!
+ Judge yourself by your actions, not your good intentions.
+ Recognize that a sense of wholeness emerges through accepting your contradictions: your shadow and your light.

Be aware of what you are already doing that supports others and lifts their spirits. *Do more of it.*

Be aware of what you are already doing that distances others or lowers their spirits. *Stop it.*

It also helps to let yourself feel your emotions. You don't have to act them all out, but know what moves you. Respect that. And trust your instincts. You may want to question them. (Sometimes they are assumptions; not instincts.) But get to know what your strongest responses are telling you.

Finally, but not least:

+ Speak up about what matters to you. *Let things matter to you.*
+ Pay attention to the small as much as to the great.
+ Release resentment. It holds you back and keeps you small.
+ Practice forgiveness.
+ Look around at the universe *of which you are a part.* Feel the wonder of it.

Visualize—and then act

Many reminders on the list of ways to develop integrity are already action-oriented but wherever one grabs your attention, take a few moments to visualize precisely how you will put it into action in your life and what positive change that will make. Then *do it. Live it. Be it.*

YOU HAVE A RIGHT TO GOOD EXPERIENCES

You want other people to love and appreciate you. You want good things to happen to you. Yet sometimes these "good things" feel as uncomfortable as disappointments.

In fact, sometimes they feel worse than disappointments. ("I have everything I wanted but I still feel depressed.")

A positive experience can lift your spirits. It can also lead you to feel unworthy, insufficient, invaded, or extremely uncomfortable. The thought may arise: "I am not worthy of this," or "I could never match what is being offered to me. I could never repay it," or "I may grow to like this. And then it will be taken from me."

To take in what life is already offering you, and to be able to enjoy what others want to offer, *you need to trust that you have a right to good experiences*. ("Good things can happen to me. I won't need to pay a 'price' for them. I won't need to 'spoil' them or distrust them.")

This sense of inner legitimacy depends on self-respect and self-acceptance. ("I am someone who is lovable. I can accept what you have to give me without feeling threatened or overwhelmed by it.")

When you are feeling anxious, depressed, or out of sorts, you will be much more inclined to doubt other people's generosity or authenticity. ("She doesn't mean those nice things she said.")

Use those painful times as a barometer. Ask yourself, "Why is it hard for me to take in good experiences right now? What's going on in my life more generally?"

Focusing on yourself in this way—rather than worrying about whether the other person "really meant it"—you can begin to see useful patterns. ("It's hard for me to accept others' kindness when I am overtired." "After Kim and I broke up, I found myself pushing other people away even though I needed their help." "When I am caught up in worrying what other people think of me, my self-doubt goes crazy.")

SUPPORT YOUR WELL-BEING

Make decisions that support your physical, psychological and spiritual well-being.

What could be simpler? Or more easily forgotten?

WHAT YOU CAN CHANGE

This is what you can change:

✦ Your mind (attitudes, thoughts, way of thinking)
✦ Your spirits (through what you cultivate and pay attention to)
✦ Your physical, mental and spiritual health
✦ Your way of living (giving attention to what matters most)
✦ What you permit—and don't—from other people
✦ The way that you regard and treat other people
✦ Your openness to life's gifts.

Does anything else *matter*?

ALL YOU ARE ISN'T UP FOR CHANGE

Standing up for who and what you are gives you unparalleled stability.

You can certainly change unhelpful patterns, broaden your focus and concerns and learn from failures.

You can round off and soften your blunt edges.

You can certainly discover and develop your talents and strengths.

But your spirit, your soul, all that you are, is not always or inevitably up for change.

Trust that.

EGO AND "SELF":
THE THREE-DIMENSIONAL VERSIONS

Ego and "Self" are technical terms that may seem irrelevant to your daily life. However, they spring into full color once you understand what a difference it makes to your happiness—to your whole attitude to life and living—whether you identify with your ego or with your Self.

Neither term, by the way, is a precise one. There are many arguments among professionals about what they mean. But what interests me is the real-life shift in experience that happens once you recognize your ego-driven and ego-defensive patterns—and realize there are other ways of thinking about yourself and other people.

A little patience leads to a lot of freedom!

Identifying with the ego (as most of us do)—which is just another way of talking about ordinary consciousness—you need lots of psychological nourishment from the outside. You draw your sense of yourself from what you *do* rather than from who you *are*. You tend to see yourself through other people's eyes—or through your own criticisms—and judge yourself accordingly. Or you puff yourself up, cultivating indifference to what other people think because you are afraid of it. The ego is hard to satisfy; it pushes you to compare yourself to other people and to think about yourself as "superior" or "inferior": it drives your sense of separation and aloneness. Identifying with your thoughts, attitudes, beliefs, emotions or personality is just another way of being ego-identified. It's "normal," but keeps you vulnerable.

Identifying with Self—or higher consciousness—you accept a profound invitation to trust your innate qualities. The universal values and strengths are Self- or soul-driven qualities; they are yours to claim. When you are Self- or soul-identified, you remain concerned about what others think of you (that's healthy), but your sense of self-worth does not depend on it. You feel connected to something larger than yourself—even if you do not call it "God." Your life is values-driven; your sense of separation from other people is radically diminished; you recognize the profound interdependence of all forms of life. That brings responsibilities, but it powerfully reduces loneliness.

Is it possible for someone who is not spiritually minded to identify with Self rather than ego?

Very few people, I suspect, are wholly Self- or soul-identified. (But when you do meet such a person it is uplifting and joyful.) Most of us are bumbling along, doing our best to come to a more generous and truthful way of living. However, even glimpsing that it is possible to detach somewhat from the ego is already transformative.

And that's where I would urge anyone to begin—"spiritually minded" or not. Start with your own everyday experience.

- ✦ Trust your inner goodness. The most practical way to do this is to practice the universal qualities: courage, tolerance, forgiveness, generosity, happiness and love. Be values-focused and values-supported. You will very quickly find yourself much less pushed around by old habits of negativity and self-denigration.
- ✦ Take the big view: no aspect of yourself is all of who you are; no incident or situation will determine your entire life. Practice "stepping back" inwardly.
- ✦ Recognize that "good" and "bad" are relative terms only when it comes to our experiences and what they teach us.

I love this quote from Martin Luther King Jr: "All men [people] are caught in an inescapable network of mutuality, tied in a single garment of destiny. Whatever affects one directly affects all indirectly … I can never be what I ought to be until you are what you ought to be, and you can never be what you ought to be until I am what I ought to be. This is the inter-related structure of reality."

That is the soul or Self speaking, not ego—that would divide and separate us and make us lonelier than we ever need to be.

- ✦ Know that when you do feel lonely, you are often lonely to reconnect with your deeper Self. Make it your business to find ways to do this.
- ✦ Resist ego-driven temptations to compare yourself relentlessly to others; to criticize or to judge; or to tell yourself how little happiness there is to go around.

✦ Give up the pleasures of self-righteousness! Nothing feeds the ego more effectively—or takes you further from the Self.

✦ Notice when you are slipping back into old habits of ego-defense: making other people wrong; falling into self-pity; feeling "small" and helpless; talking up your fears; lambasting yourself. You don't need to do much more than notice. Stop! And move on.

✦ Enjoy the fact that simply observing what's happening ("Here I go again, worrying about something that may never happen") gives you invaluable psychological distance—distance from ego habits.

✦ When you have a tough moment, or a big decision to make, ask yourself, "How would this look from the big perspective of Self rather than the defensive perspective of my ego?"

✦ Practice seeing other people as a Self (rather than as a nuisance, someone you need, distrust, adore). Focus on the big picture. Let your experience of them be accepting and inclusive. Experience how this makes a difference—to you, as well as to them!

✦ Experiment with taking questions to your inner Wise Being: a personification of Self. Get better acquainted with your own invaluable inner wisdom.

✦ Learn and practice meditation. Those who are not spiritual seekers can nevertheless experience that what you think of as "mind" is just the door, or the doorstep, to the stillness, stability and peace that lives in each of us. A "spacious," generous, inclusive view of life, as well as happiness and compassion, are the hallmarks of "Self." Making time for meditation—even fifteen minutes in your twenty-four-hour day—supports those discoveries.

Listen to Thomas R. Kelly

A twentieth-century Quaker, Thomas Kelly wrote these words in his book *Testament of Devotion* long before meditation became commonplace in the West. (Quaker worship, however, *is* meditation and has been continuously since the seventeenth century.) Kelly is speaking about meditation in a directly spiritual sense, but "Self" awareness can also be a way to experience profound inter-connectedness that is not explicitly spiritual.

"There is a way of ordering our mental life on more than one level at once ... The secular world of today values and cultivates only the first level, assured that *there* is where the real business of mankind is done, and scorns, or smiles in tolerant amusement, at the cultivation of the second level—a luxury enterprise, a vestige of superstition, an occupation for special temperaments. But in a deeply religious culture men [people] know that it is at the deep level that the real business of life is determined. The secular [ego-identified] mind is an abbreviated, fragmentary mind, building only upon a part of man's nature, powers and resources. The religious [Self-identified] mind involves the whole of man ... It knows joys and stabilities, peace and assurances, that are utterly incomprehensible to the secular mind. Between the two levels is fruitful interplay, but ever the accent must be upon the deeper level."

YOU ARE A SELF

Thirty years ago, I learned from my training in Roberto Assagioli's wonderful therapeutic approach called psychosynthesis, and have never forgotten:

> You *have* a body. You are not your body.
> You *have* feelings. You are not your feelings.
> You *have* desires. You are not your desires.
> You *have* a mind. You are not your mind.
> You *have* beliefs and attitudes. You are not your beliefs and attitudes.

Who are you?

You are a Self, observing all these realms, acting through them, but also distinct from them.

You *are* a Self. You *have* a physical existence.

"The experience of Self," wrote Jungian analyst Marie-Louise von Franz, "brings a feeling of standing on solid ground inside oneself, on a patch of eternity, which even physical death cannot touch."

TURN A DIFFICULT SITUATION AROUND

Self-respect comes to life in its full glory when you turn a difficult situation around. In fact, it's tempting to say that *you are more likely to grow in self-respect through the ways that you handle adversity* than you ever could as you coast through the good times.

This doesn't mean that you will welcome hard times. You may, however, come to be less afraid of them.

The following questions let you use your own invaluable self-knowledge and experience as a resource. Write out the questions and *write out your answers.* This is far more effective and powerful than just turning them over in your mind.

- ✦ What can I learn from this situation? What do I need to pay attention to? (This doesn't mean: "Why is this happening to me?" That question leads only to increasing self-pity.)
- ✦ What past experiences can I draw on? What's familiar here?
- ✦ What part did I play in creating this situation?
- ✦ What aspects feel far out of my control?
- ✦ What values and qualities do I need to help me?
- ✦ How am I going to put those qualities into practice?
- ✦ Do I need support? How will I get that?
- ✦ What question am I not asking? What issue am I not seeing? (These are two questions with an almost magical power to shift obstacles to insight.)

Don't expect neat and tidy answers immediately. Let your unconscious do its own work. My experience is that asking the question is frequently enough. The answer may then come when you least expect it. Even in the most testing and difficult situations, give yourself a real chance to find the jewels of your own wisdom.

Over-responsible?

I tend toward severe over-responsibility so am very sympathetic to fellow sufferers. I have certainly learned that it is possible to take some situations too much to heart. Not everything is about "you," your attitudes or your psychological processes. Sometimes tough and unwelcome things happen. *And you are not the cause.* It is easy to worry away or seek meaning from an event when it would actually be much healthier to close the door on it and move on.

SITUATIONS THAT HARM YOU

Self-respect and self-harm cannot coexist; one saves you from the other.

If you constantly or even occasionally find yourself in situations that are unworthy of you, that put you in danger, that "invite" abuse or disrespect from others, or that shame you, then this speaks very clearly of a problem with self-love and self-respect.

If you are addicted to self-criticism or self-loathing, or to any of the other addictions that are an attempt to push self-loathing away, then this too speaks very clearly of a problem with self-love and self-respect.

Should you recognize yourself on this page, be uplifted rather than alarmed! This is a pattern that can be transformed—not least, *by noticing it*. We usually go into dangerous situations, or repeat the same dispiriting scenarios, as though in a dream. And it is a kind of dream. **The dream is that we cannot save ourselves.** That someone else will have to save us. Or that we are beyond saving.

This is never true.

Look for *patterns* in the way you behave and describe your behavior to yourself. Once you see even a vague pattern, it becomes easier to step back and make more positive choices.

Pay far less attention to *why* you are behaving like this than to *how* you will make the changes that you need:

+ Monitor your self-talk ruthlessly.
+ Monitor your care of your body ruthlessly. Eating well and resting may not solve your problems, but *your thinking will radically improve when your brain is well nourished.*
+ Know that it is not a "failure" to get the help you need. It's an act of courage and love.
+ Don't ask whether you "deserve" help. Take the chance to receive it *unconditionally*. Doing that, you learn what love is.

It can be remarkably helpful to take charge of the situation by asking yourself, "If this were a dear friend who needed help, what would I suggest? What immediate change would make a significant difference?"

BE A LOVING FRIEND TO OTHERS

Your behavior toward other people is crucial in building self-respect.

When you are the one who is undermining a situation or relationship—perhaps through jealousy, possessiveness, aggression, anxiety or addiction—*seek professional help.*

Take responsibility for your behavior—and for changing your behavior. You deserve it. So do the people you care about.

"NO" IS A COMPLETE SENTENCE

It's impossible to grow in self-respect if you cannot say a clear "Yes" to what you want, and an equally clear "No" to what you don't want. (And sometimes you need to be able to say: "I'm not sure yet. I am thinking about it.")

Be unafraid to say "No" to anyone who asks something of you that feels even the slightest bit "off" or wrong.

But *check that you are not routinely negative*.

Ask for what you want

Don't expect other people to read your mind. They can't.

Ask for what you want. Know that you can survive not getting it.

SELF-LOVE AND SELF-RESPECT

Respect for yourself and others cannot be separated. Self-love and self-respect also go hand in hand.

Sometimes self-respect is easier to come at than self-love, but one doesn't exist meaningfully without the other. Both offer, paradoxically, a path away from self-absorption and not toward it. (The person who is obsessively self-focused lacks both self-love and self-respect.) Both involve all of who you are: mind, body, spirit, soul, Self. Both are essential to lasting experiences of happiness.

Loving your life, you will want to do your best by it.

Appreciating the unique gift of your life, you will also respect it.

Self-love allows self-respect to arise quite naturally. Think about the respect you would give a good friend. Think about the enthusiasm, loyalty and encouragement that quite naturally flow from that. It's that kind of attitude toward yourself that self-love and self-respect allow.

Self-respect—for all our sakes

Love and respect yourself—not for your own sake only, but also for the sake of every person with whom you'll be in contact throughout your life. This will not only make it far more natural to love and respect others. You, yourself, will become much easier to love. No one will be making up for your love deficits. Nor will you need to challenge or mistrust other people's efforts to love and respect you.

OTHER PEOPLE'S OPINIONS MATTER.
BUT LESS THAN YOU THINK

It's a good thing to heed what other people think; to be sensitive to their opinions; to be open even to their criticisms if they have validity. However, *your sense of self cannot be ruled by what other people think about you.*

Their opinions will often say far more about them than they do about you. Sometimes they want to flatter you—or to hurt you. Those are *their* impulses; you are simply the object of them.

Allowing other people's views to determine your inner well-being leaves you powerless and extremely vulnerable. It will also leave you needy for approval—because you are not giving approval to yourself.

In one of life's countless psychological ironies, *the more you crave approval from others, the less you are likely to get it.* Your neediness will distance people and put them off.

People who get most genuine approval, love, admiration and respect are usually those who care about it least. This is not because they are indifferent but because they are quietly self-assured and trusting.

They don't need to be constantly told that they are "all right": they can trust that.

They don't need to be told that they are "better than others": they would distrust that.

As you grow in self-respect, your choices and decisions will reflect that. Other people's opinions of you won't cease to matter, but they will matter far less. And when those opinions are hurtful or harmful, you will see those harsh moments not as any useful measure of your worth but as a reflection of that person's own negativity.

When my children were young it was terrible to witness their pain when someone said something cutting, mean or unjust to or about them. Children have few defenses against those kinds of attacks. Many adults continue to suffer acutely also from real or perceived attacks. So how good it is to know that as we get older it is possible to grow in self-confidence and self-trust. As we do that, we can learn to see unfair or ugly attacks as a reflection of the inner world of the person who is attacking us, rather than as a comment on our own selves.

GIVE YOURSELF GOOD ADVICE

Self-respect soars when you know that you can trust your own good advice. When you don't know what to do, or where to turn, *turn to yourself.*

Write yourself a letter: "Dear Angela . . . ," "Dear William . . ." outlining the situation and offering the wisdom of your own internal "Wise Being." Stepping back mentally to address yourself will give you invaluable perspective and a chance to see a familiar situation in a new way. "Feeling silly" is no impediment to making great discoveries!

Use these prompts:

+ The central issue here seems to be . . .
+ What's getting in the way is . . .
+ Change will come when . . .

Remember: no one knows you better than you know yourself. Value your inner wisdom.

Writing, not ruminating

This is another instance where you will get a quite different and more satisfying level of insight by writing, rather than ruminating. It takes a small effort to get started but even the person who "never writes" will be rewarded with unexpected, useful turns in their train of thought.

ENTITLED TO BE YOURSELF

CATHERINE: It's been a feature of my life—and perhaps yours, too—that every so often, someone feels entitled to sit me down and have The Talk. Usually this is preceded by a phrase that indicates someone knows me better than I know myself: "I'm mentioning this for your own good . . ." they'll say, or, "You see, the problem with you is . . ."

These talks seem to result from a judgment that I am "too something."

As a random sampling, my third-grade report card said I was "too overbearing." In high school, a fellow student told me that I was "too superficial." When I was twenty-two, my boyfriend said I was "too needy." As a twenty-six-year-old teacher in a private school, I was told by the middle-aged guidance counselor that I was "too provocative" with "too-short skirts"! When I was in my thirties, my manager at a major corporation said I was "too reticent in meetings." And now, as an at-home mother with a no-TV rule for little children, I've been called "too controlling."

Of course these comments hurt, even when they are justified. But they are only one side of the picture. I am (or was) all *these things and more*, including creative, impulsive, hardworking, anxious, a perfectionist, reliable, critical, encouraging, and warm.

People are often ready (with ammunition!) to comment on our temperaments. Some of us are naturally anxious. Or bossy. Or unwilling to speak up. There are a million ways that we find our temperament surfacing, often despite our best intentions at managing it.

As I age, I am trying to accept rather than fight my temperament and focus on the useful parts of my character. At the same time, if I let them, those "tough-to-swallow" parts of me, like anxiety and perfectionism, can really run rampant and make both myself and everyone around me quite miserable. Just ask my husband when I routinely start another serious talk about our life's direction at 11 P.M. on a Sunday night!

What I wonder is this: How can we manage to accept our own temperaments without being overrun by them? And how should we respond when others feel entitled to make negative judgments based on personal qualities that simply are a part of "who we are"?

STEPHANIE: Essential to both self-respect and respect (two sides of the same coin) is that you allow people to *be who they are.*

This doesn't mean that you can't raise genuine problems. Or, if you are a parent, it doesn't mean that you can't let your children know what matters to you and what's likely to help them become thoughtful human beings. Nevertheless, it does mean that you hesitate long and hard before "putting people right"—especially when that translates into, "Be the person I need you to be—rather than who you are!"

As I read Catherine's story, the first thing that occurs to me is that the need to have "The Talk" says more about the person who wishes to have it than it does about the person being "put right." (And if you are the one urgently needing to give someone else "The Talk," the same rule applies; you are probably doing it to release your own tension—to try to get your own way—no matter how vehemently you may insist it's for someone else's good.)

Some of those comments could have been made in ways that left Catherine feeling encouraged and supported rather than attacked. Instead Catherine remembers these hurts because she was left feeling undermined, defensive and uncertain.

Could this be because Catherine is "too sensitive"? I think not.

I have had a fair few versions of "The Talk" myself over the course of a lifetime. I was definitely too loud, opinionated, forceful and ambitious (or too "bookish," independent and withdrawn) for many people, especially when I was growing up. And some didn't hesitate to tell me. Moving from country to country, I discovered to my delight that some of this was cultural. Living in Germany (briefly) and Israel (very briefly) and traveling to New York (not nearly often enough), I discovered how someone who seems like a lion in one country can be regarded as a mouse in another. What a relief!

But Catherine's question remains complex. *Self-respect depends upon self-acceptance.* But we are social beings; more than capable of rubbing others the wrong way.

Is Catherine entitled to her "too-short skirts," her "superficiality," her "neediness," "reticence" and "perfectionism"? Is she entitled to raise serious matters with her husband late on a Sunday night? Can she be herself—and also have the approval and acceptance she wants?

What's needed here, I suspect, is the healing balm of detachment. This lets us see how subjective other people's responses are. (At the same time, if there's a common theme among those responses, for your own sake it's certainly worth examining them.)

What is also true is that every quality for which Catherine has been criticized has its "other side," for which I suspect she has also been praised. Detachment can help Catherine see this: that the same "reticence" that irritates one person could be viewed as "calm" or "thoughtfulness" by another; that her "perfectionism" could be seen as underpinning her brilliant organizational skills and persistence.

For all that, it's also true that sometimes "being ourselves" genuinely does cause problems for other people. Catherine cites "anxiety" as part of her temperament and it is probably anxiety that drives her need to have a rather too-serious talk with her husband Luther rather too late on a Sunday night.

Is she entitled to do so?

Detachment is key here also. (And easily learned. Think of it as taking a step back mentally; bigger picture, less involved; away from the heat.)

Viewing anxiety as an aspect of herself (and not *who she is*), Catherine is immediately better placed to deal with it. She may not need to act on it at all. She might remind herself that her sense of urgency rises when she's tired and subject to bad-mood (confused) thinking. *And so does her vulnerability to criticism and self-doubt.*

If she still needs to act, she could, for example, flag her late-night concerns to Luther, including her concern that they don't get enough time to talk during the day. And leave it at that.

Catherine can:

+ Step back mentally from the situation
+ Disidentify from it ("I am not my short skirts . . .")
+ Use self-awareness as her ally ("I get very sensitive around this kind of issue . . .")
+ Respond neutrally rather than defensively
+ Defuse her own emotions
+ Engage her self-respect.

And this can come about virtually on automatic.

However, underlying Catherine's questions is, I suspect, the big one. *"Am I all right as I am?"*

Like any of us, as long as Catherine draws her identity from how she is seen and experienced by other people, she will be extremely vulnerable to their opinions. She can tell herself repeatedly that their opinions are highly subjective (revealing more about them than they do about her), but *while other people's opinions remain a primary guide to her own value, she'll always be knocked around by them.*

Catherine would help herself wonderfully if she were to allow the source of her self-respect to shift from the outside to the inside. Or, more precisely, from ego to Self.

Looking at any loaded situation from the spacious, trusting perspective of Self, rather than the more prickly and defensive perspective of ego, Catherine will quickly work out which criticisms are useful and which are not. She will also see how every temperament has its strengths and challenges, and that often those are the exact same qualities just seen from different viewpoints. But the most profound change will be that Catherine's self-respect grows from the inside out and is not reliant on other people's highly variable opinions.

In her last question, Catherine asks, "How should we respond when others feel entitled to make negative judgments based on personal qualities that simply are a part of 'who we are'?"

Detachment is her brilliant ally here, too. And understanding the phrase, "Part of 'who we are'" is key. When we rush to defend ourselves, we are behaving as though the "bit" that is being attacked is everything we are. It is not.

"Thank you for letting me know" or "That's certainly another way of looking at things" are brilliant circuit-breakers.

Answering in neutral ensures that you are neither agreeing nor buying into an argument. You are not raising the energy levels around an unhelpful issue; nor are you getting more involved with it. Like the most skilled martial arts expert, you are gracefully deflecting. What might have been a blow has nowhere to land.

It can seem "impossible" not to rush to your own defense. Once again, though, it's the ego that needs defending, not the Self.

TIDYING UP THE PEOPLE AROUND YOU

As you grow in self-respect, your respect for other people will flow quite naturally.

As you learn how to be friendlier toward yourself your capacity to take pleasure in the company of other people will also flourish.

As you feel easier with yourself, it will become easier to allow others to "be themselves."

Nothing is more important than acceptance when it comes to a genuine expression of respect. What we all want is to be accepted as we are—not who we might be ten years from now!

None of us can flourish in a situation where we don't feel respected and accepted.

As you come to accept people in all their complexity and contradictions, and stop trying to tidy them up or change them, they will inevitably experience you more positively and with greater ease and trust.

You will benefit. And you will be a benefactor.

Telling people what they already know

Don't do it!

Telling people what they already know says everything about your anxiety—and nothing about their abilities.

When your mouth opens, close it. And smile.

NO BEATING UP ON YOURSELF

It's self-love, and a simple trust that we can learn from our mistakes, that allows us to be compassionate rather than ruthless as we try to lift our game, psychologically and spiritually.

There's no merit, it seems to me, in giving ourselves a hard time while struggling to be more generous to others!

Self-respect requires that we notice, learn from our mistakes and clean up our messes. It doesn't require that we beat up on ourselves, compare ourselves to other people or remind ourselves how hopeless we are.

I am twenty years further along the road of life than Catherine is. Thinking about our human potential is my passion and my work. For all that, I am still an amateur, doing my best and learning every day what "best" means. *We are in this together.* Choosing happiness as we go.

SMALL STEPS ARE PERFECT

After many months of intense work on this book, I began to notice something of a pattern in the questions that Catherine was bringing to me. What they seemed quite often to express was a gap between her expectations of herself ("I know I should be more generous . . ."), and what she was actually experiencing as her capabilities ("Sometimes I am just so tired.").

Catherine does have high standards. She is idealistic. This means that she is vulnerable to feeling very disappointed with herself when her behavior doesn't match her ideals. But what I also noticed was how often Catherine—like the rest of us—was reaching for a global change when a small change was probably not only more realistic but more appropriate. Doing this, she was overvaluing other people's mastery of the qualities she desired, while undervaluing her own efforts.

That insight was as useful for me as it is for her. I, too, needed reminding that *we don't become wise, compassionate or fully realized overnight*. In this age of "instant" everything, it's an incredible relief to know that small steps are perfect.

If Catherine, for example, wants to develop a more inclusive view of love then she simply has to pay attention to what each small situation, each small moment, asks of her. Nothing more.

And when she "fails"?

Move on to the next moment. Learning as she goes.

SPEAK RESPECTFULLY

How you talk about yourself speaks volumes about the way you feel about yourself.

It is impossible to grow in self-respect while talking yourself down—or constantly (and anxiously) puffing yourself up.

Speak about yourself with respect. And *within the privacy of your own mind, do nothing less.*

You will be guiding others unconsciously to think about you respectfully also. Consciously or not, they will take their cues from you. And not just from the way you speak about yourself, but even from the way that you present yourself physically.

This doesn't mean dressing expensively or walking like a dancer. It does mean honoring your life by caring for your physical being in a loving and self-respectful way, holding yourself well, caring for yourself and your environment.

Even in the quiet of your own mind, watch out for self-talk that is hurtful, undermining or plain abusive.

When you catch yourself using words or phrases to or about yourself that you would never use to or about anyone else, *stop.*

The way you talk to and about yourself is just a habit. If this habit is not supporting your sense of worth and integrity, it can be transformed and replaced by something better.

Self-portrait in speech

How you speak to others—and how you think and speak about them—always says far more about you than it does about them. Beware!

TRANSFORM DEFENSIVENESS

Defensiveness is something most of us know well. So it's good to know that it need not ruin our lives or run our relationships.

Defensiveness arises from wanting other people to think well of us, and wanting to think well of ourselves. Those are legitimate desires. But defensiveness gets in the way. A defensive mind-set is uncomfortable. It is highly reactive, prickly, oversensitive. And it tends to see problems even when there aren't any.

Defensiveness gets worse if you avoid acknowledging and learning from your mistakes. And it gets better fast the more "owning up" you do and the more self-responsibility you take.

These are just some of the problems a defensive mind-set causes:

- ✦ Holding on to negative assumptions
- ✦ Disparaging others, relishing their failures, laughing at their mistakes
- ✦ Ending a relationship because wrongs can't be admitted and put right
- ✦ Trivializing and discounting others
- ✦ Hurting, blaming, attacking—rather than listening and talking
- ✦ Reducing other people to the sum total of their faults.

Defensiveness is driven by fear. You may think that as a strategy it "hides" you, or props you up and puffs you out. The opposite is true. It radically undermines your self-respect, personal power and all your relationships.

Entire families, social groups or even nations can and do adopt a defensive mind-set—refusing to accept that they could ever be in the wrong or have anything of value to learn. They may believe that they are supporting one another through their defensive behaviors. In fact, they are intensifying their anxiety and limitations.

It is possible to prick the balloon of defensiveness—and let it go. Here's how:

- ✦ Use self-respect and self-trust to take a more generous and inclusive stand. This will give you invaluable distance; it will lower tension and clarify your thinking; it will move your focus from ego to Self.

- ✦ Remind yourself that other people's complexity is much like your own. This will make it much easier to accept their disappointing, unkind or incomprehensible behavior.
- ✦ Question your own assumptions. You could be "defending" against a paper tiger.
- ✦ Soothe your fears, rather than revving them up.
- ✦ Choose a tolerant and inclusive approach to complex situations.

All of these changes rapidly restore self-respect. All will significantly benefit you. Remember: *none of us is blameless.*

DETOX NEGATIVE ASSUMPTIONS

Negative assumptions savage your self-respect. And the vast majority of them are unfounded.

For at least two weeks, briefly note all the judgments that *you assume others are making about you*. Write them down exactly as you are repeating them to yourself. ("No one wants to sit with me at lunch.") Notice (and note down) when they occur.

You may find that they coincide with times of extra stress or general anxiety. It's at those times your capacity to soothe yourself will be low. You are feeling generally vulnerable. That's why this kind of recording can be so helpful.

It may be enough simply to notice what's going on more generally in your life. ("I'm actually freaked out by the number of deadlines I have before the end of the month.") At other times you might notice there's a pattern to these negative thoughts you are attributing to other people. ("I can see it's around my partner's family that I feel most sensitive.")

Once you see those assumptions written down in black and white it becomes much harder to be tripped up by them. In fact, you can step back from them and see them for what they are. ("Here it comes again, that tired old insult . . .")

Better still, it becomes much easier for you to give yourself and other people the benefit of the doubt. ("He probably doesn't think I am a total idiot. Maybe he himself is flustered about the end-of-quarter figures.")

Be aware that once you stop attributing negative thoughts to other people you not only get a great deal of personal power back, you also clear the way for easier and less defensive relationships with them.

And if you turn out to be right? If someone else really is saying something awful about you, or doing something mean that is genuinely distressing?

Let your self-respect guide you.

Their unkind words say more about them than they do about you. Which is why we should watch carefully what *we* say about other people.

If their unkind actions will continue to impact on you, speak up—self-respectfully and *with a focus on solution rather than complaint.* ("I was quite upset to find that you left me out of the management meeting again. How do we set up better lines of communication?" "I know you like to be spontaneous but I feel as though you are often calling me at the last minute and assuming that I can fit in with your plans. How do we find some middle ground here?")

Those small acts of appropriate self-assertion benefit you and often significantly change the tone and outcome of the situation that has been troubling you.

SOLUTIONS, NOT PROBLEMS

Even the word "solution" has a very different energy to it than the word "problem."

Self-respect (and respect for others) soars in any complex or painful situation when you focus on solutions rather than problems, on going forward rather than looking back, on cooperation rather than conflict.

WHEN OTHERS TREAT YOU
DISRESPECTFULLY

You can't always control the way that others behave toward or around you. You can, however, strictly limit the time you spend with people who don't treat you well.

If anyone is treating you badly *you should not spend any time with them at all.* Get professional help without delay if it seems difficult to disentangle yourself.

Consider the following strategies when someone behaves in a way that is disrespectful, harsh, rude or trivializing.

+ *Did your own behavior invite negativity?* This doesn't mean that you caused someone else to behave badly. Each person is entirely responsible for the way they behave. But so are you. **If you are disrespectful to others, it will invite a negative response**. This is something you can change. When you catch yourself behaving in ways that pull you into a spiral of negativity, stop. Walk away from the situation. Catch your breath. Center yourself.

+ *Is this person routinely disrespectful?* If so, you need to talk to them about the way their behavior impacts on you. Set clear limits: "I am not going to have these kinds of conversations when you are stressed/drunk/tired/angry."

+ *Perhaps the matter is genuinely trivial* (but it feels like the last straw on a hard day). If so, choose a cup of tea and ten minutes' quiet time instead of "having it out."

+ *Perhaps the person who is behaving rudely is simply off-loading their negativity and you are the soul closest to hand!* That's not an excuse, but it may make it easier to sidestep and pay attention again when peace is restored. If it happens routinely, speak up: "How are we going to deal with this?"

"MY LIFE, YOUR FAULT"

Self-respect—and genuine respect for anyone else—cannot grow as long as you are in victim mode.

It is too easy to distract yourself from taking responsibility for your own feelings or behavior by focusing on the faults and failings of other people. (A partner can be extremely handy here.)

Of course all the problems in your life may not have been caused by your current partner. They may have been caused by your previous one. Or by your parents, your siblings, boss or children. There are endless variations on the "your-fault" theme. They are all emotionally impoverishing.

Blame is one of the greatest obstacles to love. It denies your complexity and that of the other person. It shuts out generosity. It keeps you locked in the past.

Some of the people you are close to now, or have been close to in the past, will undoubtedly have hurt you. (And you may have hurt them.) Sometimes these hurts are outrageous and totally unjust. Sometimes it feels as though it would be impossible ever to recover.

Yet you owe it to yourself and to the people around you to make every effort to see even the most difficult situation as *something that happened to you; not as the definition of who you are.*

This doesn't mean making excuses for what was distressing, or pretending those situations didn't happen. It does mean acknowledging that you are more than your hurts and tough experiences.

You *have* hurts; you are not your hurts.

It means remaining open to your entire complex life: to the situations that did go well, to the people who did lend a hand, to the role models you do still admire; to the strength of resilience you have acquired on the way.

When your difficulties continue to preoccupy you, pay close attention to what you can learn from them. *This is key to shifting you from victim mode and key to moving on with the rest of your life.*

The learning may be quite simple: "Now I really do know what good friends I have." It may be confronting: "Now I see that I am drawn to violent relationships even though that's the last thing I consciously want."

What help do you need to move forward?
What strengths do you already have that you can call on?
What kind of future are you ready to create?

If you are currently in a situation that is causing you harm, seek professional help immediately.

Grow in resilience

Whatever has your attention will increase and multiply.

If you focus on being a victim, *you will become a superb victim.*

If you insist on rejecting yourself through harsh or punishing thoughts, *you will feel rejected.*

If you pay constant attention to what has hurt or offended you, or to what limits you, *you will feel increasingly crushed and powerless.*

Turn that around.

Pay attention to what you have learned from a difficult situation, and to the strengths and values you need to move forward. You will grow powerfully in resilience as well as self-respect.

THE POWER OF FORGIVENESS

We move through life, hurting others as well as being hurt.

We move through life hurting ourselves as well as being hurt by others.

And forgiveness is needed.

I have written extensively in *Forgiveness and Other Acts of Love* about what forgiveness achieves and allows. What follows is a summary, recognizing that when forgiveness is absent, so is self-respect and perhaps self-love.

Forgiveness is the most demanding of all the qualities; in our world, it is also the most essential. We live in a world where cycles of revenge or just plain bitterness and resentment rule in countless encounters from the most private to the most public.

Forgiveness breaks those cycles. It allows you to say, "I may hate what you have done. I may despise everything about you. But I nevertheless acknowledge that you are a complex human being, as I am, and *I do not wish you harm*."

It also lets you say, "I hate what you have done—but I want to move forward, if only for my own sake."

Sometimes the person we find most difficult to forgive is our own self. Yet, no matter what we have done, reconciliation with ourselves remains just as essential if we are to go forward in our lives in a hopeful and compassionate way. As long as we can't forgive ourselves, we will be shut off from our own respect—and from love.

There is no timetable to the process of forgiveness, especially when there has been a deep betrayal. However, these steps help both psychologically and spiritually.

Know that:

+ Forgiveness is an acknowledgment of our shared complex humanity. "*The sun rises on the just and the unjust . . .*"
+ It is irrelevant whether the person "deserves" to be forgiven. You are forgiving to release yourself at least as much as the other person. And you are forgiving *because you can*.
+ Forgiveness does not pretend that something that was wrong is now right. It is *not* condoning.

✦ Forgiveness has its own timetable; but you can make yourself ready. ("I will start by thinking more about the present than letting myself go over and over the past.")

✦ Forgiveness is an act of love that transcends the rational mind and calls on spirit or your highest self—yet has perceptible psychological and physical benefits as stress decreases and tension subsides.

✦ Forgiveness happens in small stages. It starts with a determination not to let those past hurts or betrayals dominate your entire existence.

✦ Forgiveness should not lead to forced reunions. There may be some people you are better never to see, hear from, or even think about.

✦ Sometimes our greatest rage and resentment is directed toward the people we ourselves have hurt or injured. We may believe that making them "wrong" saves us from feeling bad. It doesn't.

✦ To begin the process of forgiveness, you need to let go of the wish that the other person would understand what they have done and suffer for it. They may never understand. They may never suffer "enough." That must cease to be your business.

✦ Know that revenge and hatred weaken you. *Even to begin to forgive strengthens you.*

When the person you need to forgive is yourself:

✦ Acknowledging what you have done, making appropriate reparations, learning from it, and *valuing all of who you are* will help.

✦ Recognize that you are capable of learning from every situation that you are in—however painful. Take time to discover what you have learned.

✦ Pay conscious attention to positive experiences also (you do "deserve" them).

✦ Practice gratitude for what is good and supportive in your life.

✦ Don't keep talking about what you have done wrong—get professional help if you feel obsessed by it.

+ Support your need for self-forgiveness with clarity and compassion, not self-pity.
+ When self-hatred or self-pity fill your mind, meet them with compassion—but don't cultivate them. Pay attention to something uplifting. Focus on your strengths.
+ When you have hurt others, offer your apologies unconditionally. But know that *an apology is worthless if it is not backed up by a change in behavior.*

When it seems too hard to forgive:

+ Monitor and *strictly censor* how often you talk about the person or the offense.
+ Know that "forgetting" is part of forgiving but doesn't imply never remembering or pretending something hasn't happened. It means living without that person or event being constantly in your mind almost every second of the day. What you learn from a difficult situation, and from the process of forgiving, *is worth remembering.*
+ It can be remarkably helpful to imagine that you are putting the person who has caused you harm into a small boat, and that the boat is traveling back out onto the ocean of life. Give it a great heave! Soon it's far out of your range of vision. You are not causing that person harm; you are leaving them to their destiny. You are getting on with your own.

When someone asks you for forgiveness:

+ Accept other people's apologies unconditionally. Don't expect them to "suffer more" to make you feel better.
+ *If there are chronic cycles of hurt/forgiveness/hurt, this is a relationship problem that needs urgent professional help.*

In thinking about forgiveness, understand that it offends the rational mind. It is a Divine quality that human beings can and must learn to practice.

SHAME CAN BE HEALTHY

Contrary to popular opinion, it's a healthy thing to feel shame when you've done something wrong. (It's wonderfully healthy *to know* that you've done something wrong—and face up to it.) There are far too many people in our world who have turned off their shame switch permanently—who are aggressive, defensive or self-pitying when they should feel shame. And we all suffer for it.

Shame is a powerful warning that harm has been caused.

You do not lessen your self-respect when you feel shame. Self-respect demands that you should clearly know right from wrong, and make amends when they are needed. Sometimes it's tempting to make excuses rather than amends. ("I would never have shouted if you hadn't been mean to me last week . . .") *Making excuses diminishes self-respect.*

Self-respect requires that you:

✦ Acknowledge what you have done
✦ Take responsibility for it
✦ Express your regret
✦ Genuinely resolve not to repeat this same mistake
✦ Make restitutions when that is appropriate and move on.

Making amends doesn't mean wallowing in self-pity ("I'm the worst parent in the world . . . how could you love someone like me . . . you deserve better . . ."). *Self-pity does not rebuild self-respect. Self-pity is the enemy of self-respect.* It keeps you focused on yourself rather than recognizing how you have injured someone else—and what you must do about it.

When you have been harmed

When someone has harmed or abused you, and you suspect that you are carrying their shame, please seek professional help. *You did not cause the wrong-doing.* You can come back to the essential goodness of who you are—and move on.

GUILT

Guilt is a close cousin of shame, but it tends to linger longer.

Be clear about what you have learned from a difficult or painful situation—especially when you betrayed someone else or your own values.

Be clear if there are any changes needed in your own behavior.

Even if you cannot make it up to the particular person you have hurt or injured, make sure that you never hurt someone else in that same way.

If there is an appropriate reparation you can make, *do so anonymously*. Save yourself from the possibility that you are doing this to impress others. This should be between you and your conscience only.

Allow yourself to behave with more compassion to others when you see them making similar mistakes. Let yourself understand them in all their foolishness and complexity—rather than condemning them.

HOW TO APOLOGIZE

A genuine apology is a powerful thing. It affects both the person giving it and the person receiving it, making way for healing and moving on as nothing else can.

Here's how to do it.

Look at the person and say, "I am sorry to have hurt you."

Do not convey through your body language or tone of voice that you are not really sorry; that you resent apologizing, or that you may be apologizing but you will soon repeat the wrong.

An apology carries weight only when it is not forced, when you believe it and you also believe that you have learned something and will not do again whatever caused the hurt or harm.

Do I need to add that an apology ceases to be an apology when you tell the person that although you are sorry to have hurt them *you were quite justified because . . . ?*

An apology needs to be clean, short, simple and genuine. And it needs to be supported by a change in insight and behavior.

There may be times when someone is clearly very hurt by something you have done or that they believe you have done—but you know that they misread you or your good intentions. It may be, for example, that your best friend is hurt because when she told you about her promotion you paid it very little attention and went on to talk about something else. You were careless, but not deliberately hurtful. Or it may be that your sibling is very hurt that you haven't called them for a month, not realizing what pressure you are under at work. Or you laugh inappropriately but not unkindly at something someone says or does; or you are frowning rather than smiling as you farewell your adolescent children in the morning.

Breakdowns in good communication happen frequently. Protesting about other people's reactions, telling them that they "have no reason to be hurt," getting irritated because they are hurt, is never helpful.

It is possible to say, very simply, "I am so sorry that you are upset," without taking on inappropriate guilt or shame. You may also want to add, "That certainly wasn't my intention," but the crucial point is that you acknowledge the hurt, and express your concern that they are hurt, without attacking them or going into elaborate self-justifying.

And when someone apologizes to you?

Accept it gracefully and gratefully. Do not ask yourself whether you need to go on sulking for another week, or whether you can make them suffer as much as you have.

If others are routinely apologizing to you *without changing their behavior,* this is a relationship issue and needs urgent attention.

Apologies—given or received—weave their magic only when they bring a little wisdom and are accompanied by changed action as well as insight.

STOP, IN THE NAME OF LOVE!

It takes many of us a lifetime (or perhaps many lifetimes) to untangle some of our confusion about what we can or cannot ask in the name of love. And what we should—or should not—put up with in the name of love.

It seems so obvious that we could expect "best behavior" from the people who claim to love us.

It seems so obvious that we would want to offer the people we love our "best behavior" in return.

Yet one of the countless paradoxes of the human condition is that *so many of us offer the worst of ourselves to the people we claim to love best.*

That's bad enough. But on top of that, we expect them to put up with this—and us—*because we claim to love them.*

And then, when our loved ones legitimately protest that our behavior doesn't match our claims, we become outraged. Compounding our childishness, we become the hurt and injured ones!

Yet **love is not love until our actions match our finest intentions**—until we are living love and not just talking about it.

"Love" is *never* an excuse to abuse, bully, cajole, possess, ignore or have temper tantrums. Nor to control, diminish, trivialize, take for granted, push around or dishonor.

Behaving in ways that diminish the relationship, you diminish yourself.

Insisting that someone else should put up with this, you kid yourself.

Your self-worth, *your* self-respect and the *health of your relationship* depend on your finding out what loving behavior is—and putting that consistently into practice.

"I HAVE TO PUT UP WITH THIS. I'M IN LOVE"

If you are "putting up with" behavior that diminishes your self-respect, get professional help. No one "has to" or *should* put up with such behavior. Sticking around is a form of "rescuing" that helps no one.

Regaining your self-respect, you might find it much easier to be calmly insistent on what's acceptable to you and what is not.

It is never acceptable to be the repository for someone else's negativity.

"Love" does not demand that, and self-love certainly cannot flourish in the face of that.

When abuse happens over a long period of time it's easy to become confused about where the line should be drawn. It can help to ask, "Is this what I would want for my best friend/sister/brother?"

Accept nothing less for yourself.

Give nothing less to others.

YOU CAN ACT DIFFERENTLY

It's a glorious truth that you cannot "improve" yourself by criticizing, berating yourself or putting yourself down. (You can't improve anyone else that way either.)

This doesn't mean that you can't be real about your mistakes. Or that your mistakes don't matter. They do.

Your "mistakes" may hurt others and seriously undermine your self-respect. But it's wonderful to know that they are rarely fatal.

It is also wonderful to know that you will turn them around fast by calling upon and extending your self-respect.

Self-respect lets you own up to your mistakes without feeling shattered by them.

Self-respect lets you notice the harm or hurt you have caused so you can do something about it.

A "mistake" loses its power to diminish you when you recognize it—and recognize that you can act differently.

COPING WITH SETBACKS AND MISTAKES

CATHERINE: When Stephanie and I took the Values in Action: Signature Strengths Survey online <www.authentichappiness.org>, I wasn't surprised to find that her greatest strength was bravery. For me, bravery didn't even rate a mention. Throughout much of my life, fear has been my constant companion. I'm afraid of setbacks and mistakes, I'm afraid to speak up and offer an honest opinion, and my fear often causes me to be pessimistic. It's a downward spiral.

Luckily, I am married to someone who, like Stephanie, possesses bravery as a signature strength. Whenever I'm afraid to face a problem, my trusted adviser is my husband, Luther, mainly because of our relationship and his commitment to me, but also because he is incredibly skilled at dealing with setbacks and uncertainty. In his corporate life, he has the opportunity to work with a wide range of highly motivated clients who rely on his guidance and strategic decision-making.

Both personally and professionally, Luther has learned skills to meet fear head-on and make decisions despite it. When I asked him how he does it, this is what he shared with me.

"My experience is that it's easier to cope with setbacks and uncertainty if your personal worth isn't tied to your performance. I can still get upset or disappointed when I fail, but I don't feel deeply affected in the core of who I am.

"If you are a person who focuses on your weaknesses, then each event that has failure in it becomes overwhelming and confirms your weakness. If you choose to focus on your strengths, then failures don't confirm anything—they simply become learning experiences and another part of life.

"When I face a setback, first I remind myself that this situation is temporary. Then, based on my faith, I remember that everything will eventually work out for the highest good. I ask myself whether or not there's a lesson I need to learn. Sometimes there is *no lesson* . . . it's just life and just the way things are. If that's true, I move on—and stop thinking about the setback!

"Of course this is harder to do than say. I sometimes find myself fingering the mistake like an old scar. When I do, I consciously *stop* and tell myself, 'This is not useful at all.' In all likelihood, no one else is thinking about my mistake at that moment but me. So why should I hang on to it?

"If the event or setback has the potential to make me re-evaluate my responsibility and change my behavior, then I need to go through the whole change process.

"First I accept that this situation is happening (like it or not). Then I take realistic responsibility for my part in it.

"I grieve if I need to and I apologize and make amends if necessary.

"Finally, I resolve to 'do better next time.' I make some changes to my behavior when that's needed. I forgive myself (though sometimes I have to remind myself that I have). And I move on."

THINK, PLAN ... AND PLAY

When you are thinking about your life, don't pay attention only to your suffering or your mistakes or the things that have gone wrong or even the behaviors you believe you need to "work at."

Life is also for living. Life is abundantly and overwhelmingly for living!

Pay attention to your triumphs, your joys, your energy, vigor, your daydreams, your hilarity, exuberance, excessiveness; your capacity to sing opera in the kitchen or dance naked under the stars. Relish your choice to cook, paint or write for the sheer pleasure of it; to make love, laugh loudly, walk vigorously; to reread a favorite novel or poem or see a movie on a wet afternoon; to eat with pleasure; to talk for an hour to a darling friend on the other side of the world; to tell people how much you love them; to gaze into the sky as the sun rises or as the stars emerge, or to sit under a tree smelling sweet earth and thinking about absolutely nothing at all.

HOW TO BUILD SELF-RESPECT

Essential insights

✦ No one can give you self-respect. No one can take it away, either.

✦ Self-respect begins in your own mind: with the way you think and talk about yourself.

✦ Self-respect powerfully guides other people in how they should treat you. It also allows you to see when someone else's actions or behavior have less to do with you than with their own issues or projections.

✦ To think well of yourself, you need to behave respectfully toward other people. Self-justifying can't change that.

✦ Self-respect limits recklessness; it keeps you safe.

✦ Your life is created through millions of choices. Choosing consciously builds responsibility and self-respect. It also gives you your greatest chance for happiness.

✦ Not choosing is also a choice. Self-respect encourages an active life—not a passive one.

✦ Other people can and do help, support and inspire us. But no one can make the essential choices for us (to live well, kindly and with greater happiness and engagement). *Value your power to choose.* ("My life and attitudes are my own creation.")

✦ Self-respect and respect for others live back to back. What's more, self-respect brings peace of mind, as well as happiness.

◆ When you are wrong, say so and apologize. Self-respect allows this—and "character" depends upon it.

◆ Self-love and self-respect are closely aligned. Together they build compassion, letting you support yourself in tough moments—and other people in the ways that they need.

◆ Value self-love. It is not narcissism. Loving your life genuinely, you grow to love *life*—in all its variety and manifestations.

◆ Small changes are perfect—and soon add up.

Essential actions

◆ Encourage yourself as you would a good friend. Focus on your strengths.

◆ Speak to and about yourself respectfully. If you are putting yourself down, it becomes easy to assume other people are thinking badly of you; it also makes it harder to take in their validation and affection.

◆ Check and *challenge* your negative assumptions. Assumptions are not facts. They often begin and end in your own mind. Look for patterns.

◆ If you are letting yourself down, STOP. It's possible to regroup in less than a second.

◆ Judge yourself by your actions—not your good intentions. *Give* the benefit of the doubt.

◆ Listen to your conscience; value your intuition. Sometimes your body is your best guide when it comes to situations that you can welcome—or should turn away from.

✦ Recognize the differences between Self and ego. Aim for the "big picture" and compassionate view.

✦ Turn a difficult or painful situation around by finding and valuing what you can learn from it.

✦ Make decisions that *support* your physical, psychological and spiritual well-being. Use self-respect as a reference point. "Will this decision/choice/action build my self-respect or diminish it?"

✦ Remove yourself from dangerous, abusive or demeaning situations. Never sacrifice yourself to other people's negativity.

✦ Speak up for what you need. Don't expect other people to read your mind. They can't. Know you can survive not getting all your needs "met."

✦ Check for patterns: what do you commonly "take to heart"? Does this benefit you? Remember that other people's attitudes and opinions often say more about them than they do about you.

✦ Treat other people with respect—always. Don't wait to see if they "deserve" it. Choose your own behavior.

✦ Practice forgiveness. Make it easy also for others to forgive you.

✦ Pay attention to what increases your love of living—and brings happiness to others. "The soul is here for its own joy!" Do more of that.

Consider
others

CONSIDER OTHERS?

This book pays a great deal of attention to your development. It offers many, many strategies for you to enjoy your life more, deal with setbacks more easily, and to benefit your most valued and personal relationships.

But what about everyone else?

What about the people you work with? What about the people in your community, your neighbors in your street or apartment block, the strangers with whom you commute each day? What about the other parents at your child's school? Or the people who work in the shops, the bank, the fitness center or the day-care center? And then there are the people on whose services you depend, but whom you never see. And the people who are living on the streets in cardboard boxes who perhaps you would rather never see. *What about them?* What do they have to do with your happiness—and you with theirs?

Since I am writing a twenty-first-century book on life and soul essentials, it was not possible to leave those people out. Your happiness (and safety) depends on their well-being; more specifically, your happiness depends on how willing you are to see them as real people and not as faceless ciphers—and to take responsibility for the way that you think about and treat them.

It is so easy to say—and I do say this several times—that the happiest people in our society are also the most caring. But what does it actually mean? How does it translate into action? And how relevant is this if you feel you can hardly lift your own spirits or take care of yourself?

During the many conversations that Catherine and I had as this book took shape, this was one of the themes that came up most consistently. Catherine made it clear that while she considers herself to be a "good person" (and she certainly is), her circle of interest and personal concern was nevertheless limited. She was deeply interested in her own family and friends. She certainly actively supported a number of charities and as a Christian was engaged in charitable work through her church. But "considering others" beyond those groups felt like a leap that she didn't know if she was ready to take.

Surely, she argued initially, you need to feel good about yourself first—deal with your own issues first. And she felt paralyzed by the sheer number of problems "out there." How could she, she said, even begin to make a difference globally, to "consider others" globally? But as we worked together on this book, and sent ideas back and forth, Catherine came to see this issue quite differently.

I don't believe that I did anything to persuade her. What made the change was Catherine's own realization that *she does have a far greater capacity to care than she had recognized*, and that in "waking up" and releasing that capacity she was not only extending her circle of influence and concern, she was also becoming a more mature "self."

That potential to care is one of our most precious gifts. We may be afraid of it—perhaps afraid that if we begin to care we will be flooded with helplessness in the face of all the need that surrounds us. In my experience, that doesn't happen.

My experience is that first, we "consider others" one step at a time. We do what needs to be done, *one step at a time*. And that second, considering others offers far more than it takes.

As your world grows larger, you grow up. You grow into yourself.

As you recognize your capacity to care, you feel safer, less vulnerable and far less isolated. As Catherine said, "It makes me feel grown up, more realistic, less infantile."

"Considering others" is also a choice.

Exclusions and inclusions

It was also Catherine who pointed out that enlarging your circle of concern goes a long way toward breaking the circles of exclusion and inclusion that cause so much pain and havoc in contemporary life. Judgments about who's "in" and who's "out" are as agonizing in the workplace or neighborhood as they ever were in kindergarten or high school.

Behaving with *interest and respect whoever you are with* is one of our most essential freedoms. Oddly enough, it is also a privilege—available to all.

OTHER LIVES MATTER

Our lives are only as big as our capacity to consider others.

When our capacity to be thoughtful begins and ends with ourselves, or the few people upon whom we depend, we occupy a painfully small universe. What's more, we remain infantile. And that gets less and less attractive the older we grow.

An infant or young child quite legitimately believes that she is the center of the universe and that the people around her have no function but to please her. When they do please her, she rewards them with smiles. When they fail to please her, she howls and roars.

As we get older—if we are willing—we develop the capacity to look beyond ourselves.

We recognise that some of our needs pass—whether or not they are "met."

We recognize that we can meet some of our own needs.

Better yet, we can also meet other people's needs. And benefit from doing that.

Leaving childhood behind, we recognize that *other lives matter.*

Listen to Hildegard of Bingen

Eight hundred years before twentieth-century physicists came up with evidence for the interconnectedness of life, twelfth-century artist and abbess Hildegard of Bingen wrote:

"All things in this world are arranged in consideration of everything else. Everything that is in the heavens, on the earth, and under the earth, is penetrated with connectedness, is penetrated with relatedness."

Considering others, we also benefit.

A FRIENDLIER WAY OF LIFE

Considering others in order to feel a little better about yourself may seem like a new spin on the old narcissism. What saves it (and you) is learning to consider others regardless of how useful they are to you, how important they seem or how graciously they acknowledge your good deeds.

Freedom lies in recognizing that you can consider others as a way of life. What's more, you can do this unconditionally.

I suspect that you will always be more interested in some people than others; you will certainly be far closer to some people than others. Nevertheless, neither this nor anything else needs to stop you from considering other people routinely.

"Thinking about other people" means not losing sight of the fact that every human being you meet wants what you want: respect, friendliness, kindness and happiness. Nothing more, but nothing less either.

You are free to give that. You are free to receive it.

WHAT CONSIDERING OTHERS MEANS

Considering other people includes:

+ Caring about their well-being
+ Giving *time*, thought and attention
+ Noticing what's going on with them—not relying on your assumptions
+ Moving outside your own comfort zone, at least sometimes
+ Thinking about their welfare as you would think about your own
+ Honoring their integrity
+ Respecting *differences* as well as what you share.

Considering other people does not include assuming that:

+ They will—or should—want what you want
+ Everything you do, say or ask will be welcome
+ You know more about their life than they do
+ In return for your kindness, they should take care of your needs.

YOU AFFECT OTHER PEOPLE CONSTANTLY

It's easy to recognize the impact other people have on us. We feel it deeply and immediately when they are rude, thoughtless, critical or unkind. We nurse our wounds when someone dismisses our ideas or ignores us, or walks all over us, or speaks about us in ways that are untrue or unfair.

We also feel it deeply and immediately when other people are thoughtful, open, welcoming and accepting. We blossom when people treat us with respect. We are grateful when other people forgive us.

Even when our self-image and self-worth are not dependent on what other people think or how they behave, we are still affected by their attitudes and actions. But turn the situation around and we become confused.

Do I really have that same effect on other people?

Could they possibly be as affected by my moods, behaviors and attitudes as I am by theirs?

The truth is stark: **no matter how powerless or insignificant you may feel on any particular day, you affect everyone with whom you come into contact.** The only question is, *how* are you affecting them?

Are they encouraged or discouraged by the way you treat them?

Are you lifting their spirits or driving them crazy?

Are they better or worse off for knowing you?

Be confronted!

Many of the questions in this book are confronting. That is my intention! Think of them as the psychological equivalent of a cool shower: let yourself be woken up, stimulated, refreshed and recharged. And let them take you to new levels of self-awareness— and appreciation of other people.

TALKING WITHOUT LISTENING

Writing this chapter, I have become aware how frequently I meet people who talk a great deal about themselves and quite unself-consciously take no interest in my reality beyond "How are you?" or a few stock inquiries. I don't take it personally. I assume this is how they behave with most people. Also, I'm a good listener and sometimes I prefer to listen. It keeps me private and "safe." Nevertheless, I am well aware that *unilateral talking doesn't build intimacy*. Eventually, it becomes a demand. Or a bore.

What do you tell others in the first ten minutes?

Listening in with a little more care than usual, find out what you routinely "let people know" both through words and body language in the first ten minutes or so that you are with them.

What impression are they getting?

What information are they hearing?

Are you consciously choosing what impression you will give, what "message" you are sending, what values you are conveying?

GIVE HAPPINESS A CHANCE

Considering other people, and taking responsibility for how you affect them, can seem intimidating. But it not only has immediate positive effects on them. It also powerfully affects how you think about yourself.

It simply isn't possible to gain self-respect and self-worth if the only reality that counts is your own. Looking beyond the garden gate is essential when it comes to growing up and growing into everything you can be.

The happiest people in all societies, across all cultures, races and religions, are those who recognize their power to affect others positively—*and do something about it.*

What are you doing for anybody else?

In her wonderful book *A Return to Love*, Marianne Williamson describes a long period of depression and angst, during which she complained bitterly to a friend about how bad she was feeling.

Her friend asked, "Marianne, what are you doing for anybody else?"

You may think that was a deeply unsympathetic question. Marianne Williamson accepted it as truthful and compassionate. What's more, it prompted and provoked profound changes that eventually re-created Williamson's entire existence.

WE ARE ALL COMPLEX BEINGS

Many of us spend our lives running.

It becomes incredibly tempting also to rush our reactions to other people, sometimes reducing them to a limiting label—even when it's someone we claim to know well.

"He's a loser."

"She's a slut."

"A total rat."

"Such a bitch."

Doing this, we not only deny them even the traces of courtesy. We also deny their complexity—and their humanity. What's more, when we see them as "all bad"—or even as "all good"—we are probably not seeing them at all. What we are reacting to are our own limited inner perceptions.

Condemning some people, overidealizing others, does them no service. And it does us no service either. Our own complexity and humanity can come to life only when we recognize the complexity and humanity of other people—and respond to that.

Not just complex—contradictory

We are not just complex; we are also contradictory. We want several things, sometimes opposites, at the same time. What we want today, we might not want tomorrow.

When it's difficult to be patient with other people's inconsistencies, it helps to see them alongside your own.

OTHER PEOPLE WANT WHAT YOU WANT

Our lives would be quite different if we were able to take seriously the idea that other people want the same qualities of love, respect and happiness that we do. In fact, our whole world would be different—happier and far more peaceful—if we really believed that **every life has the same value that ours does**. In this mechanical age, we are severely tempted to treat one another mechanically; to have one set of behaviors for people who are "useful" and different behaviors for those who are not. But when we assess people only in terms of their usefulness (or status), we lose sight of what we share: *the precious gift of human existence.*

Honoring your own life more genuinely, you cannot fail also to honor other people and treat them with greater kindness and respect. Their happiness, and yours, become far more securely aligned.

Only the details change

The details of our wants and needs vary tremendously, but when it comes to the big issues, we are very much the same. You want safety, respect, kindness and trust. You want happiness. And you want love. *So do we all.*

Value empathy

The capacity genuinely to care about other people's feelings, even when you don't have those same feelings at the same time or in the same way, is what builds and develops empathy. This is a crucial attribute of emotional maturity.

If you are mean to someone, withholding of kindness, aggressive or cold and indifferent, you are demonstrating a lack of empathy. (You are also demonstrating a lack of self-awareness and self-respect.) Caring about one another not only modifies and controls our behavior; it also keeps us safe. This can only happen when we allow other people to become "real" to us. Empathy is essential to that.

DO I FEEL LIKE IT?

It's easy to consider others *when you feel like it*.

What builds character, inner stability and trust is to *consider others routinely*—and because you are free to do so—rather than being ruled by the changing tides of your emotions.

As long as you are considering others only when you feel like it, your attention remains with yourself. ("What do I feel like?" Not, "What's needed here?")

Considering others *for their sake* is not quite it, either. (It helps. But that could speak more of a need for approval than of your desire to be genuinely open to other people's lives.)

Try this.

Consider others because this best expresses your attitude to life and cultivates your highest values. Yes!

Put into practice your awareness that you are free to behave thoughtfully no matter what the circumstances, no matter how you feel, and no matter who you are with.

Tell yourself: "The choice is mine."

BECAUSE YOU *CAN*

Do you assume that other people should prove they "deserve" your kindness, thoughtfulness or consideration *before they get it?*

"Why should I be nice to her when she was so rude to me?"

"Mean old bag, never smiles, who would want to treat her decently?"

"He hurt me. I'm not going to waste my time talking to him."

Living like this—and many people do—you are letting other people decide how you will behave. *You are giving away your power to decide.* You are letting them determine how you will think and feel.

When you *treat people decently because you can* you are relying on something far more solid than other people's reactions (or your assumptions about those reactions).

You are relying on your values. And living them.

"CONSIDERING OTHERS IS FOREIGN TO ME"

Perhaps one of your reasons for not wholeheartedly considering others is listed here. Or have I overlooked it?

"I don't feel mature enough to think about other people." Maturity is gained in the midst of living. We don't get mature—and then behave well. We learn to behave with more consideration—and this matures us. (It gives us the personal power we long for.) There will be countless times when you fall into old patterns of defending yourself, your ego and even your worst actions; behaving as though you are still that infant sitting in the center of the universe. But gradually you will get used to seeing that other people also have a point of view, also have legitimate needs. And you will see how much it benefits you to notice and respond to that.

"We live in a selfish society. Why should I be different?" The miracle really is how many people in our society are kind, thoughtful, good-natured and friendly. We notice the selfish people because their selfishness offends us (even when it's much like our own). Notice the others more; praise, promote and join them.

"What will I get out of being kinder?" Happiness, vitality, interest, companionship, peace of mind, an end to inertia and boredom; feelings of safety, self-respect, self-worth. That's all.

"I don't want anyone taking advantage of me." Much better, I believe, to risk a few people taking advantage of you than to risk not giving yourself every opportunity to do and be your best.

"I don't know how to consider other people." That's honest. The Golden Rule is your best guide: "Do for others what you would like them to do for you." Be the friend you want to have; take every opportunity to see yourself through other people's eyes. When you don't like what you see, change it.

"I love my family. That's enough." Unfortunately that isn't enough. Our circles of interdependence extend way beyond our immediate interests, our immediate family. As the world shrinks, the old tribalistic ways are increasingly less appropriate. Be aware of all that you receive from the world beyond your family, how your day is changed by the kindness of a stranger. *Be* that kind stranger.

"I'm too depressed to think about other people." Thinking about others is a powerful antidote to the feelings of isolation that often precede or accompany depression. It's harder at those times to feel you have something of value to give—but even more essential. It can even be a relief to shift your thoughts away from yourself. And as your thoughts shift, your feelings will follow.

"I'm busy with my career right now. When I retire I will devote myself to other people." How many people do you affect each day? How many people affect you? Can you afford to wait?

"I was abused as a child. No one taught me how to love." The absence of love (and perhaps kindness and consideration) taught you more powerfully than most how precious those qualities are. However clumsy you feel, giving what feels awkward and unpracticed, nothing will work more effectively to show you the absolute truth: your life matters and what you have to give also matters.

"I don't want other people to think I'm needy or a pushover." You are not considering other people in order to change their opinion of you. You are doing it because you are free to choose positively and to enhance other people's lives, as well as your own. And if you are regarded as a pushover? Often the thoughts we attribute to other people are actually our own worst fears. What you are really risking is that other people will think you are good to be around, thoughtful, uplifting—even inspiring.

BEYOND THE PERSONAL

Learning how to give, you'll notice it's surprisingly unimportant whether what you are giving is personal or impersonal.

Giving to the people you know best is wonderful. It can intensify your feelings of connection and beautifully express your appreciation.

Giving to someone you don't know may be less immediately rewarding, but in terms of your psychological development, *it may be even more important.*

This version of thoughtfulness expresses your awareness that *other lives matter.*

It also recognizes that your individual well-being depends on the well-being of our whole society and wider world—not just on the few people who know your name and remember your birthday.

Remind yourself how much difference it makes even in the most fleeting encounters in stores, on the train, in the bank, as you wait for the children outside their schools, as you give way to a motorist on the freeway, when that *encounter expresses goodwill.*

In several major religious traditions, it's explicitly taught that the highest form of giving is always anonymous. Only then can you be sure that you are giving for its own sake, and not out of your need to be admired or praised.

NOT EVERYONE'S NEEDS ARE THE SAME

"Considering others" doesn't mean treating everyone in the same way. It means tuning in to the subtleties of each situation and responding appropriately.

You might, for example, consider others most effectively at work by being clear about what you expect of them, taking responsibility for your role as leader.

At home, with your partner, you might express your thoughtfulness by not taking her for granted and by being explicitly courteous even when you are tired.

With one child you might express your thoughtfulness through making more time for play and one-to-one chats; with another child what might be needed right now is that you curb your own anxiety and stop nagging about their achievements.

There is no formula for thoughtful behavior. Formulaic behavior quickly grows stale. *For people to be real to you, and for you to be real to them, each encounter needs to be fresh as well as genuine.*

Let other people be real to you

The more genuinely you can see other people as complex, evolving individuals, as full of contradictions as you are, the more possible it will be to respond sensitively and appropriately.

Push yourself hard to see the real person, and not the image of the person that lives in your mind.

GROWING BEYOND ABUSE

All too many people grow up in a household dominated by a parent's dark moods, leaving them confused about their right as an adult to assert their own needs for peaceful, respectful relationships. Shame gets in the way. So does fear. Being direct becomes difficult. It's like a language that you've never learned.

The "difficult parent" almost certainly believes that he (or she) can't control his moods, emotional reactions or perhaps his abuse of alcohol or drugs if that's also part of the picture. But whatever they consciously believe, they undoubtedly control the reactions and even the perceptions of everyone around them. This doesn't benefit them. And it certainly doesn't benefit their family members.

Pretending that things are all right when they are not, family members often find it extremely difficult to develop the clarity they need to make their own psychologically healthy choices—especially when it comes to intimate relationships. They often lack the confidence or self-respect to assert themselves appropriately. This makes them vulnerable.

Two quite distinct sets of insights emerge from this widely recognizable story.

If you grew up in a family of this kind you may seem exceptionally well equipped to "consider others." Some of you may even be professional as well as private rescuers, trained by your family circumstances to see others' needs as having greater validity than your own. For you, the challenge may be to discover greater self-love, self-respect and especially self-worth. This doesn't mean ceasing to consider other people's needs. That is never helpful. But it may mean learning to recognize which of your emotional patterns arise from fear or anxiety—the need to placate and make things "all right"—and which from self-worth and a more inclusive view of love. It may mean consciously asking, "Is this the best that I can do for myself as well as for others?" It may even mean giving up the "rewards" of being needed in an essentially unhealthy situation.

If you are brave enough to see that you are the angry, "moody," irritable or difficult person, or the person reluctant to see how your drinking or drug abuse affects the people around you, then the story is somewhat different. For you, it's vital to know that it is possible to break those patterns *for the sake of the people you love.*

First, though, you will need to recognize that your moods and needs are dominating everyone around you and probably harming them. No matter how powerless you may feel, the power you wield is tremendous. Facing up to the effect of your behavior on others, and *taking responsibility for it* will of course lead to some feelings of shame and regret. But I suspect you have those feelings anyway. I also know that treating yourself and other people differently, considering their feelings and needs along with your own, is the only way to leave those feelings behind, as well as the behaviors that cause them. "Noticing" how you are affecting other people takes true courage. It can seem intolerable. But as a route out of the self-absorption and self-deceit that underpins extreme negativity, it is unparalleled.

THERE'S NOTHING PRIVATE
ABOUT YOUR MOODS

It's relatively easy to come to recognize the effects of your actions on other people. But what about your moods?

You may choose to believe that you can keep your moods to yourself. Think again.

Moods—driven by emotions and especially by thoughts— powerfully affect other people. "Mood" is conveyed energetically. When it differs from your words or actions, it will be "mood" that will linger longest and produce the greatest reaction in other people.

When you come into the presence of another person, "mood" is what you instinctively feel. It's what opens you up. Or shuts you down. *Your moods are just as powerful.*

There is often a vast gulf between the way we read our own moods and how others experience them. We underestimate their effect routinely. And often use this as an excuse as we randomly inflict them on others.

Think about the person who controls others through their passive aggression (sulking, punishing with silence, undercutting others, spoiling other people's pleasure, stonewalling, refusing to say what's wrong). That person feels powerless. They are often consumed with self-pity because they feel so powerless. Yet they pollute the atmosphere around them just as effectively as the person who rants, shouts and raves. The impact of their mood may even be worse as they will often be strongly in denial about its effects. (Those effects *hurt*.)

Noticing the effect your moods have on other people, and taking full responsibility for them, is a true wake-up call. It can signal a miraculous change in the way you think about yourself and consider others. It can also make a powerful difference in the way that other people experience being around you.

WHAT BOUNDARIES ARE

"Boundaries" are both physical and psychological.

I may not want you to stand too close to me, talk at me or touch me. If you are not my child, I may not want you to follow me around demanding my attention while I am busy with other things. I don't want you to ignore or trivialize my reality. I certainly don't want you to assume that because you want to have sex with me I will necessarily want to have sex with you.

When you do any of those things, you are trespassing and my physical boundaries are violated. That feels very uncomfortable. It may even feel dangerous.

I may not want you to tell me your intimate secrets or demand to hear mine. I may not want you to make assumptions about me, gossip about me, tell me what I am feeling or "walk all over me." I may not want you to make assumptions on the basis of my gender, race, culture or beliefs. When you do that, you are trespassing and my psychological boundaries are violated. That feels uncomfortable at best, agonizing at worst.

Many boundary transgressions happen involuntarily. The person "walking all over you" may have no idea what she is doing. (You need to tell her; she needs to listen.) Cultural and social factors also play a part here. What might be acceptable in one culture (public kissing, talking intimately, having casual sex) is shocking in another. Temperament also plays a part. So does "sense of self."

When someone doesn't have a stable, intact sense of self they are more likely to feel unsure about what they can ask of others, what they are entitled to accept or refuse, and even what's healthy and appropriate and what isn't.

Respecting other people is central to becoming more confident about yourself.

This means:

+ Reading their signals (*especially* their body language)
+ Checking things out ("How would you feel about . . ."; "Would you like to . . .")
+ Withdrawing unconditionally when you have "gone too far"

✦ Speaking up about what instinctively feels right or wrong to you
✦ Knowing that you are absolutely entitled to your autonomy
✦ Knowing other people are absolutely entitled to their autonomy, dignity and respect.

Trespassing is dangerous

"Trespass" is a primary factor in many serious psychological illnesses. *Psychological health is possible only when boundaries are intact and well protected.* If you have any doubts about your own sense of boundaries, or you have been or are being violated or hurt in any way, *seek professional help immediately.*

WHAT BOUNDARIES ALLOW

Your sense of self depends on recognizing the "otherness" of other people.

Let yourself notice what "too close," "too intrusive," "too much" and "not okay" feel like. Let yourself know that you are entitled—absolutely entitled—to maintain those boundaries for yourself.

Respect those same boundaries in all your interactions with other people. Check out that you know:

+ Where you "end"—psychologically speaking—and other people begin
+ That you and others—no matter how deeply connected—are separate people
+ That you can be close to other people without feeling their emotions for them
+ That you can be close to other people without demanding they feel your emotions along with you
+ That you are at the center of your own world—but not other people's. (When something happens to them, you may not have "caused" it. When they are rude to you it could be because they're having a bad day—and nothing to do with you.)

When boundaries are in place, you can feel empathy, interest, delight and love. You will take responsibility for the way *your attitudes always affect other people.* But you will not assume that you are the lifeblood of someone else's existence, or demand that someone else be the lifeblood for your own.

"I can't live without you" is *not* a compliment. It's an expression of infantile neediness and fear. (If that's what you feel, it's crucial to get professional help.)

"I would hate to have to live without you" is just as loving—but far more respectful.

FORTIFY THE CASTLE

In his book *The Road Less Traveled and Beyond*, psychiatrist and writer M. Scott Peck talks about what he calls "drawbridge problems."

During his years of seeing patients he observed (as I did too, in my years of working as a psychotherapist) that many had little idea that they were in charge of their own "drawbridge."

Some were, in his words, "laid open all the time, so that virtually anyone and everyone could amble into their personal space, prowl around, stay as long as they liked, and do whatever harm they would." Other people, fearing invasion, would keep their drawbridges raised and shut all of the time so that "nobody and nothing could penetrate their isolated solitude."

I was deeply struck by his description of a situation that may be increasingly familiar, that of a woman who had no real idea that she could choose which men came through her front door, which men came into her living room, and which men came into her bedroom. *Such women (and men) are unable to consider others because they don't know how to consider themselves.*

They can certainly respond to the urgency of someone else's agenda. But until they can consciously choose their responses and behaviors, and know that they are entitled to do so, they remain vulnerable and even endangered.

Considering others can certainly include saying "no"

Tolerance or even kindness should never take you to a place where your own integrity comes under threat.

Considering others *ceases to be psychologically helpful* when you lose sight of your own needs, integrity and self.

"PLEASE WANT WHAT I WANT"

Many intelligent people feel genuinely confused and sometimes outraged when they want something and those near to them want something else. This, too, is a boundary issue.

"Wanting the same things" is part of love but the story does not end there. In fact, maturity in love is more often forged through the ways that people negotiate difference rather than sameness. And come to appreciate that.

Danger signs ahead

In any relationship, from the most professional to the most personal, it's worth noticing if there are patterns about whose agenda routinely prevails; whose "choices" count most and whose desires, needs and opinions are routinely overlooked.

Respect is developed when everyone has a voice. And when everyone learns to listen.

You are entitled to be clear

Your psychological safety depends on your being clear and assertive about what you will and won't allow.

You are entitled to this clarity. And to respect others in their efforts to establish it.

"CONSIDERING OTHERS FEELS TOO HARD!"

There are countless times when you unself-consciously consider other people. You are engaged, interested, thoughtful and encouraging. And without thinking very much about it, you recognize that this not only benefits other people, it makes you feel good too.

But what about those other times, when considering other people or being open to them feels too hard, too risky, too frightening? What about when you feel too hurt to be anything but mean? What about when other people don't deserve your kindness? Or what about when you are too exhausted to care?

Sometimes you do need to be cautious. *Considering others doesn't mean ceasing to think about your own well-being and safety.*

More generally, a *lack of confidence in yourself* stands in the way of taking an active interest in other people.

Perhaps you are undervaluing what you have to give. Or you're afraid of intruding. Or you feel overwhelmed by your own agenda and concerns.

None of these reasons makes you a bad person. They do, however, keep your world smaller than it needs to be. And they certainly keep you less confident and empowered than you could be.

This will help:

- ✦ Practice what you have to give (concern, interest, respect, kindness). As you do so, you will get better at it and value it more. It will come to feel completely natural.
- ✦ Know that considering others *may include not intruding.* Check out what's wanted.
- ✦ Be assured that lack of practice ceases to be a problem the moment you begin to live more thoughtfully! Psychological skills are always learned as you go.
- ✦ Observe that when you extend your circle of concern beyond yourself, the experience of connection you receive far outweighs the discomfort of putting your own agenda temporarily aside. *Let yourself know that.*

As you take a genuine interest in other people, *your confidence will grow,* benefiting every aspect of your life.

NO DUMPING

Awareness of psychological boundaries helps put an end to "dumping."

Dumping means that you feel entitled to criticize me, blame me, spoil my pleasure, talk over the top of me, ignore me, scream or shout at me—*because you feel "bad."*

Doing that, you are ignoring that *I am a separate person* and *you are responsible for your own emotional well-being.*

Of course if you feel bad, you may want me to know how you are feeling. It's possible to do that without dumping, especially when you don't expect me to fix you, make up to you for what's wrong, or feel as miserable as you do.

Dumping is driven by self-pity as well as rage that the external world is not following your internal agenda. The finest antidote combines self-responsibility with self-respect: "What's needed here? How can I *best help myself?*"

Empathy is clean. Dumping is dirty.

Giving and getting empathy is quite different from dumping. Empathy lets us have a real sense of what someone else is feeling. It lets us care. *But it doesn't mean that we also have to have those same feelings.* "I can feel *for* you; I don't have to feel exactly what you are feeling in order to express my care."

MONITOR YOUR INNER STATE

You can monitor your inner state in part *through the reactions you have to other people.*

> Someone asks for a simple favor. You snap. *Is it them—or you?*
> Someone pays you a compliment. You tell yourself they don't mean it. *Is it them—or you?*
> Someone brushes past you or talks over the top of you in a meeting. You tell yourself they have no respect for you. *Is it them— or you?*

Noticing how you are interpreting other people's behavior—the commentary inside on what's happening outside—offers you brilliant clues about your own fluctuating levels of self-love and self-respect. **When you feel bad about yourself, you will be far more inclined to interpret other people's responses negatively.** Wonderfully, you can bring yourself back to a state of greater equilibrium by choosing to interpret their behavior more positively and by choosing to *respond and behave more positively yourself.*

VALUE COMPROMISE

It's an insecure ego that gets in the way of compromising.

Ego tells us we can't afford to give way, to see another person's point of view, to work for a win/win situation.

Ego tells us we need to be right. And that if we are not right, then we must be wrong.

Self-respect—and plain common sense—tells us something different. It reminds us that we never have the whole story; that we can benefit from other people's experiences; that sometimes giving up a little, we gain a lot.

Your attitude to others tells a story

Your self-respect and self-confidence depend on how well you treat other people. The person who treats other people badly exhibits a lack of self-respect and even self-confidence, no matter how arrogant they may appear.

The person who feels at ease inwardly, who accepts their own inner complexity, and who is capable of humility as well as kindness, will never willfully hurt another person, and will certainly never treat them with contempt or cruelty.

For you to build self-respect, it is possible to *start* by lifting your game in the way you treat others.

IN PRAISE OF GENEROSITY

Generosity comes to life when you consider others. Generosity begins with an openness of mind and spirit.

It takes you beyond yourself.

It brings out the best in you.

It opens your eyes to the reality of other people's existence.

It lets you make connections with the most unexpected people.

It lends itself to small gestures as well as large.

It subverts greed, fear and insecurity.

It doesn't depend on learning, privilege or status.

It doesn't depend on being religious or "spiritual."

It is as vital in our public institutions as it is in our bedrooms.

It is impossible to manufacture, measure, sell or waste. (You can't trade it!)

It springs from a belief in our inborn goodness.

It is an act of faith that all our lives matter.

It benefits our minds and bodies as much as it does our spirits.

Generosity takes you beyond the self-interest that sometimes masquerades as love. Without its presence in our world, we would scarcely know what love is.

GIVING TO OTHERS

Giving to others is essential to happiness. It is beautifully achieved in these and a thousand other (free) ways.

+ Allowing yourself to be fully present
+ Accepting people as they are
+ Being courteous
+ Giving *more of your time, interest and concern* than is necessary
+ Taking an interest in others' interests
+ Valuing qualities more than achievements
+ Listening without judging
+ Paying attention to what someone needs and not what you think they need
+ Refusing to pass on hurtful gossip
+ Talking about what's positive, stimulating, uplifting
+ Giving the benefit of the doubt
+ Accepting difference—and enjoying it
+ Letting past hurts go
+ Not blaming
+ Choosing cheerfulness
+ Letting mistakes go
+ Resisting all temptation to sulk, stonewall, "punish"
+ Not keeping accounts about what you have given or what you are owed
+ Receiving gracefully
+ Limiting your demands
+ Giving all the time you have promised—and more
+ Paying attention to whoever might be feeling left out
+ Praising, encouraging, rejoicing
+ Valuing your strengths and talents—and sharing them.

What do you want most?

What do *you* want most?
Practice giving that.

WALKING THE SECOND MILE

Walking the second mile is generosity in action, springing from an ancient idea that continues to make brilliant psychological sense.

In fact, as it runs so strongly in opposition to our highly self- and reward-focused ways of thinking, it may be even more powerful, even more needed now.

When someone asks you to do something, or when you see that something needs to be done, do more, offer more, *be more* than is strictly "necessary."

- ✦ Your neighbor asks you to drive her to the hospital when she needs a check-up. You cancel an appointment to wait with her and drive her home.
- ✦ Your sister is constantly asking for favors. She needs to stand on her own two feet. You usually rush in and out again, frowning. This time you say, "How about lunch?"
- ✦ Your partner has (again) forgotten his briefcase. You are tempted to tell him that you simply don't know how an apparently intelligent person could be quite this stupid. You don't.
- ✦ Someone asks you for money for a good cause. You evaluate what is needed, not what you can effortlessly afford.
- ✦ You hate cleaning the oven, sweeping up the leaves or picking up the children's toys. You do this at half the usual pace and with total focus on what you are doing. You also monitor your self-talk. Instead of, "Why should I be the one . . . ," you try, "I am doing this for myself and the people I love."

You are not doing this for the sake of the other person only.
You are not doing this to be "nice."
You walk the second mile because this is an essential expression of your freedom to determine how you will behave, a freedom that is not dictated by other people.

Matthew's gospel

Perhaps the most famous reference to the "second mile" comes in Matthew's gospel where he quotes Christ as saying, "If someone forces you to walk a mile, go with him for two miles."

Christ was referring to the convention of his time, whereby Roman soldiers, as an occupying force, could insist that Jews carry their bags for them for a mile.

For that first mile you, like the Jews of Christ's day, are doing something because you must; for the second mile you are doing something because you can.

THE KINDNESS EFFECT

Let yourself feel completely free to be kind—truly kind—for the sake of other people. And for your own sake too.

It is impossible to stretch out to other people through your emotions, imagination, concern, interest and actions without also benefiting yourself. Your world grows larger; your problems grow smaller.

I am convinced that most people want to be generous, want to give, want to be available for others. What holds them back is often a mixture of inhibition, shyness, lack of practice. Or perhaps they find it hard to value what they have to give. Yet it is only through giving that you learn to value what's being given—while also feeling easier and lighter about giving it away!

Remind yourself always, "It is a privilege to be able to give." And it is a freedom to be able to give without demanding something in return.

KIND FROM THE INSIDE OUT

Kindness to others becomes meaningless when you are not also being kind to yourself.

Perhaps some of the most "selfless" people among us become worn-out because they are kind to everyone but themselves. (Many people still believe that it is wrong to be kind to yourself, that it will lead to selfishness or laziness. It does not.)

Think deeply about what "being kind to yourself" means to you.

We often think about doing less, or living more simply, when we begin to think about being kinder to ourselves.

Sometimes though, at least in my experience, it may involve believing in yourself more, taking more risks, standing up more confidently for what you want and what you believe in. It may mean doing more, rather than less; or doing what you do with greater confidence, curiosity and trust.

It may also mean getting back in touch with your senses; taking time to do things in a way that feels less hurried and more rewarding. Most of all, it may mean engaging with life more deeply; allowing yourself to know what your feelings are and to express them; behaving in ways that are authentic and open, rather than defensive and guarded.

Being kinder to yourself will also always include monitoring how you talk to yourself. When your demands on yourself are great, or when you are picking at yourself or putting yourself down, you will feel *and express* the strain of that. To be kind to others, and to create a more peaceful and accepting atmosphere around yourself, you need to start exactly where you are.

Use the negative moments

Sometimes your rage at what others are failing to do, or your envy of what others have, will bring you invaluable insights about what you yourself are wanting. Use those "negative" moments or emotions positively. Transform them by learning something of value from them. Then put what you have learned into practice.

FRIENDSHIP

Friendship makes a profound difference to our quality of life. Having friends can be one of the greatest joys of living. Many people will not have a lifelong sexually intimate relationship. Many have a small or scattered biological family—or no family members at all. But even when someone has a lifelong partner and a large family, friends remain precious. And learning to sustain and value friendships is crucial for emotional well-being and happiness.

Some people seek and only want fairly superficial friendships. Others want and need deeper friendships where they can feel genuinely accepted—be "themselves" in every way; share their dreams and vulnerabilities as well as lighter moments. The giving and receiving of that kind of trust should never be taken for granted.

The intimacy of friendship is as valuable as any other kind. And the foundations for successful friendships are no different from any other close relationship.

For friendship to flourish, and to be a source of comfort, delight and happiness for everyone involved, it is essential for each person to be respectful, caring and interested. It is also essential to accept differences—including differences of need.

These qualities and attributes build and sustain genuine friendship.

- Loyalty
- Trust—and trustworthiness
- Acceptance
- Interest
- Warmth and encouragement
- Discretion—never gossiping, disparaging, belittling to others
- The giving of time—friendships need time. Good intentions are not enough
- Sharing responsibility for the friendship—not leaving it to one person always to take the initiative
- Pleasure in the other person's happiness and successes. If you feel jealous of your friend, deal with those feelings—don't spoil the friendship

✦ The capacity to overlook and forgive lapses, mistakes or misunderstandings. And move on
✦ Shared "caretaking"—not one person constantly being required to care for or listen to the other
✦ Reliability
✦ Kindness.

What are the qualities of friendship you value most?

It is easy to take friends and friendship for granted. Or to give countless hours to thinking about your sexual relationships—and none to your friendships.

You may want to start with a seed meditation—using "friendship" as your seed word. You may be very surprised at some of your associations if you give your mind time to travel.

Also note in your journal the qualities of friendship you value most.

Think about what friends and friendships have given you over the years—and what you learned from the friendships that did not go so well.

Think about what you expect of friends—and whether this is reasonable or supportive.

Think about what you get from friends. Would you like it to be different in any way?

Keep this journal entry open so that you can continue to add to it over the course of a week or two. "Investment" in your friendships is crucial for happiness.

What kind of friend are you?

Consider carefully what kind of friend you are. It will be most productive to write these questions in your journal—and to take time with the answers. Return to the questions as often as needed.

Is there a pattern to your friendships?

Do you bring the best of yourself to your friendships—or only what's left over?

Do you take risks in the depth of friendships you allow yourself?

Are you forgiving when friends are less than perfect?

What do you expect friendship to give you? Is that what you give in return?

How would an "ideal friend" be different from the kind of friend you are?

What changes do you want to make?

What appreciation do you want to show?

You don't have any "real friends"

Surprisingly large numbers of people do not have any close friends. If you would like to have closer friends, consider these possibilities.

Spend time with people with whom you have a shared interest. This could be a class, a cause, a community project. When the focus is not on "friendship" you will feel less exposed and more relaxed.

Explore what "being friendly" means to you. Behave in ways that are explicitly friendly, good-humored, accepting.

Recognize that the "perfect" friend is as rare as the "perfect" lover. Accept people as they are. Most people respond well to genuine acceptance.

Check your listening skills; also check what you routinely talk about. Does it extend beyond yourself and your immediate interests?

Understand that many people genuinely have very little time. Their rebuffs may not be "about you." However, where people show some interest in developing a friendship, take initiatives.

Be a good friend to yourself. Take care of your health, well-being, interests and spiritual needs.

This may be an issue where psychotherapy can help. It is a legitimate need to want sustaining friendships.

DELIBERATE IMBALANCE

CATHERINE: Deliberate imbalance, for me, is about entering an "unequal" relationship with my eyes wide open, deliberately taking on responsibilities far beyond my "fair share" because I have the resources and the desire to help.

It can be an incredibly useful tool, but I learned the hard way that it's important to be upfront about entering a deliberate imbalance.

One of my closest friends spent nearly ten years of her life (and her fertility) in a relationship with a married man, waiting for him to leave his wife. *He never did.* Meanwhile, I spent ten years of my life on the phone and in cafés having the same conversation with her about this married man who wasn't in any way ready to leave his wife. *I really did.*

Every conversation was the same. She was distraught or depressed and I was supportive. Now I know enough to understand that what she really was, was stuck and what I was, was a Rescuer!

After that hard-won experience, I have learned to enter a "deliberate imbalance" with complete honesty—making sure that I am not on a slippery slope to Rescuing someone. Even with family and close friends, I stick to three important ground rules: that both parties explicitly understand and agree to the imbalance; that, if possible, we can agree to a time limit; and that we are both clear that the imbalance is helping significantly (and not enabling irresponsible behavior).

Deliberate imbalance can be incredibly positive. A great example of this working well for me was the agreement my husband and I had while he worked full-time and completed a graduate degree at night. Though it was tough for me to offer so much support (extra housework, receiving less help with our children), we both understood why we were doing it, and our shared goal helped us to overcome our occasional difficulties with the lack of parity. When his degree was finished (after three and a half long years ... hooray!), so was the imbalance ... at least until I start my post-grad degree!

STEPHANIE: My feeling is that what Catherine is describing is very much part of the seasonal changes in all relationships.

Sometimes other people do need more help or support than usual. If we can give it, everyone benefits. (Generosity benefits you as much as the person you are helping.) Not everyone will need to articulate limits as Catherine should have in the "best friend" example, but doing so can be particularly helpful when there is a tendency toward imbalance within the relationship or when you are, by nature, something of a rescuer or "helper."

The situation with people closest to you is always a little more complicated. This reminds us that while nothing in human relationships is static, routines can quickly become "habits" and what was a favor or extra support can quickly become "normal" and entirely taken for granted.

Sometimes you have to feel resentful before a change can be initiated! Most people will take advantage of others if the opportunity is there. You "help out" your partner while she's studying and two years after her study is completed you realize you are still doing most of the tasks. You give your teenage child permission not to help out in the house during a crucial transition year and when the year is over nothing changes.

This is not because those people are bad or lazy. It's because *we severely underestimate most of what other people do for us.* Household tasks remain "invisible" except to the person who feels responsible for them. And sometimes the more humble but necessary tasks in work life are also easily trivialized or ignored by those who *rely on them but are not doing them.*

Negotiating our relationships, we need to be clear that we can ask for help, as well as give it; that we are willing to state our needs *and* also meet the needs of other people; that we are vigilant about not making classic gender roles an excuse for exploiting someone else; that we value clarity and transparency, as well as friendliness, in all our negotiations.

WATCH OTHER PEOPLE'S REACTIONS

While I was writing this section, my good friend Esther called to tell me about a situation where she had literally fainted without silencing the flow of words from the man talking to her at the time.

What makes this story a little worse is that the man who was so caught up in his own agenda that he literally did not observe Esther growing paler, sinking into her chair, and then slumping over unconscious, is a medical doctor.

It would be safe to assume that he has had rather more training than most in observing others. But for many of us, doctors and non-doctors alike, the simple courtesy of noticing the effect of what we are doing or saying on the person we are with is shockingly elusive.

It's not possible to consider others in any meaningful way without actually noticing what's happening to them.

- ✦ Are they trying to escape as we talk?
- ✦ Is this interesting or rewarding for them—as well as us?
- ✦ Are we using them as an "ear" into which we can off-load—or are we seeing them as a real person?

This kind of "blindness" can occur in any shared activity, from cleaning house to sex, from writing a shopping list to writing a book. For the activity to be mutually rewarding each person must be willing to stay open to the other person's reality—not just their own.

INTENTIONS AND ACTIONS—MIND THE GAP

Here come the psychological double standards that most of us practice so "naturally" we never question them. Yet they cause some of our most painful misunderstandings and get us into some of our worst emotional messes.

What I am talking about is the way **we judge ourselves by our good intentions and other people by their actions.**

Judging ourselves by our good intentions:

+ We read our own minds and like what we find there.
+ We are hurt and defensive when other people don't read our minds, don't give us the benefit of the doubt, and interpret our behavior negatively.

When it comes to other people, the situation looks remarkably different:

+ We judge them by their actions.
+ We use their actions as the sole measure of their intentions. ("Actions speak louder than words.")
+ We make our judgments—and often punish—accordingly.

Here's a couple of the kind of banal examples that can doom a relationship.

You and I have arranged to meet to go out for dinner. You are home waiting. I'm late. In fact, I'm still at the office telling myself I'll be there soon. You feel hurt because I'm often late. You tell yourself I don't value you, your time or our relationship. Depending on how you feel, this may slip into more global fears that you will never be loved or appreciated adequately. I finally arrive, eager to tell you how much I am looking forward to our evening. The fact that I am late seems to me far less important than the good time ahead. (After all, *I didn't mean to be late.*) You disagree. Our evening together does not go well.

You are judging me by my actions. I, on the other hand, am judging myself by my good intentions. We are both hurt and offended—and feel entitled to our feelings.

Here's another example.

I call you, ready to have an intimate chat. You say, "Sorry, no time to speak." I think, "How dare she be so rude. I'm always kind to her. What kind of friendship is it that she doesn't have time to talk?" Hours, perhaps days later, I am still telling myself how little you care about me and our friendship. You, meantime, are totally preoccupied with a crisis of your own. And you assume that I will understand. When, a week or two later, you call me, you are at a loss to understand why I am so off-hand. The cycle of hurt and misunderstanding continues.

To give our relationships their best chance we need to:

✦ Give others the benefit of the doubt. (Assume that their intentions are good—at least as long as it's halfway reasonable to do so.)

✦ Pay close attention to the effect of our actions, taking for granted that others can't read our minds—*only our actions.*

That's all.

Mind the gap

Monitor constantly the stark gap between action and intention.
Make sure your actions bring to life your finest intentions.
Ask yourself: "What story are my *actions* telling?"

Mind your e-mails

E-mails are written at speed. And they are often read at even greater speed. Between your intention, and what the person reads and comprehends, there is often yet another painful kind of gap. *What is in your mind is frequently far from what appears on someone else's screen.* I know this, to my sorrow.

As speedy as your e-mail communications need to be, pause to ask yourself: "How will this be read?"

ADULT ACTIVITY, ADULT RESPONSIBILITY

CATHERINE: Last year my friend Beth came to town, and we had lunch together in the glorious autumn sunshine. Beth told me about her two adult children, both attending university, and she said something that I want to remember. "When my kids take on an adult activity, I remind them that they also take on adult responsibilities."

With the privilege to drink comes the responsibility not to drive. With becoming sexually active comes the responsibility to be committed, to care for another person's feelings, to be mindful of health issues, to be loving and mature.

I thought about how right Beth is: regardless of our age, we all need to be reminded of the link between our actions and their consequences.

It's so easy to get caught in the trap of our own feelings and preferences, rather than being directed by what needs to be done. We allow ourselves all kinds of childish responses: *I'll work on that hard task when I feel up to it; I'll visit my aging father when I can find the time; I'll commit to you once you make some changes to suit me.*

Similarly, it's very easy to act as if the consequences simply don't apply to us. We often spend a great deal of time convincing others and ourselves that we are somehow exempt. *I'm entitled to this affair because it's True Love,* we think. Or *I need the creative buzz that I get from serial relationships.* Or *Doing this once can't hurt.*

Stephen Covey, American writer and organizational behavior expert, gives us the metaphor of the stick: when you pick up one end of a stick (your action), you automatically pick up the other (the consequence).

In all honesty, so many of the mistakes I've made happened because I fooled myself about the consequences of my actions. What makes us ignore the connection between actions and consequences? How we can we learn to act with the likely consequence held firmly in our minds?

STEPHANIE: I like Covey's image of valuing each end of the stick—
though I would prefer to call it a branch. But of course we all
know from experience that when we pick up one end (action) we
do often ignore the other (consequence)—or hope it will take care
of itself.

Desire is the least-tamed aspect of human existence. It drives
some of our finest impulses and some of our worst. Even when we
think we know exactly what we are doing, there are potent
unconscious desiring forces at work within us. Not all our actions
are driven by desires, of course. But many are.

We want pleasure, distraction, affirmation, power or satisfaction; and we want it badly. We want those experiences to
remind us that we are alive, to distract us from meaninglessness;
to stave off death. In the wanting of them, we may not also want to
think sensibly about consequences. I am not saying that this is
right; I am describing what is.

"Consequences" belong in one part of our brain, "desiring" in
another. "Desiring" is emotional; "consequences" are rational. The
challenge of maturity is to bring those functions and levels of
consciousness together. (Just think how long it takes most of us to
learn even to clean up the physical messes we leave behind us!)

If our "wanting" is around something relatively inconsequential
and doesn't hook us in to our infantile past, we will find it
relatively easy to be consequence-focused. But when the
"wanting" is primitive and powerful we may have to go a few
rounds with it to learn *through our own experience* what the
consequences are of what we are seeking.

Philosophers throughout history have warned that we are
frequently blind to our own motives.
**The challenge of self-awareness is to "see," to discover
what your motives are, to make those motives conscious and
to express them with integrity–**for your own sake, and for the
sake of others.

Nevertheless, when desire is rising, there will be times when
awareness lags behind behavior.

Let's take sex as an example (as this is the area where most of us have probably had some of our hardest lessons to learn). What "motivates" us to seek sexual intimacy—whether this is within a devoted relationship or an ill-advised fling? Sexual satisfaction is only a small part of it. We long also for intimacy, closeness; we long to inhabit our bodies fully; we long to "matter."

We may also long to free ourselves of our everyday self-control and discipline. And, interestingly enough, some of the people who are most disciplined in their everyday lives—who think strategically and with clear regard for consequences—are most at risk of going heedlessly into situations that, unconsciously, offer them release. For many people who may be out of touch with nature or the Divine, music or poetry, sex or drugs may seem the only channels available in their search for ecstasy or transcendence.

However, it must also be said that desire is ruthlessly *self-focused*. You may be fixated on the object of your desire; but the needing of it, the having of it, *is all about you*. And that's where this topic becomes more interesting.

Welcome distance arrives when you can look at "motive" at least somewhat dispassionately, thinking not only about what you are wanting but also how you are going about getting it. ("It's tenderness, energy, excitement that I want, or an end to loneliness; not necessarily my best friend's lover.")

Catherine also questions people's "childish responses," avoiding doing what needs to be done. I agree with her. We are childish. We do put off what needs doing because we don't "feel like it." We self-justify madly. We allow ourselves to be ruled by our emotions, and rarely if ever get much benefit from that. When we progress even a little from this stage, doing what needs to be done, and setting resentment aside, we liberate ourselves significantly.

But desire takes you into territory of a different kind.

What matters least to you will always be easiest to see; the things that disturb you most will always take longer to understand. Calling on values is extremely helpful here too. As long as you remain entirely self-focused, you remain vulnerable. When you can shift your gaze to consider your values and the effect of your actions on others, your driving motivation automatically becomes clearer. And *your power to choose your actions* grows much stronger.

GIVE THE BENEFIT OF THE DOUBT
LAVISHLY

Giving the benefit of the doubt is a sublime psychological strategy.

It can heal wounds.

It can save you from the agonies of regret.

It spares you unnecessary angst, worry and self-blame.

It's extremely attractive.

It lets other people know that you trust them.

It lets you know that you can afford to be generous rather than defensive.

It brilliantly subverts feelings of anxiety and jealousy.

It restores your capacity to give and receive love.

It lets you routinely expect and look for the best, aware that if something does go wrong you can and will recover.

It lets you expect the best of the other person. And it brings out the best in you.

It frees you from the twin burdens of doubt and suspicion.

It also nicely reminds you that life is complex. Things happen that can't be predicted; people have concerns beyond those that they share with you; even with the best of intentions, agendas shift and change. You can accept that.

Respect and trust also count

In an unhealthy relationship, giving the benefit of the doubt can tip over into rescuing.

Respect and trust also count. They need to be built on actions, not promises.

"I WISH YOU THE BEST"

You may be suffering the agonies of suspicion, bitterness, jealousy or hurt.

You want to give that other person the benefit of the doubt. Somehow, though, those familiar, painful feelings keep slipping under the wire.

Try this.

Hold an image of that person in your mind and imagine something good happening to them.
See this in as much detail as you can. See the happiness on their face. See how their body reflects the happiness they feel. Stay with that happiness for as long as you can.

Perhaps you are too angry or too hurt to want something good to happen to them. But can that really help you?

Thinking about someone else negatively pollutes your inner world. You can change that.

Free from the ties

If someone has seriously harmed or abused you, and should no longer be in your life even as a constant memory, you can use your imagination a little differently.

Imagine putting that person into a small boat and sending the boat safely out into the ocean of life.
Turn them over to the universe, or God. You have no need to wish them harm—or good. They are no longer your concern.

Free yourself from those ties.

WHEN YOU'RE RIGHT ABOUT OTHER PEOPLE BEING WRONG

There may be times in your life when you are seriously betrayed.

You will not be *less* prepared to deal with those situations because you routinely offer others the benefit of the doubt. In fact, the more stable and "in charge" you feel in general, the more effectively you will deal with specific disappointments, even betrayals.

This won't make a serious betrayal easy; nothing could. But you will benefit from being true to your highest values *and to your own self-respect*, even (and especially) through difficult times.

HARMONY IN DIFFERENCE

The more self-confident you become, the less you will be troubled by other people's differences from you. (And you will increasingly appreciate the ways in which their most fundamental needs for respect, love, care and safety reflect your own.)

Opening to the gloriously varied ways in which other people see their world, your own world becomes a more interesting and dynamic place. My experience tells me that in our most sustaining friendships there will be some key values and needs held in common. But this doesn't undermine *the appreciation of difference*.

Here are some ways to express your appreciation of difference:

+ Someone disagrees with you. Rather than responding defensively, try: "I see what you mean." You are not agreeing. You are affirming a different view.
+ Someone criticizes you or someone you love. Try: "I'm sorry you see it that way. I see it differently."
+ Someone approaches a task differently from how you would. Try, "Give me some time to think this through." Doing this, you are valuing them *and* remaining open to the possibility of a better outcome.
+ Someone asks for your advice. Before giving it you ask, "What options are you already considering?"
+ Someone puts forward a political or ideological point of view that you believe is profoundly wrong. *With humility*, you say, "My experience has been that . . . "
+ You are joining a group and can see that they are approaching an urgent task in an inefficient way. *Pause.* Then try, "I can see that we're approaching this differently. Can we take some time to brainstorm? Why don't I listen to you first?"

A dash of humility keeps our minds and hearts open. It helps to remember that our opinions, insights and perceptions are never more than a work in progress. The "complete answer" is almost always out of sight.

THE "DESERVING" RICH?

Social conventions teach us to be kind to the poor, weak, sick, young or very old. Some of us (not nearly enough of us) also extend our concern to those who are suffering in countries less fortunate than our own.

That circle isn't big enough! What about the people we envy, despise, stereotype and trivialize? What about the rich, powerful and famous? Do they deserve our kindness?

What about the people whose political values we despise? Or, closer to home, what about the undeserving person who is currently our manager? Or the self-satisfied colleague who has been promoted while we languish? Or the neighbor who has the money to extend her house while we can't get our plumbing fixed? Or our ex, who's hounding us for money? Should we also consider them?

It's easy to be kind to anyone we may be unconsciously patronizing. What's far more challenging is to practice thoughtfulness to those who seem to have more power, luck or opportunity than we do.

Yet *only by including everyone in our circle of goodwill* do we allow our lives to reflect our values unconditionally.

GIVE THE LOVE YOU'D LOVE TO FIND

Over my years of spiritual seeking, I've had the amazing privilege of coming into the presence of a number of people whose very being radiated love. The glorious thing about each of these encounters was that they didn't leave me feeling like a gravely inadequate being. On the contrary, they made me feel more loving—and far more accepting of myself.

Through them, I discovered this: **love is profoundly contagious.** And unconditional love is profoundly healing.

Step into the presence of just one person who radiates love, and you, too, are positively affected. You, too, feel better about yourself.

Opening to the reality of love, refusing to limit your vision of love to one partner, three children and a dog, living fearlessly and giving your time, interest, consideration or prayers generously, may bring you that same experience of love that you would feel in the presence of a loving person. But the "reward" is probably irrelevant. Choosing to act in this way is a vital opportunity to experience love, and what love truly means.

The power of love

Considering others, never underestimate yourself. It could be your moment of kindness, courtesy or interest that makes "all the difference."

You are a source of happiness for others, as well as for yourself.

HOW TO CONSIDER OTHERS

Essential insights

✦ "Considering others" is essential to maturity. As long as your world begins and ends with yourself and the people most useful to you, you remain infantilized. *Your life is as big as your capacity to consider others.*

✦ Caring about other people is essential to your own happiness. So is letting other people care about you (and making that easier for them).

✦ Beyond the fleeting happiness that pleasures can bring comes the lasting happiness that caring about others can bring. *The happiest people are always the most altruistic.*

✦ You affect other people through words, actions, behavior, responses—and your presence. Your effect on them is as inevitable as their effect on you.

✦ The society and world we are collectively creating depends for its very survival on our capacity to trust and care for one another.

✦ Considering others makes you feel less separate, less lonely and safer.

✦ Mean, cynical, critical attitudes say far more about your state of mind than they do about the people you are attacking. A generous frame of mind opens you to the complex truth of other people's lives—so like your own.

◆ Considering others means understanding that every person wants what you want: respect, safety, happiness and love. It also means taking a genuine interest in other people's lives—and opening up to differences.

◆ Accept the reality of your profound psychological, social and spiritual interdependence with others. You cannot hurt others without hurting yourself (whatever your defenses); you cannot benefit others without also benefiting.

◆ Taking a genuine interest in other people's lives is uplifting and enlightening. It is also a powerful antidote to self-absorption and depression.

◆ You will always leave other people better or worse off for knowing you. The choice (and responsibility) is yours.

Essential actions

◆ *Live* the Golden Rule: "Do unto others as you would have them do unto you." Or, live out the attitudes and actions you'd love to find. The Golden Rule is found across all cultures and faiths. It is a profound call to psychological and spiritual maturity.

◆ Watch other people's reactions to your attitudes and behavior. Make change fast when that's needed. You grow in self-awareness *through recognizing your effect on other people.*

◆ Monitor where your "comfort zone" ends; who's "in the loop" or out of it; how willing you are to include rather than exclude. *Extending your comfort zone* and *practicing inclusion* are essential to considering others—and growing up.

✦ Routinely offer encouragement, support and enthusiasm. Don't wait to see if it is worth your while. Freedom comes from offering positive support *because you can*.

✦ Monitor the effect of your moods on other people. If you suspect you are affecting them negatively, or controlling them through your attitudes or moods, get professional help immediately. No one "deserves" to be dumped on; no emotional history, however rocky, 'justifies" harmful, miserable or controlling behavior.

✦ Is there an attitude or behavior passed on from your family that no longer fits you or never did? Make a change. Sometimes you need to do things differently from the way you were raised.

✦ Limit your criticisms and complaints. Other people are often most "unbearable" when you yourself are out of sorts. Find effective ways to limit stress and release tension.

✦ Envy? Jealousy? Bitterness? Challenge your scarcity mentality. Remind yourself, "There are more than enough of the good things to go around." As your own life and strength develop, it becomes easy to appreciate and encourage rather than envy and disparage.

✦ Value and respect psychological and physical boundaries. Do not "trespass" by disrespecting others, trivializing their concerns or disregarding their integrity.

✦ Give *more* than is needed. Walk "the second mile" not because you must—because you can.

✦ Practice courtesy and gratitude always. Especially to people not "useful" to you and, above all, when you don't "feel like it."

Honor the people you love

ALWAYS IN RELATIONSHIP

Nothing in your life is more valuable than your capacity to give and receive love.

Don't limit your thinking only to the people with whom you have or have had a sexual relationship. That's one kind of love. And it can certainly be extremely precious. But there are many other kinds of love. With or without a sexually intimate relationship, with or without living parents, siblings or children, you are "in relationship" all of the time. *You are capable of giving love and being loving all of the time.*

Valuing all of your relationships, you'll ask far less of any one relationship, no matter how precious. And your vision of love will become much more truthful.

START WITH YOURSELF

The most crucial ingredient in any relationship is not what you say or do; it's who you are.

You build more loving relationships with other people by developing a healthier and more trusting relationship with yourself.

As you trust your values to support you, as you develop your strengths and grow in independence, you will also become comfortably interdependent—capable of building enduring, rewarding, varied relationships with other people.

It's this trust in yourself that lets you accept people as they are; that lets you delight in their differences from you while also respecting deeply your shared desires to love and to be loved.

HONORING LOVE

It is an extraordinary honor to become close to another human being, to glimpse their inner reality, vulnerability and tenderness.

Taking this honor seriously, you experience the wonder of it. "This person has opened their life to me. They are allowing themselves to be vulnerable in my presence."

You are formed and shaped, illuminated and chastened, supported and cared for by the people who know you best and who allow you to know them. Opening your heart and mind, you see how deeply those people affect you. With luck, you also recognize how deeply you are affecting them.

This power to affect others positively is your greatest blessing. It is also your greatest responsibility.

Listen to May Sarton

May Sarton was a poet and one of the great journal writers. These lines are from her most famous book, *Journal of a Solitude*.

"Growth is demanding and may seem dangerous, for there is loss as well as gain in growth. But why go on living if one has ceased to grow? And what more demanding atmosphere for growth than love in any form?"

HEALTHY RELATIONSHIPS BUILD A HEALTHY SOCIETY

I am all too aware how many people mock psychotherapy or regard it as a self-indulgent waste of time to read books like this one.

Some of their criticisms may be valid. Many are not.

When self-discovery is pursued intelligently (with a willingness to act on your insights), then the self-knowledge and self-awareness you gain inevitably benefits all your relationships. And healthier relationships profoundly benefit society at large.

> *It's impossible to think deeply about your relationships* without also reflecting on your part in those relationships—and understanding yourself better.

> *It's impossible to think deeply about yourself* without also thinking deeply about your impact on other people—and understanding them better.

> *It's impossible to understand humankind* more deeply and not want to play your part in creating a society that benefits everyone.

Sometimes you will focus on understanding your relationships through greater self-understanding. Sometimes the reverse is needed. Either way, it's only a shift in emphasis.

You are in a constant dance of relationship between self and others. The more confident you are in your capacity to give and receive love, the less you need to control and cling and the more graceful the steps.

GAY, STRAIGHT OR CELIBATE?

Even in these relatively inclusive times, we pay far too much attention to issues of sexual orientation—and to sex—and far too little attention to understanding the transformative power of love.

Rather than worrying so much about who might be doing what to whom, we would do far better to ask *ourselves*, with a dash of humility: "Do I know what love is?' And, 'Am I living lovingly?"

Our finest and most invaluable relationships—the relationships that benefit our whole society as well as the individuals directly involved—are those where love is honored and lived out. Period.

Happiness forecast

Esteemed researcher David Myers points out, in *American Paradox*, "There are few stronger predictors of happiness than a close, nurturing, equitable, intimate, lifelong companionship with one's best friend."

This depends not on sexual orientation but on a willingness and capacity to give and receive love.

INVEST IN YOUR RELATIONSHIPS
(AND YOURSELF)

Can you imagine how different our world would be if we hovered over our relationship investments with even half the interest we pour into thinking about our mortgages or movements in the stock market?

Relationship investment is fail-safe. Can any other investment category claim that? Whatever we put in, it will be returned tenfold.

You might be saying, "But I was so nice to my last three partners and they left me anyway!"

And I would have to reply, "What did you learn from that? What are you still learning from it?"

Even from relationship "failures," there is always much to learn. Sometimes, for example, you give what you want to give, not what's needed. There's learning in that. *Each and every relationship can help make you a wiser and kinder person, if you let it.*

As you learn to give more generously, consider others more routinely, look at the world from other people's point of view, *you contribute to the sum total of human happiness.* And you grow as a human being. No "downturn" can take that from you.

WHAT ARE YOUR RELATIONSHIPS FOR?

Have you ever wondered what your relationships are for?

You are likely to think about your relationships differently, and behave differently too, if you see them as bestowing status, keeping the wolf of loneliness from the door, giving you financial security, providing a housekeeper or playmate, or as a means to discover what love is.

I suspect that women and men alike want many things from relationships, including companionship, understanding, warmth, affirmation, kindness, stability, excitement, stimulation, continuity and meaning. Sometimes what we want changes, or is even contradictory.

Nevertheless, wherever we are heading, *it helps to know what we are looking for and most passionately desire.*

When we want our closest relationships to make up for something that we (perhaps unconsciously) believe we lack, we may be hurt or angry when ordinary human beings can't or won't provide that. In those circumstances we might come to believe that we are "failing" at love. Or that love is failing us.

Paradoxically, the bigger our view is of love, the less likely it is to be disappointing. This would mean that we are alive to what we can give— as well as receive.

We are alive to what we can learn, even from "disasters."

Our vision of love is not limited to those closest to us.

We are less seduced by the "ideal" and more awake to the "real."

What am I looking for?

Give yourself time to turn this question over in your mind. Take time, too, to discuss it with a trusted friend, or in your journal.

You might want to apply it to a particular relationship or to love in general.

Knowing what you are looking for, it may become easier to find. It may also become easier to see what you are most ready to give.

LOSING YOURSELF IN OTHERS

You and I are social beings. Whether you are shy or totally extroverted, connection with other people brings crucial meaning to your existence. But to women especially, "feeling connected" may also bring boundary problems that can severely mar your experiences of closeness and intimacy—and disturb your feelings of self-respect.

Perhaps you can't easily distinguish your needs or feelings from those of other people. ("Do I want to go away for the weekend or do I think Nic would like to get away?" "When Eva doesn't seem to be enjoying herself at playgroup as much as the other children, then I feel really helpless and sometimes I feel angry with her.")

You may sometimes lose track of what you want in your efforts to find out what other people want. ("I thought she wanted to have people over to our new place but in fact it was the last thing she wanted and she ended up furious with me.")

You may be more dependent than you would like to be on others' opinions of you. ("Do I really look okay in this?" "Are you sure my report is good enough?")

You may regard differences of attitude or experience as threatening and defend yourself against them. ("I can't stand it when you disagree with me in front of your friends.")

You may be unable to confront others and to say what is on your mind. ("It just seems so mean to say that I would like a night out on my own with my friends.")

Losing sight of your own needs for the sake of other people can seem noble and selfless. And sometimes it is. Yet when genuine choice is lacking, then it becomes limiting and defensive. It may also be a means to avoid facing your own fears of loneliness or emptiness. Either way, it undermines your essential feelings of self-respect and choice.

Risk the big picture always: self and others; others and self.

CLOSE *AND* SEPARATE

Closeness to others works best when you are also clear about being a separate person. What this means depends very much upon context. When you have vulnerable people to care for (little children, the elderly, the very sick) your "needs" will look very different from when you are sharing your home with healthy adolescents or young adults, or an adult partner or friend.

Monitor what is appropriate right now. Meeting people's needs at your own expense can be a way of controlling them or the relationship. This is usually not done maliciously; on the contrary. But *intimacy and interdependence require that you look honestly at issues of power and control*—and adjust your behavior accordingly.

THE INTIMATE RELATIONSHIPS MOST LIKELY TO SUCCEED

It will come as no surprise that the intimate relationships most likely to succeed are those where both people feel pretty good about themselves as well as one another; where both feel able to encourage, support and delight in one another—rather than focusing on having "their needs met."

A loving relationship also supports the development of those strengths.

Ideal relationships are not achieved instantly. Nor are they ever static. Even when two people come together with high levels of self-awareness and generosity, there will be unexpected challenges of many kinds throughout the lifetime of the relationship. It is in intimacy that some of our least conscious needs and desires are projected and lived out; sometimes this causes us problems. Often this causes our loved one problems. The issue is not whether there will be problems; it is how those problems or issues are dealt with. And, alongside that, how joy and delight and encouragement are cultivated and expressed.

I have seen couples who, after decades together, still listen to one another with interest and great good humor; still "light up" when they see one another after a day apart; still talk about one another with interest and unfailing respect. These are the people who are friends as well as lovers, who have interests in common as well as interests apart; who are unafraid to be separate—sometimes for significant periods of time—but also truly enjoy coming together.

Shared values (not just views or opinions), a positive self-image and confidence in your strengths make a terrific start. Trust is also high on the list: trust that the other person will have *your best interests at heart always,* as well as trust that you can be yourself and accepted and loved for who you most deeply are. That's the great demand of intimacy: to be yourself in the presence of another person. It supports maturity to risk it—and offer it.

Because good relationships don't happen by magic, psychological research shows that people also do best who are willing to give time to developing relationship skills. Learning to be a partner is different from being a friend, lover, child or parent. Communication is key; so is learning to see your own needs not just alongside the needs of the other person, but *alongside the needs of the relationship.* This may seem to be a gender issue, with many more women than men initiating personal and relationship development. Yet so much of this "skill development" is in fact highly informal. Using a book like this one as a catalyst, couples can have all kinds of conversations that not only add to their repertoire of relationship skills, but also give them greater depth of understanding of themselves as well as one another.

Tenderness grows as two people understand one another more deeply. Open, curious, trusting communication is essential for that.

Making time for one another, respecting each other's friends and family, negotiating the big issues around work and family, money and housework, short- and long-term goals: these all matter. But so do the (not-so) little things: taking time to ask your partner about their day; taking an interest in their interests; respecting their need for physical or emotional "space"; being creative about fun times, surprises and treats; kissing or hugging as a greeting and kissing goodnight; calling when you will be home late; asking, not demanding, if something is needed; dealing with your own frustrations and bad moods and not dumping them; encouraging, appreciating, loving, delighting.

And the absolute essentials?

- ✦ Recognizing the person as much loved—but also as a separate individual whose needs and wants may not always coincide with your own. *And accepting that*
- ✦ Unfailing courtesy—especially when you don't feel like it
- ✦ A capacity to compromise and to resolve conflict
- ✦ A shared enthusiasm for life and living
- ✦ Shared interests beyond yourselves.

CAN THIS MARRIAGE BE SAVED?

My experience is that when any couple—gay or heterosexual—is at the point of deciding whether to stay together or split up, these factors are decisive.

+ You feel emotionally and physically safe.
+ You care more about making the relationship "right" than being "right" (and making your partner "wrong").
+ You share sustaining values.
+ You value concern and kindness over self-righteousness.
+ You still *value the relationship* (and the people it affects, especially where there are children).
+ You are willing to see the other person's point of view and respect it.
+ Your friendship is intact. (It may be battered—but you can still listen with interest, feel relaxed at least sometimes, take an interest in each other, *care what happens*.)
+ You have—or could imagine having—some sexual desire and certainly physical ease with each other.
+ You can acknowledge your part in hurting the relationship as well as the other person.
+ You value and can practice forgiveness.

KINDNESS AND CLOSENESS

Sometimes it is easier to be kind to those you don't know, or barely know, than to those closest to you.

It is a far greater test of your sincerity, and your character, to be kind to those who know you best, even when you are feeling at your worst.

Use honesty as your ally here. When you do feel bad, or you are anxious, tense, disappointed or depressed, speak up about that—even very briefly—rather than acting it out through unkindness, hostility, irritation or plain mean-spiritedness. ("Sorry to be grumpy. Feel rattled by the day and need some time alone.")

Clear the air—and keep it clear.

Respect others' needs

When someone needs or wants time or space to deal with their tension or stress in their own way, *respect that.*

Don't add to their stress by insisting that they should behave or respond as you would (or believe they should).

Allowing people to be themselves in these ways—assuming no harm is done—builds respect and expresses love.

CAN YOU READ MY MIND?

At the heart of intimacy is a belief that we can and will understand one another.

That's lovely.

Rather less lovely is your assumption that because you and I are in an intimate relationship *I will know what you want without your having to tell me.*

And when I fail to read your mind? When I don't know what you want or need or feel or think without you telling me?

You are not just angry. You may even feel betrayed. Or you may feel that love itself has failed. ("You should have known . . . "; "I shouldn't have to tell you . . . "; "How could you . . . ?")

This pattern is as hard to catch as it is common.

Risk being direct (*kind* and direct).

Play clean. "Point-scoring" is manipulative and unproductive. It is also unloving.

Enjoy your separateness

Intimacy is not "about" sameness. Intimacy thrives as much on difference—and especially appreciation of difference—as it does on shared interests and closeness. This is what enlarges your life.

LOVE YOU TODAY, LOATHE YOU TOMORROW

Our reactions to the people we love or are close to can fluctuate wildly. We might like to think they have caused this; that they are, indeed, angels one day and mere humans the next. This isn't true.

Their behavior and moods may well vary. They probably do. What varies far more, however, are our reactions to them. We see them as we are; not as they are.

When you are out of sorts, you will find the people closest to you most irritating.

Your partner can never make up her mind what movie she wants to see. Today it drives you crazy. Your children whine. Today it's unbearable. Your dad always "knows best." Today you take it as a personal offense.

Use this knowledge like an alarm bell. Next time someone you are close to seems irritating, unappealing or intolerable, ask yourself, "What's going on with *me*? Why am *I* feeling so uptight and critical? What am *I* not coping with? What am *I* unhappy about—or not resolving?"

Let other people off the hook. Re-own the emotions you are projecting outward.

Displaced emotions

Displaced emotions can cause havoc, especially in intimate relationships.

You are angry with your colleague, but you yell at your daughter.

You are frightened about losing your job, and accuse your partner of extravagant spending.

You are feeling exhausted and unappreciated, and greet your friend's good news with a snarl and a whine.

When your own responses are emotionally fraught or inappropriate, ask yourself again, "What's *my* issue?"

And when you have taken out your feelings in the wrong place and on the wrong person? Apologize. Clarify. Acknowledge the hurt you have caused. Move on.

NO INTIMACY WITHOUT LISTENING

Three kinds of listening matter. (And really couldn't matter more.)

+ Listening to your inner self-talk
+ Listening to the way you speak to others—tone of voice as well as content
+ Listening to other people.

Intimacy—taking another person's separate inner reality seriously and honoring that—depends entirely on your capacity to still your own urgent concerns and tune in to another person.

Listening with care and interest, you are saying to that other person, "You matter to me. You interest me. Tell me more about what it's like to be you. I care about you."

Listening with care and interest, you are also allowing yourself to get to know that other person more deeply and truthfully. It is listening that takes you into their world—and expands your own.

Listening with care and interest, *you are seeking to understand.*

Too often, listening is merely a prelude to speaking. It expresses a desire not to understand but to be understood. You speak—and I can't wait to interrupt, tell you what I think of what you are saying, top your story with my own . . . cut you off or put you right. *This does not build intimacy.*

When you are seeking to understand—and what would love be without that?—it is wonderful to know that you can learn to listen with greater care and interest. It may feel clumsy at first. And it helps to know that it's not constantly required.

What matters is that *you can listen when listening is needed*; that you read the clues; honor the urgency or depth of someone's need—and take that seriously.

Quite soon, with more awareness of the other person—and more interest in their interests—careful listening will become natural. It can even become relaxing to listen deeply rather than shallowly; to take in all of what someone else is saying without constantly reviewing your own pressing contribution.

Careful listening is achieved through the quality of your attention. It doesn't direct. It asks how things were, what feelings were felt, rather than "Why?"

Careful listening saves relationships. It is what people hunger for most desperately. It's what allows people to feel met as well as heard. It is also profoundly consoling. And it need not take hours.

People who talk incessantly usually do so both because they are not listening to themselves—and they do not feel "heard." Careful listening can be brief; focus is everything.

Timing is everything

Asking anyone to listen deeply, or bare their soul, *when they have no choice about the matter*, is rarely productive.

Whether it is your child, friend, aged parent, boss or partner, let yourself get to know what their rhythms and patterns are when it comes to talking and listening. Many parents value car trips for the talking it allows with their children. Some couples know that they need time alone to talk productively; others do best if they go out to a crowded pub or restaurant.

Trying to force someone to talk—or to listen—when the timing is wrong adds to stress; it doesn't resolve it.

If the matter is exceptionally urgent, be clear about that. "I know this isn't a great time for you but could we have just fifteen minutes? I'm under pressure to make a decision by tomorrow."

When one person is not routinely driving the talking/listening agenda, compromise is usually possible.

Valuing talking

Not everyone values talking (or listening) in the same way. This seems obvious, yet it can cause tremendous grief, especially in an intimate relationship where one person wants or expects to be able to talk often and intensely, and the other person doesn't believe that's necessary or welcome.

People's "talking patterns" arise partly from their own temperament and are also very much shaped in their family of origin. Culture also plays a part.

When one person feels that they are getting too little intimate talking in the relationship, this is a legitimate thing to raise—but it needs to be done tactfully. Often the person who is not talking "enough" is genuinely perplexed by the complaint and at a loss to make change. When any of us feel defensive, we are less likely to welcome change.

It's often more productive to think laterally. Perhaps it's easier to talk when there are more people around, or when you are doing more stimulating things together? Perhaps you can increase those social activities, rather than asking for "more talk" in an abstract way.

It is also uplifting to honor the genuine non-verbal "languages of love": the gestures of kindness, the acts of thoughtfulness, the smiles, touches and hugs.

Don't trespass

When listening, never deny the other person their own experiences. ("You couldn't possibly have felt that," "I don't see what the fuss is about," "We all have our problems.")

This is a form of trespass that hurts feelings and destroys truthful communication.

Listening to yourself—to your own inner talk and to your reactions—is key to careful listening to others.

WHAT ARE YOU WILLING TO GIVE?

It's easy to say what you want love to do for you.

Take stock of what you are willing to *give*—for love's sake.

Love is expressed through the small gestures: kind words, genuine courtesies; criticisms swallowed back and forgotten; delight in the moments of greeting; sweetness in the moments of saying good-bye; time spent on a shared activity that might not have been your first choice; thoughtful encouragement; a delicious meal; a hug held for several moments; flowers next to the bed; a candle lit by the bath; fewer demands; delight in someone else's pleasure.

What comes gift-wrapped can be gorgeous. Far more sustaining are the priceless gifts of good humor, reliability, thoughtfulness, kindness, awareness, accepting, listening, care and presence.

Well, what *are* you willing to give?

What you are willing to give—and to whom—is worth writing down. (Record practical, physical, constructive, emotional, intellectual and spiritual gifts. They all count.) Often it is not until you see the "facts" recorded in black and white that you can also see what's missing.

What have you received?

Take stock, too, of what you have *received* in the name of love.

Write this down, covering all the years or decades of your life. Take weeks or months to expand your list. Reviewing what you have received provides vitamins for the soul. It can also be extremely humbling—especially when we have trained ourselves to focus on what we haven't got, or what other people haven't done, or what's missing rather than what's gained. Every day you are the recipient of other people's kindness. *Notice that.*

HOW TO LOVE GENEROUSLY

Love is not love except when it is generous. To become generous, your relationships need *fewer demands and greater acceptance.* Love is never less than friendly. If you are unsure, ask yourself, "Is this the best that I can do?" Or, "Is this kind?"

Here are some key ways to express and deepen love.

+ Let minor irritations go. *Speak up about what's pleasing.* Making this change alone could save many relationships from resentment.
+ Be slow to blame, quick to forgive.
+ Monitor the tone and content of your most routine remarks. *Listen to your tone of voice.* Watch your body language. Recognize what emotions they express.
+ Be sensitive to people's individuality. Know which expressions of love work best for each person and in varying circumstances.
+ Release others from your hidden demands to behave in certain kinds of ways so that you can feel all right about them (or yourself). *Accept them as they are.*
+ Respect other people's choices—even when you would have chosen differently for them. Take a lively, non-judgmental interest in their choices.
+ Don't require other people to read your mind. If you want someone to know something, be direct about it. Speak up.
+ *Express* your feelings of love. Don't assume they know you love them. *Say aloud what you feel inside.* "I am so glad you are in my life, Jane." "Our early morning walks give me a magical start to the day." "There's nothing I like more than seeing my family and friends sitting together at this table."
+ Every day, *see the people you love through new eyes.* Remind yourself, "This could be my last opportunity to show concern or express my love to this person." Take that opportunity.

If you did nothing else but take seriously these practical ideas about loving more generously, your relationships would change for the better. *And you would be happier.*

GOOD MANNERS

CATHERINE: It's 3 A.M. when I sense a face beside mine. Four-year-old Luke is in our room again, asking if he can sleep with us for "just a teeny little time."

We move over. Luke and I lie there, fully awake, while my husband—trained from years of sleep deprivation during his previous career as a naval warship navigator—returns happily to slumber. Minutes later he begins to snore. I tell him to stop, which he does. For twenty seconds.

I try again, louder this time, my voice charged with authority. "Luther, you have to stop snoring *now*, or we'll never get any sleep."

"Okay," he mumbles, 'I can't help it . . . but I'll try."

That's when I hear it—the little voice of my son, piping up, implying that I'm being more army sergeant than loving partner. Implying that I should practice a little of what I preach to him all day long—that we need to speak respectfully to people, even when our requests are legitimate and our irritations well founded.

"Mom," Luke whispers, "you shouldn't talk to Dad like that. You should talk with good manners."

"You're right," I say. "Luther, would you please try to stop snoring?" Which he does, and eventually we all go back to sleep.

Luther and I chuckle over this exchange at breakfast the next morning. But part of it pricks me like a thorn. Once again, my four-year-old has reminded me of the most important rules to play by with the people I love.

It only takes a moment to be respectful. Respect lets people know they are loved.

Even if it's "family shorthand" or a legitimate complaint, we're responsible for what we say . . . and how we say it.

And always our behavior speaks louder than our words.

STEPHANIE: We frequently behave as if we had all the time in the world to re-establish closeness and affirm love. This isn't always true. *Never miss a chance to give and express love.*

LOVE FOR LIFE?
THE FUNDAMENTAL QUESTIONS

We prepare for weddings, but not for marriage.

We prepare for childbirth, but not for becoming parents.

And we get seriously involved without having any real idea of who it is we might be getting involved with!

Contemplating "the relationship of a lifetime" most people do not spend a single hour exploring the most basic questions—some of which I have outlined below.

If you are contemplating making a commitment, or reviewing a commitment within an existing relationship, give yourself the luxury of time to go deeply into these questions.

You are not looking for the perfect person or total reassurance. What you are doing is giving yourself a chance to choose more consciously and wisely, and to assess more realistically what the strengths and challenges of the relationship might be.

You may want to use your journal to explore these questions—or talk them through with a trusted friend or counselor.

- ✦ Does the idea of being in love make me happy—or is it this actual person?
- ✦ Am I willing to accept this person—and not attempt to change him (or her)?
- ✦ Does he (or she) want to change me?
- ✦ What values do we share? How are those values lived out?
- ✦ What interests do we have in common—beyond the interest of having a relationship?
- ✦ Is there anything that fits a less than positive "pattern" in my relationship life?
- ✦ Do I like his friends, family or lifestyle more than I like him?
- ✦ Do we share a sense of humor?
- ✦ Do we share a view of what commitment means?
- ✦ Have we talked about the big issues: children, families, money, housework, home/work balance?
- ✦ Do I know what gives his life meaning? Do I respect that?
- ✦ Does he know what gives my life meaning? Does he respect that?

✦ *Do I feel totally safe?*
✦ Can I be myself sexually, emotionally, spiritually?
✦ Do I feel loved? (This may be different from feeling wanted, needed, even adored.)
✦ Can we solve problems cooperatively?
✦ Do we need drugs, alcohol or other people to have a good time together?
✦ Do I feel safe to contemplate these questions?

You may even just want to ask, "Am I hoping for the best? Or do I dare expect it?"

"Help! I don't feel sure."

If serious concerns arise when you consider this list of questions (or your answers), then use your discretion. If it makes you doubt your own feelings, I would suggest that you make an appointment with a counselor who is experienced in relationship issues. If it makes you doubt the other person's feelings, find a good moment to ask if you can talk about it. It may also be that when you take a little time to go on thinking about it, the answer will become clear. ("We don't have many interests in common but our daily life together is still really enjoyable." "I think he has been trying to change the way that I look, but that's something I can set limits about and I feel confident he will accept that.")

LOOK AT THE PEOPLE YOU LOVE

We spend large chunks of our busy days with our minds far away from where our bodies are. Rushing toward the next moment, this present moment passes us by. And it will not come again.

Often this means that we are "too busy" to look at people—even at the people we love. Even when we are sharing good news, we frequently do this without making real contact. Yet it's the contact we make that keeps our relationships alive.

It takes only a few seconds to pause—and connect. Doing that, you may realize that what you have been responding to is not the real live person in front of you, but a rather limited "image" inside your own mind. (Or perhaps to the complaints inside your own mind.)

Make it a habit to look at the people you love when you talk to them or when they are trying to talk to you. Send love through your eyes. And even when you are not talking, make eye contact when you greet them or say good-bye. Take time to look into their eyes as you smile or before you kiss or hug. Celebrate and enjoy moments of closeness.

The eyes truly are the windows of the soul. We can give so much love to another person through a simple glance; we can let someone know that they are loved or understood or valued without a single word being spoken.

Avoiding the eyes, you risk missing the essence of who that person is; you miss the soul. You miss a chance to give and receive happiness.

Making this small change will soften and open your heart. And it will feed your relationships powerfully.

EXPECT TO BE LOVED

For many people—and you may be one of them—it's a radical notion to expect to be loved.

While it could be because you have been loved so inadequately in the past, life is not always that predictable.

Sometimes it's because you have grown used to responding to the criticisms in your mind—and to projecting your fears outward. Sometimes it's because you have allowed your idea of what love is to narrow to the point of invisibility.

Broaden your vision of love. Value loving friendships, passionate interests, a love of nature, deep talks with people you trust and care about.

That you will be loved (or liked) is the most supportive of all expectations. Cultivate it.

Your positive expectations can't guarantee results. Other people have their agendas also. But having positive expectations radically lifts your chances of getting the warmth and affection you want.

OF COURSE COMPLAINING RARELY WORKS

We all hate complaints from other people, especially when they attack our sense of self or are unjust and unfair.

We all flourish when we are praised and encouraged. So isn't it a little odd that we spend so much time complaining to or about our loved ones? Or that we verbally demolish and undermine, even when there is little chance that our complaints will bring out the best in them, lead to greater mutual understanding or bring the changes that we so urgently want?

We keep doing what makes the situation worse. Then we complain even more because it's not getting better.

In the early days of a relationship, we are usually more than willing to put a positive spin on what our loved one says and does. We may even find their vulnerabilities touching and appealing. Further into the relationship, however, this often changes. Enthusiasm gives way to irritation; support gives way to undermining. And everybody suffers.

Complaining (whining, picking, undermining, teasing) can play such a powerful role in a relationship that each person is unconsciously defensive virtually all the time.

Some complaints are driven by a belief that whatever is felt within a relationship should be spoken. This isn't so. Sharing feelings and experiences, looking together at what is happening and working on strategies when conflicts are causing pain are worthwhile ingredients in any loving relationship. But there is also a place for restraint, for holding back that impulse to make someone else wrong—often because you feel wrong yourself.

You contribute most to your relationships by rigorously examining your impulses to complain, recognizing how often you may be projecting your own inner negativity onto those closest to you. When you do have an issue that genuinely needs airing and discussion this will be dealt with far more effectively in an atmosphere of minimum defensiveness and maximum trust.

Why complaints hurt

Complaints and criticism hurt—and stay in our minds long after encouragement has vanished—because *they so often match the worst things we feel and fear about ourselves.*

As we come to feel steadier inside ourselves we also become less reactive and defensive, able to see which complaints are useful and which simply describe and reflect the disgruntled inner world of the critic or complainer.

HOW WOULD YOU LIKE ME TO BEHAVE?

We rarely ask the people we love how they would like us to behave.

Perhaps we are afraid to ask this. Or the people we love may be afraid to tell us.

Maybe in the past—in the middle of a fight or when tensions are running high—they have told us (exactly) how they would like us to behave. Maybe we felt overwhelmed, criticized, insulted, attacked. Maybe we reacted defensively.

It is quite a different experience to take your power into your hands and ask whether there is something in your behavior that is jarring or abrasive; whether you are causing hurt or harm unintentionally; whether there is something you could do that would be more considerate and more loving.

Some questions are powerful enough to change the way you see your life. This could be one of them.

A SPONGE WRUNG DRY

CATHERINE: This morning we had World War III in our kitchen. It isn't often that my husband and I argue, but when we do it's always over the same old issue: time. Who has it, and who doesn't. Who can work for hours in peace and quiet with a skim latte at his desk overlooking the Sydney Opera House—albeit at 3 P.M. on a Saturday with impossible deadlines and enormous pressure—and who works with earplugs and a laptop at the kitchen table, overseeing a surprisingly mobile baby Elijah and four-year-old Luke armed with Play-Doh and baking tins.

Our arguments start out as discussions, usually initiated by me because I am feeling too stretched. This morning it was the culmination of months of sleep deprivation, with writing deadlines looming and a sinking feeling that the likelihood of getting some respite from all the endless household chores held as much promise as Anne Boleyn being pardoned while marching toward her execution.

Granted, I am a tiny bit dramatic. And I am also capable of being grossly unfair. So many times I forget that *I chose* to stay at home and work simultaneously. My husband chose to take on a great deal of pressure to make most of the money to keep home and hearth together while we live in one of the most expensive cities in the world. Neither one of us has an easy time of it.

And I suspect that if you have a partner, neither of you do either.

My friend Sue, who has a career, a husband and four children from a blended marriage, says that after a day of work she feels like a sponge wrung dry. Don't we all? Most days, we start out with a fair bit of energy and enthusiasm, but each encounter can leave us feeling a little more depleted until at the end of the day there's not much left for those we love the most.

When a marriage consists of two dry sponges, who does the cleaning up? And how is it possible to fight fairly when you really don't feel like being fair, or even being *there*?

STEPHANIE: The instant answer is that when you feel wrung out, *this is the worst possible time to fight.* What you will be fighting *for* is some recognition of how burdened and maybe how unappreciated you both feel. But you won't get that. And you especially won't get it when what you are fighting *about* are the superficial issues ("What do you mean you have to work overtime for the third time this week and it's only Tuesday!") rather than the deeper ones.

Catherine (honest Catherine!) is quick to chide herself, reminding herself (and us) that she chose her situation. Her subtext is clear: having chosen it, *she has no right to resent it.* But "choosing" is a complex business, socially as well as psychologically. Socially, it is complicated by roles and the expectations we have of those roles (none more so than "mother"). Psychologically, it is complicated because we are not all of a piece: we have conflicting desires and needs—some of them unconscious.

We can choose according to our values, *but still be in conflict.* Catherine loves being a mother and has fantastic support from her husband and her own mother. Because she is so fortunate, she doesn't feel entitled to want more time for her own work, more choice about her routine, more time to think. These are luxuries that she has sacrificed willingly, but it doesn't mean that every part of her feeling self has caught up with the new agenda.

The kind of morning that Catherine describes should be taken seriously. It's not disastrous. But it is a call to reassess. *We don't fix a painful situation by telling ourselves that we shouldn't be feeling what we are feeling.* Instead, we need to look at those feelings and ask ourselves what needs attention.

When two people want to be less burdened and more appreciated, and when at least one of them wants a little more self-determination about how she spends her days, those are genuine issues.

Fighting can't produce a solution—because what they are fighting about is not what they are fighting for.

I suspect that the biggest issue here—at least for Catherine—is one of entitlement. ("Am I entitled to feel what I am feeling? Am I entitled to want something to change? Am I entitled to raise this?")

Catherine speaks for countless couples when she says, "At the end of the day, there's not much left for those we love the most."

This is serious. Who is running our lives? Who is determining our agendas? Who is getting what we most want to give? Are we giving all our love to the marketing department? All our creativity to accounts? All our hope to the bottom line?

Thinking of an issue like this as "one person's problem" is no more helpful than fighting. *Whatever affects the relationship must be seen as a relationship problem.* That calls for two people putting their heads together to ask, "What's going on here? How can we see this situation in a more productive way? How can we give each other *the time and appreciation we both need* when we feel, as Catherine put it, like "two dry sponges"? How can each of us get to the end of a day still with something to give to the people we love best?"

Feeling entitled to have this conversation—without blaming herself for wanting it—will itself be healing for Catherine. So will accepting her inconsistencies, even when they occasionally disrupt the picture she would most like to have of herself.

And there's more good news. When any two people who are close—and they could be siblings or an adult child and parent—solve an emotional issue jointly *the relationship as a whole invariably benefits.* So do each of the individuals.

The tools are straightforward:

+ Careful listening
+ Respect for each person's experience and feelings
+ Time to listen
+ A willingness to save the argument for later (when it can probably be a discussion and not an argument)
+ A willingness to state the issues honestly
+ A willingness to compromise
+ A willingness to accept that each may see the issue differently and no one person needs to be "right"
+ Confidence that each wants the best possible outcome *for the other person.*

BETTER THAN FIGHTING

I believe that aggression is the enemy of love. Passive aggression—
sulking, stonewalling and punishing with silence—also swiftly
undermines goodwill and love.

Nevertheless, people do fight. And it is possible to do this more
skillfully rather than less. But first:

- ✦ *Never fight when you most feel like it.* At those times, when you are
  most agitated and least rational, do anything but fight. Go for a
  walk, take a shower, go to another room and shut the door—
  saying "I just need time out." This will seem extremely difficult
  initially. But it is possible and it is wonderfully empowering to
  know that you are not a slave to your emotions.
- ✦ *Never fight when you are drunk,* drugged, tired or seriously
  depressed.
- ✦ *Never pick a fight because you are in a bad temper* and want to pass
  your misery on.

You also need to remind yourself what you know about this person. If
they are under pressure, have low self-esteem, are easily irritated, keep
your own needs as low-key as possible, especially in those grim
moments. *Soothe yourself before raising "issues" or responding to them.*
Making someone "mad" is never a victory.

If something must be said, it is also and always essential to state
your position clearly, using "I statements," sticking to the point and
resisting any temptation to rerun old battles or grievances.

Ask yourself: "What do I want to get out of this? What is it that I
actually want to communicate? *Is "fighting" the best way to get the results
that I want?"*

Of course, sometimes arguments erupt despite your best
intentions. Once you do get started, you have to accept that it's not
only you who wants to be heard; it will also be the other person. If
you can't walk away, you will have to accept that you may hear things
you don't want to hear, as well as say things you don't want to say.

Hurt is minimized when each of you at least practices self-control
around listening. This means you are as prepared to listen as to speak.

(If you have heard people fighting, you will know that minimal listening takes place and what there is tends to be painfully distorted.)

If you can step into listening in a real way, the need to fight may dissipate. Often what is "fighting to emerge" is a communication issue, with *both* people feeling hurt and misunderstood and *not heard*.

If you can bring yourself to recognize that you probably *both feel tense because you both feel hurt*, then whatever the real issues are will be much easier to clarify and resolve.

If you have a serious conflict with someone, or there is tension between you that is not getting resolved, these basics will also help:

+ Listen while the other person speaks. This might resolve the problem right away. Let them say everything that they need to.
+ Even when you are sure that fault lies on one side only, think about what they are saying. Accept the possibility you could learn something.
+ *Never* make a personal attack. If you say something regrettable, apologize immediately.
+ *Check out your assumptions.* "Did you think I was saying you should never go out on your own with your friends?"
+ When you have both been heard, ask, "What do you think the real issues are here?" Use collaborative language. "How can we best deal with this?"
+ Look for concessions you can make *for the sake of the relationship.*

Putting your values into practice, you will often find that even in a tense situation you are supporting rather than undermining each other. This is more likely to happen when you step beyond the right/wrong mind-set to discover that both people can be "right," and that anyway "who's right" is not the issue.

And on the basis that whatever affection you have for each other counts for more than your differences, I can't help but add the old adage that you should never go to bed, leave the house, or end a phone call without making peace and affirming the other person. Do this for your own sake as well as for the other person; do it for the sake of love.

RECEIVING LOVE FEELS TOO HARD

Giving and receiving love are not two puffs of the same breath.

Receiving love—opening yourself to the risks and rewards of intimacy—you must first regard yourself as worthy of love.

Positive self-regard is directly related to your capacity to receive love and affection from other people. Without that, you are likely to denigrate what's offered—and the person offering it.

You need to discover that love is not frightening. (Love is not love when it's anything but kind.) When it has been frightening in the past, or when painful or even cruel demands have been made under the guise of love, then professional support is needed. Get that support.

You need to know where your boundaries are, how to ask for what you want and refuse what you don't want.

And you need to accept people as they are and accept their way of loving you—as long as you can trust their good intentions.

As an infant, love and helplessness were inextricably entwined in your mind. When love didn't come as and when you wanted, perhaps it felt terrifying. As an adult, with far more choices available to you than an infant has, you can loosen that equation. You can learn to see how variously love is expressed—and value that.

Your capacity to receive—and give—love is not limited by what has happened in the past.

Identify the problem. Then focus on the solution.

Wanting too much from love?

You may be frightened of wanting too much from love, of revealing your great hunger not just to someone else but also to yourself. Developing an inner sense of stability is crucial for you, too. Focusing on your strengths, trusting your capacity for resilience, learning from your mistakes rather than fearing them: all of this will help. It will also support you to think about love more broadly. Love is not one person, one relationship. *Love is a quality that can be present in everything you do, everything you think, everything you believe, everything you are.*

ABOUT RESCUING

Rescuing is a huge issue in close relationships, yet it's rarely talked about. Not all of it is bad; the experience of love is itself "rescuing."

So how do we work out when our rescuing undermines the people we love—and when it genuinely supports them? How do we get to know how much rescuing *we* need or demand?

I see rescuing as an impulse to save another person from hurt, disappointment, suffering or harm. Sometimes that's what's needed. You tell your daughter not to run on the road. She runs. You pull her back by the arm (and probably yell). You don't leave her to "learn a lesson" by risking her life.

Lots of rescuing goes on when we "quite naturally" compensate for our partner or children: remembering people's names; making sure homework reaches the teacher on time; inviting friends over when they are down; networking; listening, coaxing, encouraging, *making people feel better.*

No harm there.

Rescuing becomes less healthy when you are compensating for other people, shielding them, discouraging them from living fully— and not trusting that they could learn from and survive their own setbacks or mistakes.

Your partner can't land a new job. You tell him how unfair this is and that no one could be better qualified than he is. What you don't tell him is that his attitude is aggressive and off-putting. Or that his CV is sloppily written and unimpressive.

Your best friend is constantly depressed. You find her quite depressing yourself but you love her and believe that "being there for her" is kind. She isn't willing to consider change. She certainly isn't willing to get help. She has you. As long as she has you, she'll "manage." You spend countless hours together, hovering over her miseries. They grow and multiply.

Your son is clumsy and dreamy. He forgets everything. If you didn't make lists for him, pack his bag every morning and unpack it each evening, put out his clothes and pick up and wash them, you and he both know that he'd barely make it through the day. Your son is thirty.

You've been with your girlfriend since you were both in your early twenties. She's often "worn-out." You take amazing care of her. Over the last year, she has been angry more often than tired. Now she wants to enroll at university. You know she gets "worse" when she's stressed. You want her to give up this mad idea—for her own sake.

Your husband has no idea how to bathe the baby. He can't be trusted with the four-year-old either. While he's doing deals on his phone, she could wander off. You would like to have the occasional lunch with a friend on the weekend. But you could never leave the kids.

Taking other adults' lives seriously, trusting that they can and indeed must look to their own issues, make their own decisions and learn from their own mistakes, is not only respectful, it is also essential to the experience of intimacy.

You are grateful that your wife "thinks of everything" when it comes to the children, the house, your parents, her parents and your friends. Should she also remember your dry-cleaning, school reunion, her birthday and your health check-up? *Some of that is "rescuing."*

You worry that your husband will one day meet someone at an important meeting who is clever, slim and doesn't have baby food on any of her clothes. Your husband has told you countless times that you have nothing to worry about. He does this patiently. Nevertheless, you insist on raising this again and you demand that he comforts you. *Some of that is "rescuing."*

You are beautiful, talented—and temperamental. Your life is running at an incredible pace, so fast that you cannot keep track of your diary, appointments, keys, credit card payments or car services. Fortunately you have a partner who "adores" you. *Some of that is "rescuing."*

You are an average student living in a high-achieving family. It doesn't hurt, you reason, if your mom does a little thinking for you, reads a few books for you, searches the Internet for you. And because you can't yet type efficiently it makes perfect sense that when it comes to important assignments she would also do your typing for you. *Some of that is "rescuing."*

To avoid being rescued in ways that are unhealthy—*you need to take responsibility for your own attitudes and action.*

To avoid rescuing other people in ways that are unhealthy—*you need to offer trust in their resilience and capacity to learn from their mistakes.*

Take codependence very seriously

Rescuing can be even darker: "not noticing" that your partner is bullying or sexually abusing one of your children; making excuses when your partner bullies or abuses you; ignoring drug or alcohol abuse; financially supporting a loved one's addictive behaviors. When rescuing tips into codependent behaviors, and the fear and paralysis that accompany them, professional help or structured help through a twelve-step program like Alcoholics Anonymous offer crucial support to create lasting change.

TAKE A LOAD FROM YOUR PARTNER
(AND YOUR BEST FRIENDS)

Your partner and closest friends know and love the best of you. And also see the worst of you. While familiarity is part of the joy of a committed friendship or relationship, it also makes it easy to slide into something less than "best behaviors" and even to ask more of that person than is reasonable—and certainly more than helps support the relationship.

Be aware of what you didn't get in childhood as well as what you most resent. Use that awareness to be especially sensitive about not unconsciously demanding that your partner or closest friends make up for that.

Know—and continue to get to know—what your emotional history is; know what issues from the past are most likely to be affecting you in the present; know what makes you feel especially vulnerable, sensitive, needy or demanding.

We frequently transfer emotions from past relationships (especially childhood) into present close relationships. When you suspect that's happening (or when someone tells you that you are routinely overreacting), take it seriously. The more conscious you are of what will stir you up, the more likely it is that you can respond appropriately to what's happening right now.

It also helps to talk about your expectations of what each person can or should provide in terms of emotional support. Your expectations may be unreasonable—even outrageous! Sometimes we not only project past emotions into our present relationships but also unconsciously expect our closest friend or partner to take on the role of parent to our "child." This desire may be expressed through demanding that they take responsibility for us, make allowances for us, or protect us even from the arduous reality of growing up. An adult-with-adult relationship can never flourish while one person remains a child.

Do I also need to add that no relationship should be required to meet all your needs? We all know this; yet often our behavior says something quite different.

Take some of your emotional needs outside the relationship: to friends, family or even a therapist when something painful limits or haunts you. This takes a load from your partner; it also significantly helps you.

Encouraging and cherishing the ones you love

You will want to add to this list, I hope. And share it.

Believe in each other's strengths. Focus on them.
Take advice from one another.
Show interest in each other's feelings, perspective and vision of the world.
Read and think broadly so that you have something stimulating to talk about.
Limit the time you spend "spaced out" in front of a screen.
Make time together a priority.
If you are a couple, cultivate mutual interests (other than running the house and looking after the children).
Take an interest in each other's friends, family, colleagues.
Make it a high priority to have fun together.
Be direct about asking for what you want. And grown up enough to survive not getting it.

Also, don't assume you know everything about each other. That is never true.

LOOK CLOSELY AT THE PICTURES YOU HOLD IN YOUR MIND

Often, perhaps more often than not, we respond not to the person standing in front of us, but to a limited picture inside our own minds, made up of past experiences and present assumptions, heavily laced with our own needs and emotions.

It takes effort to keep up to date in our relationships, especially our closest ones. But that effort is essential.

What I am describing is perhaps most dramatically illustrated when you think about how children replace the highly idealized "picture" of their parents that they hold through most of childhood with the highly critical "picture" of those same parents that they maintain through the years of adolescence. *It is in part that "picture" that they respond to.* Their parents will inevitably change during that time, but not nearly as much as their children's perception of them. And then that "picture" will change again, both when those children move from adolescence to adulthood, and perhaps even more so when they become parents themselves.

Even in our relationships with other adults we can all too easily respond to unexamined internal images, rather than to the real live person changing and growing in front of us. This always limits the relationship; it may even defeat it.

Deep communication saves relationships

Sharing time together, listening deeply, caring, taking an interest in where the person is heading, emotionally and intellectually: these are not simply relationship skills. They are also the essential life-savers that keep a relationship fresh and alive *in your own mind*—as well as in the outer world you share.

Having fun is every bit as essential.

"I AM PAINFULLY DEPENDENT ON THE PERSON I LOVE"

Your capacity to love others honestly and generously depends on:

✦ Your self-respect and feelings of self-worth
✦ Your willingness to see other people as treasured—but separate from you
✦ Your determination to want the best for them always—even when this "inconveniences" you.

This becomes difficult when you believe that your world will fall apart if your partner rejects or leaves you.

This belief—and it's painfully common—keeps you infantilized and in a state of fear. It probably pushes you to make demands that are unrealistic, overwhelming or even frightening.

When you were a baby, you were indeed dependent on your primary carer for your survival. That carer, probably your mother, really did have life-and-death power over you. This meant that all your feelings about her were extremely heightened; from bliss to rage, you felt them at full volume.

If you have similar feelings now, as an adult in a relationship with another adult, it is crucial to know that they are not "caused" by that other person. You may think you have these feelings because the other person is so special and you are so much in love. Or because the other person is so unreliable and you can't trust them.

In fact, the feelings you have are not love. And the person you can't trust is yourself.

Your feelings are not "about" the other person, even if you do feel them only in this relationship. They are "about" you.

When you feel highly possessive, or desperate in relation to another person, it is almost always because you have not yet developed your own inner feelings of safety. Put bluntly, you don't yet know how to be your own inner "mother," how to soothe yourself, meet your own needs and remind yourself that you are lovable.

It's possible that you do also love the other person. It's certainly possible that you value the relationship. But what is urgently needed is that you learn to soothe and especially value yourself.

You may need help. This is a situation where intelligent psychotherapy can make a huge difference.

It will certainly mean monitoring your own reactions and behavior ruthlessly. *It is an act of desperation, not an act of love, to demand that another person give your life meaning.*

When those impulses arise, pay attention to them, inwardly. Reassure yourself, inwardly. Resist the temptation to project them onto your partner or make demands "in the name of love."

Know, too, that if you are brave and honest enough to recognize your life in this description, you are already on the path to creating positive and significant change—and finding freedom.

CHILDREN ARE NOT POSSESSIONS

Your children are not your possessions. They should not be required to reflect well on you, give you status, live out your dreams for you, or bring meaning to your life.

They don't benefit from being petted, paraded, or overpraised.

They do benefit from being loved fiercely and unconditionally; accepted and cherished for who they are; listened to with interest and spoken to with respect.

Each child requires you to be a different parent. And to be a different—but consistently loving—parent through each increasingly complex stage of their development.

Each child comes to this life with lessons to learn. Encourage all their strengths, not just those that fit with current educational criteria. Encourage them to learn values—most crucially through observing you live them out.

Each child comes to this life with lessons to teach their parents. Understanding this helps to make our relationships with our children more honest, more truthful. Sometimes a "difficult" child or a "different" one has something very special to teach. Be open to that.

It is the greatest possible privilege of love to be a parent. It is what drags you into maturity with greatest speed. It teaches you humility on a daily basis. The rewards of parenting are extraordinary. This doesn't make it easy.

Everyday parenting

As a mother, I know it's not the dramatic events that let our children know how much we love, value and trust them. *It's the everyday interactions that count.*

It's also the way that we think about our children. And think about ourselves as parents.

Paying attention to the small moments, one by one, dramatically reduces the anguish of, "Am I a good-enough parent?"

Staying in the present is what children need. *It's where they are.*

WHAT YOUR CHILDREN NEED

Your children need you to be a parent.

+ **They need you to be the grown-up so that they can be the child.**
+ They need you to measure the consequences of what you are doing, to stand back from some of your own emotions and deal with their emotions with equanimity—however raw.
+ They need you to be able to meet their needs whether or not you feel like it.
+ They need the safety of boundaries and values.
+ They need you to be able to see them as separate from you, however precious.
+ They need you to show them sufficient respect so that they can make their own mistakes and (eventually) their own decisions.
+ They need both space and support to discover their strengths.
+ They need to learn that how they treat other people will dramatically affect the quality of their lives.

Your children can eventually find other people to be their friends, coaches or therapists. That's not what they need from you.

Parenting is not optional

Parenting is not optional. It's not what we do when we feel like it. Our children are not someone to fill in empty moments in our lives—to be dropped when something or someone else comes along.

If your child has two living parents, parenting is also not something to be done by women only.

Children deserve our loyalty, along with our good humor, interest, curiosity, delight—and infinite time and patience.

RESCUING OUR CHILDREN FROM OUR COMPETITIVENESS

An attitude of competitiveness dominates our society. Many of us view even our own children through this prism.

We tell ourselves that we want the best for our children. But the truth is, we often want our children to be *seen to be the best,* in large part to reassure ourselves.

When our children "do well" this may reassure us about our adequacy as parents. More seriously, it may silence our fears about our own self-worth.

Having positive expectations for our children can be loving and supportive. But when we *need* our children to do well, and especially when we need them to do well for *us*, we place a huge burden on them.

Even thinking and talking about our children competitively sends them a powerful and painful message. It teaches them that despite what we say ("I love you for who you are"), what engages and excites us most is "performing well."

In this situation the child will inevitably confuse their value as a human being with the value of their achievements. They will also come to value other people on the basis of their achievements— measured by the standards of a highly anxious and competitive society.

It takes maturity to become aware that you may be inadvertently using your children to reassure yourself—and to resist this persistently

.

Positive expectations all round

Our children's strengths, gifts, talents and challenges may well surprise us. We support them most effectively when we encourage through example and interest a high level of engagement in whatever they do, emphasizing the joys of discovery, cooperation and evolving skills, rather than "instant success" or the need to be "the best." "Doing your best" then becomes an exciting and realistic possibility, rather than an early burden or an implicit demand.

TAKING THE PRESSURE OFF YOUR CHILDREN—AND YOURSELF

Give yourself a break (or a whole series of breaks):

- ✦ Develop an attitude about your own self that *values your life rather than your achievements.* (Enjoy your achievements; don't be ruled by them.)
- ✦ Develop rewarding interests so that your children don't have to compensate you for a shallow or disappointing life.
- ✦ Know which of your own dreams have not yet been lived out. Don't expect or hope that your children will live them for you.
- ✦ *Demonstrate* that you can learn from mistakes and setbacks and grow in resilience.
- ✦ Pay far more attention to qualities than achievements.
- ✦ Let yourself see which of your decisions are status-focused rather than child-focused.
- ✦ Use your values as a guide when making decisions, not your anxieties.
- ✦ Delight in the ordinary.
- ✦ Treasure enthusiasm.
- ✦ Resist parenting "gossip" that brags. This reflects parents' anxiety, and it creates more anxiety both for parents and for children.
- ✦ Show that you can afford to *be pleased for other people.*
- ✦ Value and practice creativity.
- ✦ Value friendliness and kindness. Talk about these qualities. Practice them. Praise them.
- ✦ Consider what you enjoy most about being a parent. Do more of that.

Give your children a break:

- ✦ Keep in mind that your children are separate people, however dependent and beloved. They are not you; you are not them.
- ✦ Remember that you are a parent, not a coach. A coach praises conditionally; a parent loves unconditionally.
- ✦ Be pleased for them when things go well; be confident in them when things don't go so well.

✦ Encourage through your interest, time, commitment, trust; not excessive praise.

✦ Notice how much of your "encouragement" is focused on performance rather than process. (Try: "I could see how much fun that game was," rather than, "I'm so thrilled you scored." Or just ask, with loving enthusiasm, "How was that?")

✦ Get to know each child and what their needs are. Don't assume they will always fit the script you have.

✦ Don't compare your own children, even in your own mind.

✦ Don't compare your children to other people's children. *Accept their individuality.*

✦ Don't make too much of "successes"; nor too much of failures.

✦ Give your children plenty of opportunities to witness you enjoying things you don't do particularly well but that you truly enjoy.

✦ Be clear about what supports each separate child's happiness, contentment, confidence and joy. Create opportunities for more of that. Share their happiness.

✦ Value simple pleasures, easy sharing, quiet talks, lots of cuddles, play and laughter.

Rhythms and routines

With young and not-so-young children, rhythms, routines and rituals create a structure for childhood that is profoundly reassuring. They "settle" children—and their parents.

LEARNING SLOWLY

My son, Gabriel, who is now an adult, went to a Rudolf Steiner school. It's a big school and caters well for a wide range of talents. It also has values that reflect my own. For many years I was extremely happy Gabriel was there, although I was aware that as time went by some of my peers were quietly critical. "Could such a cooperative school, which didn't rank students or reward them with prizes, possibly provide a realistic preparation for the tough, competitive world outside?"

When Gabriel was at the end of ninth grade, and a little more than fourteen, my own anxieties began to trouble me. I wasn't concerned about the lack of prizes or the absence of ranking. I was concerned about Gabriel's work ethic. Did the school demand enough from him to help establish this essential attribute? Or was this attribute essential only in my own eyes?

Having survived a number of earnest conversations in which I would cajole and Gabe would promise . . . I insisted that he sit the entrance examination to the most academically demanding boys' school in Sydney. I convinced myself that this would give him an enhanced academic experience and set aside my internal rumblings about the school's social values. He sat the exam. And passed.

At that point, Gabriel asserted himself. He didn't want to change schools, he told me. He liked his school. What's more, he saw himself as a "Steiner" boy and definitely did not see himself as a prospective student of the school I had chosen. He promised (again) to work hard. In fact, he assured me, I had absolutely nothing to worry about.

I backed down.

Three years went by and Gabriel finished school. He never did keep his promise to work hard (enough!) but he did perfectly well in his exams and extremely well at what he was most interested in. More to the point, he left school relaxed and confident, and with a group of talented, interesting friends who may well last a lifetime.

Was he prepared for the hard, competitive world outside?

My hunch is that staying at a school where he felt instinctively at home intellectually as well as socially, and which valued people rather than prizes, thoroughly prepared him to feel good about himself, interested in others, and alive to his own creative interests. Could anyone ask for more?

Perhaps those same qualities would have emerged wherever he was, but looking back I think two things were important. Most crucially, I listened to him and trusted his instincts—and he felt respected. But what also mattered was that I was pushed by his decision to honor my values rather than my anxieties. We both benefited.

CHECK YOUR PRIORITIES

To honor the people you love, you need to spend real time with them. And be mentally and emotionally present, as well as physically.

This is true for friends, extended family, neighbors and community. It is certainly true for lovers and partners. And it is truer than true when it comes to children.

Nothing matters more to your children than your willingness to be present (and your cheerfulness when you are present).

Have the courage to work out what matters. **Say no—without apologizing—to what is less important than your relationships.**

You can still work hard, pursue independent interests and spend valuable time alone. (Spending time alone may be essential to a healthy relationship with yourself.) But there are countless moments when you have a real choice whether to spend extra time at the office or go home; when you could read the Saturday paper from end to end or go to the park with your children; when you could take a call in the middle of a family dinner, or turn off your phone; when you could talk about your clients' needs or listen to a friend's experiences.

You are choosing.

What was it like to be your parent?

If your parents are still living, consider asking them what it was like to be your parent. You are not asking what kind of child you were, but what parenting you was like for them in the context of their whole life. This can make them and their experiences real to you in genuinely fresh ways.

You may also want to ask your siblings similar questions, but generally the leap is greater in understanding your parents with a truly "adult" mind. It can also be challenging to ask a partner or close friend, "How is it for you to be my partner (or friend)?"

TRUST IS ESSENTIAL FOR LOVING RELATIONSHIPS

We know the value of trust instinctively. We feel its presence or absence in and through our bodies: tensing and contracting when trust is absent; expanding and relaxing when trust is present. *Becoming a person whom others can trust, you create a life of integrity for yourself.*

Trust asks that you:

✦ Keep your promises
✦ Respect other people's values and point of view
✦ Hold their interests in mind
✦ Behave consistently
✦ Respect boundaries
✦ Practice empathy
✦ Work through conflict.

These are hugely significant factors in whether a relationship rises or falls. (And in whether you take on the challenge of growing up.) What's more, trust becomes more and not less important when a relationship enters a less idealized phase, perhaps when two people divorce but remain parents to their children, or an adult child leaves home, or an elderly parent goes to live in a nursing home.

Your inner integrity is directly reflected in how you treat other people.

Trust is not something that other people have to win from you. Trust is something you have and can learn to give—generously.

We can get through this

Most people can work through even quite serious difficulties far more easily and with far greater insight when they trust and can say, "We are in this together." In those situations people may emerge from conflict feeling more and not less positive about themselves, each other and their relationship. When people are afraid that conflict will end their relationship, difficulties are perceived as extremely threatening. *Trust is crucial in changing this dynamic.*

RESENTMENT BLOCKS LOVE

In countless relationships, resentment blocks the path of love.

Resentment can severely limit your ideas about who has a "right" to your kindness—even to your courtesy and consideration. It can mire you in childish helplessness. ("Why should I be the one to make the effort?") And **resentment is highly contagious.**

There are few situations as bitter as when each person in a relationship is consumed by their own resentment. (And this can happen as easily between colleagues as family members or lovers.) It blinds them to the other person's reality. It also blinds them to the truth and complexity of their own situation: that the person who has failed or betrayed them is also someone with whom they have shared tender moments and genuine hopes. And that's what hurts.

An abusive or truly miserable relationship may never get beyond resentment. But in the relationships where some goodwill survives, *it can literally be the difference between life and death to discover how possible it is to set resentment aside.*

Gratitude is the most powerful antidote to resentment. Notice what you can and do appreciate.

These strategies also help:

+ Silence some petty complaints. (Most complaints are petty.)
+ Look at the bigger picture and pay conscious attention to what is going well.
+ Focus on the present moment rather than the past.
+ Monitor your self-talk. (Do not nourish and rehearse your resentments.)
+ Be prepared to listen afresh and with an open mind to the other person's point of view.
+ Practice encouragement constantly and consciously and censor discouragement.
+ Express your enthusiasm and delight even around small things.

Resentment *can* go back into the past where it belongs. Forgiveness and forgetting are possible. Love *can* come back to life.

HOW DO YOU THINK ABOUT SEX?

The way we think about sex probably corresponds pretty closely to the way we think about ourselves.

If we are casual about the value of our lives, we may be just as casual about what we do with our bodies.

Disconnected sex is one way of looking for love, but I suspect it makes love hard to find. My own life has shown me clearly that when we are out of touch with our essence, when we have little love for ourselves, then we are likely to take risks that we would not take once we recognize how intrinsically precious our own existence is.

Loving ourselves more, valuing ourselves more, taking better care of ourselves, we can take sex more seriously, knowing that this seriousness is what will bring us playfulness and laughter, commitment and intensity.

I think the "best friend" test works extremely well when it comes to thinking about our own choices and behaviors around sex.

"Would you want this for your dearest friend?" is a powerful question. It can also be an unusually compassionate and helpful one.

Celibacy is also a choice

Celibacy is a valid choice for long or short periods of life.

Obviously it makes a huge difference if your celibacy is voluntary or not. But celibacy can be a genuine liberation, freeing you up to be open with a whole range of people in warm, affectionate, sensual but non-sexual ways.

"SEX DREW US TOGETHER
BUT NOW IT'S A PROBLEM"

"I used to find him so attractive ..." The most common obstacles to sexual desire are too little rewarding time spent together; too exhausted; stale resentments. If the relationship is worth saving, and especially when children are involved, look frankly at the obstacles. Then take action.

"He's the one who doesn't want to have sex with me more than two or three times a year." My years as a psychotherapist showed me that women are as likely as men to complain about their partner's waning desire. And that sexual desire can die as easily in gay or lesbian relationships as in heterosexual ones. The man who is not feeling desire is, however, a little more likely to feel shamed by this and is definitely less likely to want to talk about it. He may be depressed in general, as well as around this issue. Depression can be significantly helped with appropriate therapy or medication. Otherwise, the common obstacles above apply.

"He says that he cherishes me as a wife and mother but now he needs someone else as a lover." This is a problem of "splitting." He sees you not as *a* mother, but as *his* mother. This definitely kills sexual desire. Maturity demands that we accept our various roles as expressions of a whole self and accept that same complexity in our partner. Get professional help. There is hope.

"She critizies everything I do. It puts me off." Tell her you adore her but that your bedroom is a criticism-free zone and that only loving, kind, enthusiastic and outrageously encouraging words are to be spoken there. Extend your encouragement "pact" to every area of your life. Criticism is a habit; it can be broken.

"We always have sex in exactly the same way. I can't stand it." He's nervous, anxious and perhaps unimaginative! He may also be stubborn and aurally challenged (doesn't listen to anything you say). Nevertheless, you love him. *That's where your focus needs to be.* Talking about sex makes him more nervous. Talking about him, his interests and where you are going for your next weekend away may be more helpful. When someone is "stuck," we often mirror them with our own stuck responses of frustration. When your responses ease, he may also relax—

and may even be open to more adventurous and good-humored lovemaking.

"I have never been faithful." That's because you love to try something new. Now try fidelity! Better than that, try the genuine challenge of keeping life fresh with the one you love.

"He wants me to do things that make me uncomfortable." A little bit "uncomfortable" could, with trust and a sense of adventure, become fun. (Sometimes this means having a spa bath together.) Something you believe is morally wrong, or that is humiliating or offensive, is *never fun* and it's your absolute right to say no.

"We never have sex together and neither of us really cares." This may be true. If it is true, there is no problem. The litmus test really is whether you are relaxed, affectionate, easy together—or whether tension emerges in chronic nit-picking, undermining, etc. In the latter situation, all is not so well and broader issues may need attention.

"How often is often enough?" You need to ask each other, then pick a number in the middle. Meanwhile, increase your hugs, cuddles, relaxing time together; make more time for whatever gives you both pleasure; relish everything about your relationship—and life.

"I was abused as a child. I'm ambivalent about sex." This is definitely a situation where some serious healing needs to take place. Your serious healer should be a therapist and not your partner, however loving.

"He's nice to me only when he wants to have sex." This is not a sexual problem. It is a relationship problem. You aren't relating any longer and you need to take this seriously. Sex works best and makes both people happiest when it reflects the way that they think about themselves, each other and their relationship. When sex simply passes time, fills a need or meets a hunger, each person is using the other, or being used, and mutual delight is lost. Time to look at the big picture. What do *you* want?

"Since we had the baby she has lost all interest in me." She is exhausted. And overwhelmed. She may be suffering a real sense of discontinuity between who she used to be and who she is now. Giving more and

demanding less are perfect at this time. Get into the sensuality of massages, hugs, foot-rubs, plumped-up pillows, little treats and notes. Value your new role as protector–father. Keep telling her how gorgeous she is without asking for anything in return. Sexual desire does return. When it does, it will reflect your new depths of love and mutual understanding. When the baby is older (before he graduates!), spend some regular time away from the baby and with your partner. Just as crucially, make sure she gets time alone if she needs that. And that you get time alone with the baby.

"I never meet anyone that I'm attracted to who is also attracted to me." Try for six months or so to focus on friendship exclusively. Give yourself a refreshing break from the agonies of sexual inspection and judgment. There could be many reasons why these sexual connections are not happening but, rather than focusing on them, tell yourself that even if you meet someone perfect during this six-month period you are most unlikely to be available. Freed from the grip of worrying about sexual desire, you will be far less self-judgmental and stressed, more relaxed and certainly more available to all sorts of other adventures of a non-sexual kind. Your sensuality will bloom. But remember what you are available to are the boundless joys of friendship.

HOLDING BACK

It has taken me years to learn how powerfully love is expressed in the moments when we hold back from taking action for the sake of someone else (and for the sake of love).

Sometimes *not speaking* is perfect.

Sometimes *not advising* is perfect.

Sometimes *not pushing* is perfect.

Sometimes *not gossiping* is perfect.

Sometimes *not holding on to the past* is perfect.

Sometimes *relinquishing your agenda* is perfect.

TALK LESS

I love to talk. I also need silence. But in the relationships I value most, lots of talking goes on. My closest relationship is built on talk and the absolute confidence that we will always have lots to say to one another and can delight in listening.

Nevertheless, in intimate relationships talk can be wounding. Even "helpful" talk can become repetitive and unhelpful. Often our talking is not much more than a rehearsal of what's wrong. It doesn't take us toward insight or "solutions"; it doesn't shift our feelings. It doesn't do anything much at all except increase our sense of helplessness and frustration.

When a close relationship is stuck, "going nowhere," or feels as though it's going round in circles, talking—and "having things out"— is often *not* the best place to start.

What helps most is to start with yourself. Take time to go inward. Dive deep, writing out your questions and then your answers.

Simple questions are most useful: What's familiar here? Have I been in this place before? Am I feeling out of sorts? Am I focusing on the relationship when something else needs attention? What am I blocking—within myself or for the other people involved? What outcome do I want? What would achieve it? What qualities do I need to call on?

ARE YOU HAVING ANY FUN?

Relationships are the source of our greatest delight and pleasure. *They are not mini-companies to be run with maximum efficiency.*

For us to receive what they can give (what we can give each other), we must make ourselves available. We need to relate intuitively, creatively, sensually, playfully. We need to save at least some of our best energies for our relationships.

Put the relationship first

Often we put the relationship last when we are trying to achieve something. It might be something as banal as getting the house in order over a busy weekend. Asking, "How can we do this so that everyone will benefit?" may produce a quite different set of insights from when you are making the tasks your priority, rather than the people.

It can be wonderfully liberating to sacrifice some efficiencies for the sake of love.

AN OUTBREAK OF COURTESY

A simple renewal of good manners can profoundly change the way that people feel about one another. Paying attention, expressing gratitude, looking at one another, holding back and stepping forward appropriately: *this makes a difference.*

In each of our close relationships, we have so much power to hurt.

In each of our close relationships, we have so much power to heal.

HOW TO HONOR THE PEOPLE YOU LOVE

Essential insights

✦ "Relationship" extends way beyond sexual relationships. Whatever your circumstances, you are always "in a relationship."

✦ It is an honor to be emotionally close to another human being; your behavior can reflect that.

✦ You express love—and gratitude—through your choices and behavior. No point claiming to love, but behaving unlovingly.

✦ Possessiveness is not love; being unable to live without another person is not love. Love honors separateness as well as togetherness.

✦ As you grow in self-awareness and self-love, you will inevitably ask less of others, give more, and your relationships will inevitably benefit.

✦ To grow in generosity and love, your relationships need fewer demands and greater acceptance. Acceptance is a vital precondition to lasting happiness.

✦ Close relationships need the basics: time, interest, attention, good humor, forgiveness and love. *They are not mini-corporations to be run with maximum efficiency.*

✦ The people you love will profoundly affect your happiness, but you are responsible for it.

✦ You are also responsible for the effect you have on them: lifting their spirits through your own care, affection and good humor.

✦ Children need you to be the grown-up so that they can be the child. They also need to be loved and cherished for who they are and not for how impressive or talented they are.

✦ Your partner (and closest friends) also needs you to be a grown-up. Relationships do best when they are based on mutual respect, shared interests, love, joy—and shared responsibility.

✦ In all close relationships, the little things *add up to* the big things.

✦ Your capacity to give and receive love is not limited by your past. "Attitude" counts as much as history.

✦ Be aware of what you didn't get in childhood as well as what you most resent. Don't expect the people you love to compensate for your past.

✦ Recognize that the people you love may not always want what you want. This challenges your egocentricity, not your relationships.

✦ Love is not love except when it is generous.

Essential actions

✦ *Give of yourself*. Give time, interest, respect and love to the people who know you best. If you are "fitting them in," re-work your priorities.

✦ *Be* the partner/friend/parent/lover you would love to find.

✦ *Know* what lifts the spirits of the people you love. Care about that. Do it.

✦ To improve a relationship immediately, be courteous and grateful. And *listen*.

✦ Value difference.

✦ Check out your unspoken assumptions about what a relationship "should" provide. Check out what you are prepared to offer. When change is needed, write that down as a promise to yourself. Also write down how you are willing to make it.

✦ Look at your own behavior from the perspective of the people you love.

✦ Ask the people you love how they would like you to behave. You might want to ask them what you should *stop*, what you should *start*, and what you should *continue* to do. Listen with interest—even if it's tough.

✦ Respect other people's choices—even when you might have chosen more wisely for them.

✦ Let yourself be inspired by the people you love. Tell them how they inspire you.

✦ *Receive* others' love gracefully. When it doesn't fit your ideal, focus on the intention.

✦ Take a genuine interest in the interests of the people you are close to; know what gives their lives meaning; know what their passions are; show how you value their enthusiasms. Demonstrate that you love them *for who they are*.

✦ Never assume that you know everything about another person—even your partner or child.

✦ Choose just one or two relationship skills to practice (listening carefully, smiling when your loved one enters a room, speaking with respect). Behaving well is not always "obvious." And even when the behavior that's needed is obvious, often we don't do it.

✦ When you desperately want to criticize someone you care about, STOP. *Let minor criticisms go*. If something is genuinely important, raise it when you are *not* irritated.

✦ Recognize that on your bad-mood days, the people closest to you will seem most annoying. When you feel irritated with them, *ask yourself*, "What am I not paying attention to?"

✦ Keep yourself in the present moment. Look people in the eyes. Let them be real to you.

✦ Know that any day could be the last day. Make it count.

✦ Practice forgiveness.

Think and act positively

HOW DIFFERENT WOULD YOUR LIFE BE?

How different would your life be if you could trust yourself to meet more or less any situation as it arose? You may well prefer some situations to others. But you would know that you could at least cope with whatever comes—and most often do better than merely cope.

How different would your life be if you could trust that you can give and receive love?

How different would your life be if you could count on your moods being stable—that you could feel good pretty much all of the time? And that "feeling good" did not depend on events going your way or other people treating you appreciatively?

How different would your life be if you were confident that when you do feel depressed, pessimistic or anxious you could change your state of mind?

How different would your life be if you could look out at the world around you and feel uplifted by what you find?

The life that these questions are inviting you to imagine *is not out of reach*.

Some have it quite naturally. Others of us have to work a little harder: give up some old habits and create some new ones. *But the rewards are tremendous.* In fact, I would go so far as to say that the rewards are literally life-saving.

They buy you what money can't: not only happiness but also peace of mind, tolerance, kindness and genuine engagement with life.

WHAT A POSITIVE ATTITUDE WILL GIVE YOU

Claim these gifts as you dare to think and act positively:

+ Self-acceptance
+ Stability of mood
+ Better physical health
+ Access to your inner strengths
+ Enjoyment of others' strengths
+ Increased emotional, moral and spiritual intelligence
+ A radically heightened sense of possibility
+ A willingness to experiment, make mistakes, recover
+ Happiness

And what will a more positive attitude take away or lessen?

+ Anxiety
+ Depression
+ Mistrust
+ Procrastination
+ Bigotry
+ Self-righteousness
+ Fear
+ Loneliness
+ Despair

THOUGHTS ARE THE CRUCIAL FACTOR

Even if you pride yourself on being highly "rational," you probably suspect that your emotions are the strongest force in your existence.

Emotions are incredibly strong, incredibly powerful. In fact, they color everything. But an emotion doesn't exist without the thought or circumstance that drives it. What's more, emotions can't be changed because you decide they "ought to be." But thoughts—or where you place your attention—can be changed.

As thoughts change, mood, feelings and emotions will follow. So will actions and behavior.

+ *Change* your thinking—and you will also change the way you feel.
+ *Challenge* the beliefs that hold you back or harm you—and you will change the way you feel.
+ *"Notice"* that you are falling into dreary or pessimistic thinking and take positive action—and you will change the way you feel.
+ *Limit* the attention you give to what's disappointing or hurtful—and you will change the way you feel.
+ *Increase* the attention you give to what is positive, uplifting, hopeful and supportive—and you will radically change the way you feel.

This all seems so obvious! So the big questions are: Why don't we automatically weed out the thoughts that hurt us and cultivate the thoughts that support us? Why don't we act decisively, knowing that our feelings will change as we do so?

This entire chapter is an answer to that question. However, the short answer is that most of us don't realize that thoughts are driving our emotions and limiting our behavior. Nor do we realize that we can do something about those thoughts; that **we can direct them rather than being directed by them.**

BEYOND BANAL AFFIRMATIONS

I spent years resisting the insights of the "positive thinking" movement.

I told myself that it was superficial, mechanical and banal.

I was wrong.

There is plenty of banality available. Life is not just one long opportunity to rehearse your affirmations. And sometimes "looking on the bright side" or catching the silver lining in each passing cloud isn't nearly good enough. However, wade in a little deeper and you will make some startling discoveries.

✦ You can learn to observe your thoughts and stand back from them.

✦ You can learn to experience that you are more powerful than your thoughts. (When they are undermining or depressing, *you can change them.*)

✦ You can *use your own thinking* to access your innate strengths and qualities, putting you in touch with your true inheritance.

✦ You can profoundly influence your own life for the better—and be a source of inspiration and support for other people.

What's more, you can do this whatever your emotional history has been to date. Forget the proverbial glass: half-full or half-empty. Trust these skills of emotional intelligence. They ask nothing of you but your willing engagement.

A positive life is not naïve

You do not need to exclude your awareness of suffering or disappointment, injustice or social discord to lead a genuinely positive life. The issue is *how* you see suffering. And what qualities you are prepared to bring to relieving it.

A POSITIVE ATTITUDE CONNECTS YOU TO LIFE

A genuinely positive attitude needs to be inclusive: self, others, life itself. It needs to *free you from self-absorption, not intensify it.*

As anyone knows who has suffered from painful bouts of anxiety or depression, **when you feel worst about yourself, you also feel most disconnected from other people.** You feel as though you have nothing worthwhile to give. And you doubt that anyone else can give you what you need, either.

When you feel good about yourself, you feel and *are* far more open. Your levels of trust soar. Your face expresses this; so does your body.

A positive attitude allows you to be truly interested in what's going on around you. It engages and connects you.

It moves you away from simplistic black/white thinking. It lets you see how much beauty there is in the world, how much kindness and good humor, even when you also see what's difficult and dark.

It lets you open up to what is wondrous.

It supports you to respect life in all its forms.

It means recognizing that you are part of something miraculous.

Listen to Albert Einstein

I love these words from Albert Einstein, scientist and great humanitarian, and keep them on my noticeboard to remind myself of what's most true about existence.

"A human being is part of the whole called by us a universe—a part limited in time and space. He experiences himself, his thoughts and his feelings as something separate from the rest, a kind of optical delusion of his consciousness. This delusion is a kind of prison for us; it restricts us to our personal decisions and our affections to a few persons nearest to us. Our task must be to free ourselves from this prison by widening our circle of compassion to embrace all living creatures and the whole of nature in its beauty."

YOUR THOUGHTS MATTER
MORE THAN ANY EVENT

Human beings are the only species on Earth whose inner lives are so powerful that what we think about a situation, how we describe it to ourselves, what meaning we attribute to it or draw from it, matters more than the event itself.

And who is doing the thinking, describing and attributing of meaning?

You are.

Listen to Proverbs

"As [a man] thinketh in his heart, so is he."

Listen to the Buddha

"We are what we think.
With our thoughts we create the world."

BITTER ROOTS

CATHERINE: Several years ago I was given an opportunity to work on a challenging series of customer communications. I think the client was expecting a black-clad, bourbon-drinking, twenty-six-year-old advertising agency copywriter to turn up for the briefing meeting. I walked in wearing a camel-colored twin set and pearl earrings. To say the least, the fit wasn't exactly right.

As the meeting progressed, the client briefed me on writing hip, irreverent, in-your-face customer communications. I argued that people want letters that are respectful and reassuring. She disagreed. Street smart was what people wanted, she told me; writing that was funny, edgy, off-key.

Even though my gut said no, my pride accepted the job. I convinced myself that it was an opportunity to grow as a writer. Surely I could do this, I reasoned. I was a professional! I had never before missed my mark with a brief. I would just assume the voice and style she wanted and make it work.

It was a disaster. For the first time ever, I couldn't do what my client expected. I ended up with hours of wasted time, confrontational meetings, a bruised ego, and a huge invoice for my work that, in good conscience, I didn't feel ethical about submitting. I spent days agonizing over the experience, feeling like a failure because of that one failed job.

Eventually I realized that nurturing my hurt wasn't affecting anyone but me. I was the one losing sleep by night and agonizing by day. I finally decided that I had a choice—to be bitter or to grow.

I used the experience to learn that I could survive failure, act out my values, and let the negative experience go. I didn't send the invoice. Instead, I sent an e-mail explaining that I wouldn't be charging my client for the unsuccessful work and why.

Nonetheless, it was hard to accept that I had failed, and I'm still embarrassed by the memory. In general, our society seems so hung up on success, and so afraid of failure!

Why do we work so hard to pretend that we never fail? Why are we so embarrassed when we do? And how can we learn to just move on?

STEPHANIE: I'm fascinated by this story. First of all, here we see Catherine ignoring her instincts. What she describes as her "gut" told her that working on this account would not go well. Yet, when her instincts turned out to be correct, she's still blaming herself. (Which part of her knew best? The part that told her she "ought" to be able to do any job; the part of her that "knew" this would never work out?)

In the list of what she has learned from the experience she includes her capacity to "let the negative experience go" – but I am not sure that she's done that.

Catherine—like so many of us—sets herself extremely high standards. And why not? But at the same time her measure of success is narrow. The combination is lethal.

When we measure success narrowly, and give failure the power to embarrass us and make us feel less than we are, or when failure hangs on long after success is forgotten, then of course success will become elusive and failure will become something to fear and dread.

But is this situation a genuine failure? Could Catherine think and act positively in the face of it?

She has already described what she learned from the situation. What she hasn't done is given what she has learned a higher value than she is giving to her sense of embarrassment and "failure." She's brushing aside those invaluable gifts, and taking herself back to the "what-if's" and the "I shouldn't have's."

Yet, from this kind of "failure" any one of us could potentially learn:

✦ That there are certain kinds of jobs that we may not accomplish well enough to satisfy ourselves as well as the employer. (Catherine was fortunate that she doesn't have to take every job just for the money.)

✦ That we *can* afford to assert ourselves firmly and pleasantly—and that this is best done sooner rather than later.

✦ That we can learn something invaluable from our "mistakes"—and reframe our idea of what a "mistake" is *once we gain insight from it.*

We could also come to discover how often our instincts are guiding us effectively, and that we do ourselves a disservice when we let our self-talk—or our worries about what other people will think—override them.

Extracting this much learning from a "failure," and *valuing that learning*, the experience may not become positive for us, but it certainly ceases to be bitter.

We are, as a society, "hung up on success," exactly as Catherine describes. But once we recognize that almost every situation yields up something of value (perhaps saving us from a worse disaster a month ahead), limited notions of both "success" and "failure" lose their punch. We can then move on more genuinely. And with a little added wisdom, to boot.

PEACE IS JUST A THOUGHT AWAY

Thoughts don't travel in one direction only. We don't only take in thoughts; we also "send them out."

The psychological description of this is that we project the contents of our minds onto the world outside ourselves. *Whatever we enact in the "outside" world has its origins in the "inside" world of our minds.*

Understanding this, we come close to a real understanding of what self-responsibility is. We are collectively responsible for the world outside ourselves. Everything in the world—good and bad—begins with a thought.

The spiritual description of this same process takes it a step further, reminding us that we are actually creating the world outside ourselves through the power of our thinking. The wars, violence and injustice, as well as the goodness, kindness and mercy, all begin in our minds; they are all states of mind that originate and are sustained by thought.

It is through our thinking—and the actions that flow from our thinking—that we allow ourselves to add to our collective well-being, or not.

I suspect that this is the true measure of "positive thinking": that it positively benefits you and all of humankind.

Bringing peace

"Peace is just a thought away" is a bumper sticker used by the Brahma Kumaris World Spiritual University, worldwide teachers of "peace of mind" meditation.

Take a moment to imagine how exquisite our world and all our lives would be if we let ourselves believe and experience that with our thoughts we could create peace, have peace, and offer peace to one another.

DEPRESSING THOUGHTS
CREATE *DEPRESSING FEELINGS*

In the course of a single day, you will have about 50,000 thoughts. (We have clinical psychologists to thank for this useful statistic!) Sometimes, though, it may feel as though you are having the same thought 50,000 times.

More worryingly, when you are depressed or anxious, or "just" in a bad mood, 90 percent of your thoughts may be miserable, anxious, self-defeating or depressing. That's a lot of thinking. *That's a lot of your life.*

Is it any wonder then that you will feel awful or even increasingly awful? How could you feel any other way when what's grabbing your attention—when what's *getting* your attention—is almost entirely bleak and dispiriting?

Just remember how exhausting it is to spend an hour or two in the company of someone who has nothing good to say about anyone or anything; who moans and complains incessantly; who goes on and on about unfair and disappointing things that happened years ago or might never happen; who is self-pitying and blaming of other people—and pays no attention whatsoever to what's going well.

You would want to escape their company as soon as possible, I suspect. But when you feel grim, *that's close to what you are doing to yourself.* You are having thoughts that *screen out the good and focus on the bad.*

You are not only having those thoughts; you are inviting them in. You are offering them the best seat in the house, bringing them refreshments, telling them that your house is their house. And you are doing this *through the power of your attention.*

You may believe that you have every reason to be depressed. You may believe that the reasons for your depression live outside you. And it's true: there are always many valid reasons to be depressed: some personal, some universal.

You may also believe that you will no longer be depressed when something outside yourself changes. You may live for tomorrow because today seems so intolerable. And it's true: tomorrow you may get the job you want, the lover you dream of, the acknowledgment you crave or the therapist who is, finally, capable of truly understanding you. And that may help.

What will certainly help, right now, in this moment, are these active changes.

- *Change your body posture.* Almost inevitably as your thoughts bring you down, your body will reflect this. Moving your body may not solve everything but it will certainly support a more positive, uplifting outlook. Your body *reflects* your emotions, and sends powerful messages *to* your mind.
- *Shift your thoughts, your attention, away from the "causes" of your depression*, from the justifications for your depression, and from fantasizing about what you need in order for your depression to disappear.
- *Engage with something beyond yourself.* Whatever your activity of choice, let it be as demanding and engaging as possible. Often a change in physical environment will support a significant inner shift.

From "why" to "how"

Pay less attention to *why* you feel so bad (there are always reasons) and far more attention to *what* will make you feel better and *how* to achieve that. Ask, "What's needed here? What can I do to help myself?"

IS NEGATIVE THINKING HARMING YOU?

You may not easily recognize the patterns that undermine or even defeat you. But until you recognize them (and the power they have over you), you can't undo them.

If you do have any of these habits (and most of us have some) know that recognizing them *they already lose their power.* Their power is sustained *only as long as you believe in them.*

Remember that these are patterns of thinking only; they are not set in stone. They probably began as ways of trying to defend yourself against hurt. Or because this is how your original family thought or behaved. But my hunch is that they have outlived their usefulness.

Do you see yourself in any of these patterns?

+ Hovering over disappointments, failures and setbacks. Focusing on the 1 percent that went badly; ignoring the 99 percent that went well. Rehearsing and replaying mistakes constantly in your mind.

+ Interpreting neutral remarks negatively. ("I am sure she meant that I should never call her again.")

+ Believing that other people can read your mind. Blaming and punishing them when they can't.

+ Looking for reasons why you feel so bad (they are always there to be found—they just don't make you feel better).

+ Justifying your bad moods, self-pity, even your loneliness, anxiety or despair as something that other people are causing.

+ Being extremely sensitive to betrayal or criticism. (Remind yourself that this says more about the person doing it than it does about you. Look at the big picture, at what's gone well, at the qualities you know you have.)

+ Catastrophizing. (Your partner is late home. They are having an affair or dead.)

+ Believing your own delusions. ("No one cares about me.")

+ Calling yourself names: loser, fat, ugly, hopeless. This is guaranteed to make your feelings plummet.

- ✦ Paying more attention to other people's lives—envying them, disparaging them, wishing them harm—than to your own.
- ✦ Discrediting what other people give you, do for you and offer you. (The antidote is gratitude.)

It's incredibly helpful to see whether and how these common patterns affect you. And to know that however powerful the emotions that accompany them, these thoughts or patterns of thinking *can be changed*.

Remain solution-focused (and creative)

Remind yourself: "I can think differently—and my moods and feelings will follow." Or "This is dead-end thinking. I can take a different path."

The minute you recognize that you are caught in a negative pattern, take action. Engross yourself in something else; change your surroundings; remind yourself that you can choose what you will pay attention to, and how that will affect your moods.

Listen to Norman Vincent Peale

Long before bookshops offered their current vast array of motivational and self-help books, Peale wrote his gold-standard book, *The Power of Positive Thinking*.

He most usefully points out: "A positive thinker does not refuse to recognize the negative, *he refuses to dwell on it* [my itals]. Positive thinking is a form of thought which habitually looks for the best results from the worst conditions."

GRIEF AND SORROW ARE NOT
"NEGATIVE" FEELINGS

Events occur in all our lives that are profoundly distressing. A friend dies. One of your parents has a stroke. Your house burns down. You are diagnosed with a degenerative illness. You lose a second breast to cancer. Your partner leaves or betrays you. You discover that the youngest of your five wonderful children is using hard drugs.

These are not moments to snap into "positive thinking" mode.

There are certainly ways that you can support yourself. There are qualities of courage, tolerance and generosity that you can call upon. You can treat yourself kindly. You can refuse to ask, "Why me?" You can refuse to criticize the way that you are "handling it," even to yourself.

Spending time in good company with loving family or friends, divesting yourself of all but the most essential tasks, taking time to be in places of natural beauty, paying attention to what you eat, praying or meditating: these all help.

But sorrow and grief, even rage, are quite natural at these times.

Rushing past your genuine emotions, feeling not entitled to have them, denying, trivializing them or retreating into cynicism is never "positive." It cuts you off from your own truth. It makes it difficult for you to relate in a genuine way with other people.

It is a precious thing to learn that you can survive even the worst losses. *You will be changed. But you need not be diminished.*

This learning should neither be rushed nor imposed. Grief can break our hearts wide open. It can shatter our myths of self-sufficiency and show how deeply we depend on one another.

These are hard lessons to learn. My experience is that they are best learned in a spirit of gentleness. When we feel most broken, kindness is everything.

THINKING HARDER DOESN'T DO IT

It's not possible to think your way out of a depression or low mood by *constantly returning to whatever made you depressed or upset in the first place.*

I know that's extremely tempting. In fact, it is the psychological equivalent of picking at a scab. (*Very* tempting.) Yet each time you pick, the wound reopens. And healing is further postponed.

Often we tell ourselves that if we really understood what had caused the wound in the first place, the scab would fall off and the skin would be healed. This isn't necessarily so.

Returning repeatedly to the thoughts that already make you feel low can only make you feel even lower. This doesn't mean that insight is not useful. It can be extremely useful. *Insight can also change your feelings.* But often when we go searching for insight we are doing nothing more than reliving past distress. What we gain is more misery, not relief and not insight.

Insight is more likely to be available to you when you feel calm and even a little detached.

Take charge!

Thinking is what you do *to* yourself.

Changing your thinking is what you can do *for* yourself.

This may mean changing your physical environment, as well as the way you talk about your issues, whom you talk to (some people attract and adore endless complaining), and—most crucially—how you direct your attention and yourself.

NOT EVERY PROBLEM HAS A SOLUTION

Not every problem has a solution. Not every setback has a remedy. Some situations have to be outlived—maybe with lessons learned.

Often a more constructive and less destructive way of thinking is possible.

Focus on *what's needed* rather than on the problem.

Even the most intelligent among us, and sometimes especially the most intelligent among us, *return again and again to what's wrong.* On top of the pain we originally felt, we now also feel helpless, hopeless, frustrated and anguished. We are dancing on quicksand. And getting sucked in.

"What's needed here?" is a question that's deceptively simple. It arouses hope. It also wakes up your will.

Whatever is needed, *take the first small step.* Taking action is itself energizing. You cannot get a grip while you remain on quicksand. Taking action, or *choosing to move on and leave the problem behind*, will always lift your spirits.

HOW TO THINK MORE POSITIVELY

Take your time here! A little revolution could be about to happen.

Experiment first with the idea that thoughts are not something that happen to you. They are what you do to yourself. This will help you to discover that *negativity is a learned response.* You may believe that it saves you from disappointment. It doesn't. It invites disappointment and it solidifies it.

Positivity is also a learned response—and grows with practice. Coach yourself; talk yourself up; encourage yourself; remind yourself of what you know, what you can do.

Funnily enough, you might start thinking more positively by thinking less. Certainly by ruminating far, far less. (Having the same thought many times rarely lifts your spirits.)

In learning how to think more positively, pay more attention to your body than to your thoughts or feelings. **It's impossible to think positively when you are slumped in a position of helplessness or hopelessness.** This tells your body-mind that life is hopeless. Shifting and activating your body is a crucial first step; sometimes it is all that's needed.

Eat and rest well. This will immediately enhance your brain function and lift your thinking.

Pay less attention to why you feel so bad (there are always reasons) and far more attention to what will make you feel better and how to achieve that. Accept that life is unfair. Or that it's "fairness" is certainly not available to our rational minds. (Don't allow yourself to be outraged or even surprised when everything doesn't go the way you want it to.)

Remind yourself what your strengths are, what you know about yourself that is uplifting and positive. Use your strengths—including strength of mind. *Use your power to choose.*

Know that when you are in a bad mood, you will not think effectively (never mind positively). The worse your mood, the less seriously you should take your thoughts—and ignore all your "conclusions."

Get involved with something that requires your concentrated attention *in this present moment.* Let yourself be challenged, stimulated,

447

absorbed. Sometimes this will require you to switch your attention; sometimes you will benefit from new surroundings, or people who are uplifting or distracting.

This will also help:

- ✦ Monitor closely what you pay attention to. Whatever you pay attention to will occupy your mind—and determine your mood.

- ✦ Monitor how you are describing the situation to yourself: whether you are telling yourself how hopeless it is, or how hopeless you are. You cannot begin to feel better until you challenge self-defeating thoughts—or cease paying them attention.

- ✦ If there is a problem, look for a solution. If there is no solution, accept that and move on.

- ✦ Don't grab on to fruitless or self-harming thoughts, however seductive. *Let yourself know that whatever you are currently feeling and believing—good or bad—will pass.*

- ✦ Cultivate your capacity to learn from every situation. Once you have learned something of value you will be less stuck emotionally and mentally.

- ✦ Give up the pleasures of self-pity or resentment. They hold you in the past. You may not think of your resentful thoughts as pleasure-producing but they are certainly giving you something. Perhaps they are justifying a limited view of yourself? Move on.

- ✦ Practice gratitude. It is hard to feel grateful for your life and helpless at the same moment.

Pay less attention to your thoughts—and *much more attention to your behavior and actions.* Getting on and doing something shifts your thinking and feelings effortlessly. Whether it's calling a friend, checking out plans for an event you would enjoy, doing a tough but absorbing piece of work, finally sorting the linen cupboard, dancing to loud music, singing Gospel: *act.* And never wait until "you feel like it." As you take action, your feelings will change.

DISPUTE YOUR THOUGHTS—SOMETIMES

Disputing negative thinking (arguing with the illogic or emotionality of your thoughts) can be powerfully effective. As a beginner, you may need to write down your most preoccupying thoughts, then write down your challenge to them. As you become more practiced, you can do this fairly automatically.

However, sometimes your thoughts don't need (or deserve) that much attention. "There I go again, creating monsters in my mind," can be enough to spur you to place your attention elsewhere or switch to more constructive thinking.

The choices are yours.

A POSITIVE LIFE CAN STILL HAVE PROBLEMS

Regarding your life positively doesn't mean that you will no longer have any problems. Such a life does not exist, even in fairy tales. (In fact, most fairy tales are accounts of overcoming problems and experiencing transformation through courage and tenacity.)

However, thinking about life more positively, *you will see your problems differently.* Some of them will appear (and are) trivial. You can move on from them fast. Some you will recognize as serious and deserving of your attention. Those you will face with courage— learning as you go.

I am only too aware that most of the worst and most unwelcome situations in my own life have taught me a great deal. I have not been a willing learner. I would have done anything in the world to avoid those situations. But it has only been when I have been most desperate that I have called out to God for help, or turned to other people for help, or plumbed my depths to find qualities I did not believe I had.

Through the way that you deal with difficulties, you will grow, psychologically and spiritually.

This doesn't mean that there is a "perfect" way to deal with tough situations. You can give yourself more pain on top of your suffering if you imagine that there's only one way to be brave or positive.

In this, as in everything else that is significant in your life, allow yourself your own timetable, your own set of strengths, your own moments of weakness. Don't berate yourself for those times; learn that you can treat yourself gently—and more easily face another day.

Affirm yourself

It's not possible to embrace life fully without also facing your difficulties—and doing your best with whatever arises. *Trusting that you can meet whatever comes is at the heart of genuinely positive living.* That takes you way beyond "cheerful thoughts." It is a profound affirmation of the complexity of life. It is also an appropriate affirmation of yourself.

YOU ARE MORE POWERFUL THAN
YOUR THOUGHTS

As you are getting clear about who (or what) is really running your life, it's miraculous to discover that **you are more powerful than your thoughts.**

Even when your thoughts are crowding or seemingly crushing you—you have more power than your thoughts.

Your thoughts only have as much power as you are prepared to give them. You give them power by paying them attention.

A thought that's getting no attention has no power! (Where does a thought go when you are not thinking it?)

You may believe your thoughts are immune to change. This is especially true when you feel down. Being depressed not only distorts your thinking, it also makes it horribly convincing. However, even the most stubborn patterns of thinking can be viewed and experienced differently. Watching your thoughts, looking for patterns in your thinking, you will discover, "I have thoughts. I am not my thoughts."

"I am the thinker. I am not my thoughts."

Recognizing that you are more powerful than your thoughts, you will also recognize your power to *give and withdraw your attention, to send your life in the direction you most want it to go.*

HOW TO OBSERVE YOUR THOUGHTS

Your mind plays many tricks on you. How nice to discover that it's possible to use some of its "tricks" for your own benefit.

"Watch your thoughts."

"What a ridiculous idea," *is* a thought! So is, "I am not having any thoughts."

Once you get the hang of it—in seconds—you will observe that if you have thoughts, and can mentally step back and observe them, then you can't also *be* your thoughts. This tiny insight may come as a shock to those of you who are highly identified with your intellect. Even for you, however, and perhaps especially for you, this insight can be a relief.

That power we have to think, reflect and remember can be our greatest blessing. But it can also torment us. It can limit us. Crush us. Drive us crazy. Deceive us. Overwhelm us.

Discovering that you can direct your thoughts and choose to think more productively, you grow in freedom.

You don't have to pay attention to a memory that is haunting you, a fear that is preoccupying you, a suspicion that is enraging you. It *is* possible to direct your attention elsewhere or to look at those same situations more productively.

As you watch your thoughts, you may also be criticizing them. ("I'm so hopeless. . . . I'm such an idiot. . . . How could I be thinking about him again?")

Intensify the game. *Observe the observer.*

Shift your inner perspective "higher" until you experience you are looking at your life and yourself from a genuinely spacious and compassionate viewpoint. And only then ask, "What's needed?"

A SKILL OF EMOTIONAL INTELLIGENCE

Observing your thoughts—and detaching from them—is a skill of meditation and of emotional intelligence. The more you practice it, the more readily available it is to you when you need it most.

This skill doesn't turn you into a robot. On the contrary, when you feel less pushed around by your thoughts, you can engage more wholeheartedly with whatever needs your attention. And you can perceive what positive actions are necessary to support you. Remind yourself: "These are only thoughts. *I* am directing them."

A sea change

You can have a sea change without ever leaving home.

A positive life is clear and simple.

It means reaching for the best in yourself, always.

And believing that the best is there to be found.

It also means discovering that *to be your best does not involve being "better" than any other human being.* No worse, either.

BAD-MOOD THINKING

Even optimists have fluctuations in mood.

In fact, the only people I know who have very little fluctuation in mood are those who have been meditating faithfully for many years and have established an inspiring stability of mind and deep inward confidence. This is lovely to be around and provides yet another reason to meditate regularly. (Your thoughts affect the world around you, as well as the "world" inside your mind.)

For the rest of us, who are not quite there yet, it is extremely useful to know that our "good-mood thinking" is very different from our "bad-mood thinking."

Recognizing how unhelpful our "bad (depressed) mood thinking" is, we are far less likely to be seduced and convinced by it.

This simple recognition can save us from all kinds of interpersonal difficulties at home and work. It can also save us from prolonging our bad mood by thinking more and more bleakly.

Depending on how bad your bad mood is, the effects can run from irritability, oversensitivity and touchiness to irrationality, rage and paranoia.

None of that is good for problem-solving, seeing clearly, or enjoying the present moment! It's not good for your physical or mental health. And it can be disastrous for your relationships.

Also, *this kind of thinking prolongs your bad mood.* In fact, depressed people are in a fairly continuous "bad mood" state and people in a "bad mood" are in a temporarily depressed state. (Depression can be expressed through rage and addictions—including an addiction to negative thinking—as well as through collapse, emptiness, despair and withdrawal.)

When you are in a bad mood, *pay least possible attention to what your thoughts are telling you.*

Do not:

+ Make important decisions
+ Pay much attention to or act on your own thinking (especially to your suspicions and paranoia)
+ Dump on other people

- ◆ Fight with anyone—however tempted you may be
- ◆ Blame someone else for the way you are feeling.

Rest for some, greater stimulation for others; wholesome, nourishing food; good company; reading something uplifting; physical exercise; time spent in nature; absorption in something that genuinely engages you: all of these simple changes can shift a bad mood or relieve it.

All my thoughts are utterly convincing!

We are all sorely tempted to believe our own thoughts. It takes character and courage to accept that your own bad mood is distorting your thinking.

If you find this hard to believe, write down some of your thoughts when you are in a bad mood—then check them out when your mood changes. Or just reflect on some of the things that you and your loved ones say when your mood is low and your thinking plummets.

It helps to remember that a bad mood hurts only when you act on it—or out of it. Otherwise, it will simply pass (especially when you pay it little or no attention).

GOOD-MOOD THINKING

Good-mood thinking has wonderful characteristics.

I guess there are always dangers of extravagance, risk-taking, even mania. But more generally, what follows are the characteristics of how we think when "all is right with the world."

+ Generously and inclusively
+ With less prejudice and more capacity to be open to new information
+ With a willingness to listen and accept—rather than impose
+ Creatively
+ Optimistically and enthusiastically
+ Energetically
+ With wisdom and common sense.

Good-mood thinking is "can do," "willing to," thinking. It expresses confidence in yourself and it also engenders it.

When those characteristics are lacking in our thinking, a "macro-survey" may be needed, looking not so much at what thoughts might be getting in the way as at larger and more encompassing beliefs.

Sometimes the obstruction is even closer to home.

If you are exhausted, overwhelmed by demands, stretched in too many directions at one time, short of sleep, eating poorly, not exercising, drinking excessively or taking recreational drugs, your thinking will deteriorate.

So will your mood.

MORE ON MOODS

Moods are a fact of life. Like seasonal changes, they remind us that nature lives within us, not just outside us. Understanding that moods come—and go again—you are already soothing yourself and turning your attention beyond yourself and your "mood."

Couples beware

Because we tend to take out our moods on the people closest to us, it's good to recognize when someone you love is in a low or bad mood.

The best thing you can do is not take that mood too seriously; don't pay it too much attention; don't react and cause them to spiral into a worse mood; don't spin off into self-righteousness; don't take their "bad-mood" thinking to heart.

The things people say when they are in a bad mood are far less likely to be true than those they say when in a good mood.

Of course when a "bad mood" firms into depression or becomes a way of life, this is a much more serious problem. Close attention then needs to be paid to the thoughts, assumptions and beliefs that are driving a consistently low mood—and professional help may need to be considered.

INSIGHT IS NOT ENOUGH

Seeing clearly where you are sabotaging yourself through the ways that you think, and understanding that you could think more positively, is helpful. But insight is not enough.

To live more positively, you must act more positively. And don't wait to "feel better" before you start. *Start.* "Feeling" better can then take care of itself.

Behaving more positively might include:

+ Catching yourself (and stopping) when you describe yourself negatively
+ Making decisions that reflect a positive view of your own capabilities and strengths
+ Carrying through your best intentions
+ Refusing to take on other people's negativity. (This is tough, but exceptionally worthwhile)
+ Doing something about it when your mood is low
+ Finding and cherishing positive company.

Virtually any meaningful, self-directed activity will lift your mood. Think about what gives you energy and lifts your spirits. Do this when you are in a relatively good mood. At tough moments, use your self-awareness.

The power of positive action

Just recognizing that you can act differently is energizing.

Ask yourself, "What's needed?"

Visualize yourself doing that.

Then do it.

CALM YOUR MIND

When you are training yourself to think and act more positively, it's invaluable to remember that you can learn to switch on the part of your brain that soothes you, overriding the "fight or flight" response that automatically gets your heart racing, your palms sweating and your stress and tension escalating when even a remote crisis comes into sight.

Feeling relatively calm, alert and competent is essential to happiness. *Discover for yourself what soothes you most effectively and practice it faithfully.* This is a skill that could add years to your life, make you far easier to be around, and dramatically improve your quality of life.

Soothing yourself could include any or all of these positive actions:

- ✦ Paying attention to your breathing. Slowing your breathing calms you
- ✦ Checking your posture. "Fight or flight" puts you into a state of tension—and eventual adrenal exhaustion. **Calming your body also calms your mind.** Sometimes this is best achieved by physical exercise; do anything but "slump" into a position of hopelessness
- ✦ Reassuring yourself with supportive self-talk. "I can deal with this"
- ✦ Refusing to be hurried (unless it's a life-and-death situation)
- ✦ Trusting that you can assert yourself when that's needed
- ✦ Writing down the problem. Writing down possible "solutions." Use your journal. Activate your inner wisdom
- ✦ Recalling what similar situations provoked similar reactions— that takes the urgency out of this one. ("I often get in a panic when we are going to Ella's.")
- ✦ Recalling what has worked in the past. Note in your journal what has worked. Make it concrete
- ✦ *Paying much more attention to soothing yourself than to the problem.* Once you begin to feel better, you will take care of what's left of the problem far more effectively.

Use as your reminder: "Switch on soothe."

Look at the big picture

When I feel especially anxious or reactive, I have learned to ask myself, "What's going on in my life more generally?"

When we overreact, or get in a panic, or become disproportionately upset, it is almost always because we are doing too much, have become overtired, or have a significant issue that needs our cool, collected attention but isn't getting it.

Use those "panic moments" like a beacon.

This provides invaluable distance. It takes the sting out of what's right in front of you. It saves you from self-blame ("I can't deal with this . . . I'm so hopeless"). And it can lead you directly to the heart of the problem.

BE AN OLYMPIAN

Positive self-talk is an essential part of the training of every elite athlete. Visualizing themselves succeeding, using their imagination to position themselves where they want to be, meeting their fears confidently: all of this plays an incredibly significant part in their exceptional achievements.

Your goals may be different. But the power of positive self-talk is just as helpful. You can talk yourself into or out of almost any kind of attitude, positive or otherwise.

You welcome some thoughts, not others.
You encourage some thoughts, not others.
You hover over some thoughts, not others.

Whatever gets most attention from you will grow stronger and more powerful in your mind and in your life.
Pay attention to your fears and you will grow more fearful.
Pay attention to what uplifts you and you will feel strengthened.
The more consciously you choose, the more stable you will feel.

+ Notice not just what you are thinking—but what emotions accompany your thoughts. (It's hard not to feel miserable if you keep replaying the moment when your boyfriend told you he didn't love you.)
+ Experience for yourself how some thoughts lift your spirits, others do not.
+ Make your own decisions about which thoughts, or habits of thinking, support your well-being.
+ Be honest about where change is needed.
+ Practice thinking *forward* rather than *backward*.

It is impossible to move into a more positive, hopeful frame of mind as long as your body is collapsed and slumped, or you are holding yourself in a tight ball of tension.

Support your changes physically. When you relax your body and face, put your shoulders back and sit or stand "tall," your entire body-mind benefits.

461

A CURE FOR WORRIES

A skilled worrier can turn almost anything into a worry, even something positive. ("I got the job! But maybe I am not as smart as they think I am." "I've met a wonderful new friend. He's probably not nearly as interested in me as I am in him.")

Worry can be a way of life—and is for countless people. (Stand on any street corner in a busy city and watch people hurrying by, consumed and driven by worry.) Vast numbers of us live and breathe worry. We worship at the altar of worry. And we do this knowing that worry—as a way of life—is rarely productive. It may even be fatal.

Paying attention to what's needed, feeling concern in a serious situation, taking account of what's needed: all of that can be productive. Worrying constantly is not productive. It is not healthy. It is not necessary. Use your capacity to observe your thoughts to take stock of what worries you. Without worrying about whether or not my suggestion will "work," try this:

- ✦ On a blank piece of paper, write down in reasonable detail what it is you are currently worrying about.
- ✦ Ask yourself what needs to be done.
- ✦ If the answer is nothing, tear the paper into small pieces and enjoy disposing of it.
- ✦ If the answer involves some action, *write down exactly how you will carry this out.*
- ✦ Make a commitment to yourself to let go—or move forward. Refuse to stagnate.

A tiny exercise like this one accomplishes a lot.

- ✦ It allows you to take charge of the contents of your mind (and lift your emotions).
- ✦ It supports you to take action where action is needed.
- ✦ It literally "clears space" for more productive thinking.
- ✦ It supports loving self-discipline and self-respect.

END PROCRASTINATION

Procrastination can collide in dramatic fashion with your finest intentions. It is a powerful habit and an extremely common one. It arises from stress and causes stress. Yet it can often seem extraordinarily difficult to change. Other people telling you briskly and self-righteously that you ought to just get on and do whatever needs doing is rarely helpful.

Understanding the causes may be a little more helpful. They include:

+ Overestimating what needs to be done
+ Underestimating yourself
+ Fear of failure; fear of other people's power to judge you
+ Perfectionism
+ Taking on something because you didn't know how to assert yourself and say no
+ Resentment and passive aggression ("Why should I be the one who . . . ")
+ Misunderstanding other people's expectations
+ Low frustration tolerance
+ Feeling depressed, hopeless or helpless ("everything" seems impossible)
+ Self-blaming ("I'm so hopeless . . . ")
+ Undervaluing the rewards
+ Fear that success will bring more demands.

Have I left something out?

Resentment can play a highly significant role here—even when people generally have a positive attitude and a capacity to cope. Often resentment builds up imperceptibly when too many assumptions are made, too little gratitude is shown, too many demands are made and too much is required. "Good, kind, positive" people are highly vulnerable to resentment when they don't assert themselves early enough.

Whatever the reasons for your procrastination, *you are influencing yourself through negative, defeatist thinking.*

If you suffer from a general fear of failure, or from perfectionism, know that you will deal with those fears most effectively by facing them, doing what needs to be done, absorbing yourself in the process, encouraging your own creativity. Accept that some tasks are difficult and challenging. Regard this as a learning experience rather than as an insult.

Be aware, too, of what you can influence—and what you can't. You may, for example, do your best, but the person who eventually responds has their own agenda. Perhaps their ideas are different from yours; perhaps they are having a bad day. *All you can control is your own input and process—not other people's reaction to it.*

Assess whether this is something that genuinely does need your attention. If the answer is yes, and especially if the task looms large and you feel small, plan it in detail.

This plan of action will help.

+ Visualize the "end"; have it in your sights. Once the goal is clear, and you know where you are heading, *focus on process.*
+ Begin. Don't wait to "feel like it"; your feelings will change as the task proceeds. *Motivate yourself by doing.*
+ Do the part of the task first that bothers you most. Dread absorbs energy.
+ When thoughts of other people's judgments or potential criticisms intrude, let them pass. Maintain focus.
+ Let yourself know that you are actively choosing (walking the "second mile"), not dancing to someone else's tune.
+ When possible, intensify your focus by doing one thing thoroughly. Then the next.
+ When you complete the task, enjoy your feeling of satisfaction. Too often we rush from one task to the next, starving ourselves of simple encouragement—and delight.

Visualize a positive outcome

I don't have a problem with procrastination but I can certainly feel painfully overwhelmed by the enormity of what I take on. What helps me most is to combine intense focus on each tiny part—what needs my attention *in this moment* gets it—with a clear vision of where I am eventually headed.

For example, with each book that I have written, including this one, I have had a picture in my mind of the book long before I know what will go inside it. I start with the end in sight, then give all my attention to the journey.

A NATURAL OPTIMIST?

I don't regard myself as a natural optimist. Perhaps like many people, I am more a "patchy" optimist. I am certainly able to believe fiercely in the good that's in humankind. I certainly know that people feel best when they are living in ways that bring out the best in themselves and other people. (And that's the essential message of all my books.)

However, I am also aware how deep the pattern is in me to "prepare myself for the worst." I could do the psychoanalytic thing and explain this is in large part because I did get more bad news when I was a little girl than I could possibly process or cope with. (My mother was diagnosed with cancer when I was six and died when I was eight. My sister, upon whom I depended, was herself only three years older.)

I could also stand back and look at my temperament and see that "worry," intensity and anxiety were part of my genetic inheritance. On the other hand, I also inherited and have developed a strong drive to engage, speak up, "get out there," intellectually and spiritually.

I can, finally, believe in myself, as well as in other people. But I am still subject to self-doubts, insecurity; the whole shebang.

This mix of emotions and emotional responses makes me an excellent guinea pig when it comes to learning how to think more positively. (I include here how to worry less—or worry more effectively; how to let unwelcome thoughts pass; how to visualize where I am going with greater confidence; how to recover from setbacks and learn something from them.)

The greatest benefits for me in exploring "positive thinking" have been these:

✦ *Discovering that it's possible to overthink.* Going around and around in circles makes an issue worse, not better, as your sense of hopelessness or self-blame grows.

✦ *Learning to ask: "What does this situation need?"* (It's hard to believe that such a simple question would not always be immediately obvious. But I am not the only person in the world who focused intensely on the problem without looking to see what was needed to relieve it or move on.) Now I know that the qualities needed *live in me.*

+ *Understanding that thoughts drive feelings*, not the other way around.

+ *Recognizing how useful writing is* in any tough situation. I am not talking about the professional writing that I do. I mean the kind of free writing that you could do in your journal, writing out in detail a situation that is haunting you. Writing something down is always far more clarifying than keeping it in your mind. But beyond that, writing it down also magically clears space for fresh and often more helpful thoughts to arise.

+ *Acknowledging that offering hospitality to harsh, unkind, self-punishing thoughts does not improve me as a human being.* This doesn't mean that I want to deny that there are times when I let myself down or when things go "wrong." But in thinking about them and learning from them I can offer myself the same courtesy and respect that I would offer anyone else. That was revolutionary for me.

+ *Discovering that "positive thinking" can embrace genuine sadness*, sorrow, grief, regret. However, what I don't need to add to that potent mix is self-blame; only kindness.

There are still times in my life when old self-defeating patterns of thinking reassert themselves; so do the painful feelings that come with them. Now, though, I can see those patterns for what they are. When they are especially powerful or convincing I know that I am under excessive stress. *And I need to do something about that.*

For me, that's the essential gift of positive thinking: recognizing the stress that unbalances my thinking and that "I need to do something about that," trusting that I can.

ANY EXCUSE FOR A PARTY

STEPHANIE: Practice giving far more attention to what is positive in your life than to what is disappointing or painful. When there is any excuse to praise, affirm, celebrate—take it!

Create a sense of abundance with the phrase, "I can afford to . . ."

CATHERINE: In my twenties, I watched my friend Ashley celebrate any good thing that came her way. Graduations. Promotions. Holidays. Kids' birthdays. End of school and start of school. A cruise party (after returning home from a once-in-a-lifetime vacation), New Year's Eve, romantic takeaway dinners at home with her husband after the kids were in bed. Nights out with female friends. Dessert parties featuring her incredible chocolate pâté! Even Easter egg hunts and Oktoberfest. With Ashley, it really was any excuse for a party.

I used to think Ashley celebrated because her life was easy. Now that I'm older I know how naïve that was. Of course she had her share of disappointments, family struggles, health problems, and money worries. But she also had a very clear sense of gratitude. And that inspires me.

Like the fix that a navigator takes to mark the ship's position, to calculate speed, to understand how far the ship's company has traveled and how much farther they need to go, I have come to see that I, too, need to mark occasions.

It doesn't matter about the size of the celebration. For my family right now, a "celebration" means sparkling apple juice for one son and a teething rusk for the other, sparkling wine for us, some snacks, a good CD, and lots of positive conversation. The whole thing can be assembled in a few minutes, but the effect (I hope) will last for our lifetimes.

I suspect that we are all good at forgetting what's positive and dwelling on what isn't. I know that when I deliberately fix the good occasions in my mind, I am tapping into my spirit-side, however briefly. I'm remembering what's wonderful about my life, and focusing only on that.

A sweet celebration:
Catherine's "Any Excuse" Chocolate Pâté

300 grams or 10 ounces of good quality bittersweet chocolate
1 cup whipping cream
2 cups fresh raspberries

Chop chocolate. In a heat-proof bowl set over hot (not boiling) water, stir chocolate with cream until melted. Place plastic wrap directly on the surface of the pâté and refrigerate until firm. The pâté can be refrigerated for up to six days. To serve, scoop pâté onto plates and garnish with fresh raspberries.

TAKING IN POSITIVE EXPERIENCES

Holding on to positive experiences is no small thing. It builds resilience. And trust. It's essential to self-love and self-respect. It makes you less anxious, less needy.

It also strengthens you to cope better with tougher times.

However, it's one thing to have positive experiences. It's another thing altogether to "take them in," internalize them and let them become part of you—and not trivialize, discount or spoil them.

We do this "spoiling" to ourselves. We also do it to other people.

This behavior reflects a lack of kindness that may arise from something as simple as exhaustion, or it may express something as complex as self-pity or envy.

"Spoiling" a positive experience, *you are stealing something of value.*

Self-awareness is needed here: to curb the impulse to spoil someone's pleasure, and to ask yourself, "Why do I feel so irritable, ungenerous, unkind? What's *my* issue? And how can I deal with it myself rather than dumping it on someone else?"

And when you are stealing from yourself?

+ Pay attention to your thinking. Notice that *it's your own thoughts that are cutting you down, discounting the good, focusing on the bad.*
+ Step back from those thoughts. See them as an old habit in its dying phase.
+ Remind yourself of what's good and true. "These good things happened to me."
+ *Write them down.*
+ *Notice them all over again. Honor them.*

This will not only transform your own feelings of entitlement; it will also transform the way you value what you are giving to others.

RETHINK FAILURE

"Failure" can be transformed when you learn something of value from it. Every experience—unwelcome as well as welcome—contributes to the discovery of your destiny: what you are in this life to learn; what you are in this life to give. Even the most insightful among us find it difficult to predict which events in our lives will ultimately turn out to be significant—or our greatest blessings.

Do. Don't "try"

When you need to make a change, do it.

"Trying" may express a fine intention, but it doesn't arise from genuine trust and confidence in yourself; nor does it build it.

Choose to be self-supporting rather than self-defeating. Next time you hear yourself say, "Yes, I'll try," switch to, "Yes, I will."

YOUR HAPPINESS SET POINT

You have a happiness "set point," a genetically influenced level at which your happiness—or subjective well-being—tends to settle, almost regardless of what happens to you. (You win a million dollars. Two years later you feel much as you did before you won. Why? Because the change came from outside yourself; nothing has changed within.)

This set point determines about 50 percent of your disposition to happiness. That leaves another 50 percent for you to influence!

So, even when life is not ideal, when none of your dreams are coming true, when no one is coming over the horizon to save you, you can still give yourself a huge boost in the happiness stakes. You do this not by winning a million dollars (a gift from outside yourself), but *by making changes from within*. Those are priceless.

YOU DON'T HAVE TO PAY FOR
YOUR HAPPINESS

From years of listening to people's stories, I've discovered how many people carry with them from their childhood a deeply held belief that they may in some way have to "pay" for their happiness.

'If something good happens to me . . . something bad will follow."

These thoughts may be totally illogical. It doesn't make them less convincing. I suspect that this kind of thinking makes it difficult for many people to enjoy good experiences or trust whatever happiness they could experience. Like any attitude, this one grows in power *the more attention it gets*. And it diminishes in power, *the less attention it gets*.

These small steps will help.

- ✦ *Refuse to blame yourself for having these thoughts.* See it for what it is: a "thought," a conditioned belief—not reality.
- ✦ *Remind yourself that life is complex:* no "accounting method" could ever contain it.
- ✦ *Identify and claim a fundamental attitude to life* that is more trusting. ("I can risk reaching out toward and claiming happiness. I can risk some disappointments. I know that I can survive them. I will pay close attention to what's happening today rather than living in the past or dreading the future.")

Take time for this, acknowledging that the search for a more positive ethic is itself fascinating, allowing you to view your inner world with enhanced interest and curiosity.

A GRATITUDE JOURNAL

For people who have a hard time sustaining feelings of happiness, it can be most helpful to keep a gratitude journal, noting on a daily basis every small thing that has been pleasing.

No writing skills are needed, just commitment.

Writing in a gratitude journal for ten or fifteen minutes each day trains you to turn your attention away from what's chronically dissatisfying to what can please and uplift you—and join you more securely to life.

Cultivating gratitude reminds you of the intrinsic interdependence of your own existence. We do, truly, stand on one another's shoulders.

Everything that you take for granted—from the power for your computer, to the train that takes you to work, the clothes you wear, the food you buy, the talk on the radio that makes you laugh—is cultivated or facilitated by other human beings.

Notice, too, how amazing nature is in all its moods and variations. Give yourself permission to notice this even when you live in a crowded city. *Pause,* and notice.

Out of many hundreds of thousands of stimuli available to you each day, your attention will alight on very few.

Choosing to pay attention to what's uplifting by writing about it, and living it "twice over," can radically improve your mood, well-being, self-respect and trust.

It can also radically improve your relationships with other people—regardless of whether they are friends or strangers.

Gratitude is energizing, contagious—and deeply attractive.

And don't overlook expressing gratitude for everything that you are able to do for others. Every opportunity to give time, service or money is also a cause for thanksgiving.

HAPPINESS IN A SINGLE MOMENT

Happiness can come in a single moment. And in a single moment it can go again. But a single moment does not create it.

Happiness is created through countless choices made and then made again throughout a lifetime.

You are its host as well as its guest. You give it form, shape, individuality, texture, tone. And what it allows you to give can change your world.

Happiness can be stillness. But it isn't still. It wraps, enchants, heals, consoles, soothes, delights, calms, inspires and connects.

It is on your face and in your body. It is in your life and being.

THIS IS WHAT IT TAKES TO BE HAPPY

Happiness is available to you, whether or not you are practiced at it. It is not something that external circumstances create. *It is something that you allow.* Here's how.

Emotionally:

- ✦ Think well of yourself. And give yourself plenty of reasons to do so. When you let yourself down, learn something, make the change that's needed—and move on.
- ✦ Pay attention to what's uplifting—and be uplifted!
- ✦ Regard your life as a gift.
- ✦ Value what you can give others.
- ✦ Value everything that others do for you.
- ✦ Discover and value all your strengths: intellectual, emotional, spiritual, social, creative and moral.
- ✦ Let go of resentments.
- ✦ Cultivate tolerance, patience and good humor.
- ✦ Practice forgiveness.
- ✦ Express gratitude. Find increasing reasons to be grateful.

Socially:

- ✦ Find and focus on the positive qualities of other people.
- ✦ Value simple pleasures.
- ✦ Discover what makes others happy. *Do more of that.*
- ✦ Give time and attention to your close relationships.
- ✦ Think and speak positively about yourself and others.
- ✦ *Be* the friend you would most like to have.
- ✦ Practice tolerance through deeper understanding.
- ✦ Try new things or do familiar things in a fresh way.
- ✦ Give something practical to your community.
- ✦ Choose work that supports your integrity.
- ✦ Be a peacemaker.

Physically:

- ✦ Sleep and eat well. (This has a dramatic effect on well-being.)

+ Limit alcohol (or give it up entirely if you are irritable, angry or depressed). Abstain from recreational drugs.
+ Exercise every day.
+ Appreciate and relish the gifts of your health, body and senses.
+ Take regular breaks.
+ Cultivate beauty in all your environments.

Spiritually:

+ Consider that you are a soul, a living spiritual eternal being.
+ Consider that every other being is also a soul.
+ *Believe in something greater than yourself.*
+ Respect other people's paths.
+ Practice kindness. *Live* kindly.
+ See yourself in others and others in yourself.
+ Focus on the present moment (that's where happiness is experienced).
+ Spend time with people who inspire you.
+ Celebrate and create beauty.
+ Value silence.
+ Learn to meditate and still your mind.
+ Explore prayer—especially simple words of gratitude.
+ Read what's uplifting. Listen to music that soothes.
+ Recognize your interdependence with all living forms.
+ On a daily basis, relish the wonders of nature.

Spread happiness

It gives me the greatest possible joy to imagine you sharing this list with the people you love, adding to it, making it your own, encouraging one another, applauding one another—delighting in the other's increasing happiness, as much as your own.

FUN AND CREATIVITY

CATHERINE: Recently I attended a women's breakfast at a beautiful conference center overlooking the sea. The guest speaker stepped up to the podium with a huge smile. *Good morning, everybody!* she said, "*I just wanted to ask . . . are you fun to live with?*"

Everyone breathed in sharply, then laughed. The speaker's question may have been a shock, but her point was obvious: it's so easy to want to *have more fun*, without considering how to *be more fun*.

By temperament, I'm nearly always serious. I know that my family and friends would benefit from me being more fun ... and I suspect that I would really benefit as well! But where do I start?

STEPHANIE: The speaker asked a wild question—and a wonderful one. It's easy to see that we can never be fun to live with unless *we ourselves are having fun*.

We can never be interesting to live with, much less fun, unless we cultivate and encourage passions and interests that stretch and activate our minds, that engage all of our senses and lift our spirits.

Of course it is possible to reduce stress, take time to relax and rediscover simple pleasures. Those things matter. It's hard to have fun without them. But I suspect that what Catherine is after is something that "clean sweeps" an entire life; the answer to that is creativity.

Positive living is creative. It's about putting your mark on your own life, not living second-hand to someone else's prescription. It's about daring to be yourself, daring to be original, daring to dance to your own tune and to write the tune while you are dancing!

There's a wonderful Jewish saying, "If I live someone else's life, who will live mine?" *Living your own life is creative.*

+ Each time you try something new, different, challenging, adventurous, *you are being creative.*
+ Each time you invite people home for dinner without any preparation, or accept an invitation at the last minute, or change your plans for the better because it's raining, *you are being creative.*

+ Each time you turn off the television to talk with real attention and intensity, *you are being creative.*
+ Each time you bring a fresh thought or insight to an old situation, or swallow back a tired response, *you are being creative.*
+ Each time you bring a note of beauty, originality or celebration to a mundane task, *you are being creative.*
+ Each time you appreciate that this moment has never been, and will never come again, *you are being creative.*

INTENSIFY YOUR POSITIVE MOOD

Sit somewhere beautiful and comfortable. Take in your surroundings. (Recognize that your choice is creative.)

Switch on the right side (the creative side) of your brain by envisaging yourself as relaxed, open, daring. Enjoy what you see!

Ask: *What's the most outrageously beautiful, original, atypical thing that I've not yet done?*
Ask: *What would most magnificently express my love for life and gratitude for my own life?*
Ask: *Whose permission do I need?*

Listen to Katherine Mansfield

This writer has been an inspiration to me throughout my life. My daughter's name—Kezia—was inspired by her exquisite stories set in our shared home country, New Zealand. Here she is at her sensual and inspirational best.

"The mind I love must have wild places, a tangled orchard where dark damsons drop in the heavy grass, an overgrown little wood, the chances of a snake or two, a pool that nobody's fathomed the depth of, and paths threaded with flowers planted by the mind."

Cherish your own sensuality

Find passages like this one that heighten your own awareness of the beauty of existence. Write them out in your journal or on a card that you can prop up by your computer or bedside. But "read" nature itself also—in all its moods.

NO END TO JOY

Positive thinking and acting is never about "you" only. It profoundly affects the people you directly influence, and changes the world around you.

When you think laterally, you create positive change.

When you resolve conflicts, you create positive change.

When you look for the best in other people, you create positive change.

When you bite back an ugly remark, you create positive change.

When you uphold peace in any small way, you create positive change.

When you stand up for social justice, you create positive change.

When you see your desire for happiness reflected in other people's lives and act more compassionately, you create positive change.

When you appreciate and rejoice in difference, you create positive change.

When you look at the world from other people's perspectives, you create positive change.

When you take care of the physical environment, you create positive change.

When you grasp your interdependence with all living forms, you create positive change.

When you give up a little tension and gain a little humor, you create positive change.

When you refuse to be hurried, you create positive change.

When you give thanks for the blessings of existence, you create positive change.

HOW TO THINK AND ACT POSITIVELY

Essential insights

✦ Know that your moods and feelings are driven by your thoughts. And thoughts can be changed.

✦ As thoughts change, mood, feelings and emotions will follow.

✦ You are more powerful than your thoughts. You *have* thoughts; you are not your thoughts. Observing your thoughts and feelings, you will no longer be at their mercy.

✦ You can limit the attention you give to unproductive and depressing thinking. You can STOP painful ruminations. You can consciously *increase* the attention you give to what is nourishing, sustaining and hopeful.

✦ What you think about an event is more important than the event itself. Better still, while you cannot control the events in your life, you can take charge of your thinking.

✦ Positive thinking and attitudes go way beyond "cheerfulness" and upbeat affirmations. They honor your gift of life.

✦ Positive thinking is a skill. It can be learned and shared. You can become more positive as you age—and also increasingly flexible and open in your thinking.

✦ Optimism is an attitude that even a pessimist can learn and develop. It opens you to a sense of hope and possibility; it supports your creativity; it broadens your horizons.

✦ Happiness is a state of mind. It is also an attitude. Frequently, it is a choice.

✦ Acting "as if" you were feeling positive will almost magically change your feelings. Changing your physical circumstances, using your body, moving into a more uplifting and stimulating situation will also change your feelings.

✦ Your thoughts (and moods) profoundly affect other people—even when you don't say a single word.

✦ You can afford to be less judgmental. Even the most insightful people will find it difficult to predict which events turn out to be their greatest blessings.

✦ Not every problem has a solution; some problems just have to be survived.

✦ Grief, sadness or loss are not "negative feelings." Respect them.

Essential actions

✦ Value and develop your own creativity. The more engaged you are with what you do, the more of "yourself" you bring to it, the more satisfying it will be. This is true even of the most humble tasks. Leave perfectionism behind.

✦ Recognize how powerfully happiness can arise—and fall—within your own mind.

✦ Strictly limit the attention you give to what brings you down.

✦ Let yourself "take in" happiness, affection, encouragement, enthusiasm.

✦ See yourself as a source of happiness for others. You
can't "make" them happy but you can certainly affect
their quality of life through your own good humor
and goodwill.

✦ Experience the difference between good-mood and
bad-mood thinking. Do not make important decisions
when bad-mood thinking dominates. As you grow more
familiar with those different levels of thought, your
sense of choice will radically change.

✦ Begin with the way you talk to yourself; pay attention
also to what you talk about to others; what you
encourage through your attention. Encourage yourself
at least as much as you would encourage a friend.

✦ Talk to and about yourself like someone who can *learn
and grow from every situation*, not be crushed by it.

✦ Listen to the background commentary in your mind.
Are you routinely negative about yourself and your life?
Do you put yourself down? What are you saying to and
about yourself? Speak to and about yourself
encouragingly.

✦ Practice gratitude as an antidote to chronic inner
complaining or dissatisfaction. Start with two moments
each day that you can give thanks for; build up
gradually. Record your progress in your journal. Train
yourself to "notice" differently.

✦ Recognize your inner obstacles to a more positive way
of thinking and living. Go around those obstacles. Or
leap over them. They are only habits. And habits can be
changed.

✦ When you are feeling low, change your environment or your posture. Get moving. Give your attention over to something uplifting and engaging.

✦ In tough moments, remind yourself truthfully, "This will pass."

✦ Regardless of your circumstances, you can choose happiness (contentment, serenity, good humor, gratitude) and positively affect the well-being of everyone around you.

✦ Discover the space and stillness of your inner world through meditation, journal writing, reflection, appreciation of nature. Let yourself know your own depths. Continue to find the books, teachers, friends who can support you spiritually.

✦ Changing your attitudes for the better, you are also changing our world.

Acknowledgments

Stephanie Dowrick

The insights, enthusiasm and support of a number of people have enhanced this book. I would particularly like to acknowledge Caroline Ward, Luther Poier, Wendy Weiser, Greg Andrews, Amara Sherson, and most especially Kezia Dowrick, Gabriel Dowrick and Aokie Thonsaeng, as well as Jane Moore and Geraldine Killalea for loving and sustained support. Geraldine, Jane, Greg and Luther offered close, sensitive readings of an early draft and made invaluable suggestions for which I am most grateful.

This is in many ways a culminating psychological book for me. So I want to thank those people who have inspired me in the many workshops that I have led; the clients who shared their inner worlds over many years, as well as the readers, editors and publishers who have given me priceless feedback during my writing career. I want to thank, too, those who have guided me as spiritual teachers, as well as the Australian Quaker community for two decades, my Brahma Kumaris friends, especially Charlie Hogg, and, most recently, my deans and classmates at the interfaith New Seminary, New York. In this context, I again want to thank Jane Moore for a decade of inspirational conversation and shared prayer.

Many thanks to all at Allen & Unwin, led by the talented and unfailingly kind Sue Hines, and with particular thanks to Clare Emery, Andrea McNamara, Karen Williams, Lou Johnson and Nada Backovic, and, not least, those exceptional directors Paul Donovan and Patrick Gallagher.

Finally, I want to thank Catherine Greer, whose good humor, faith, enthusiasm and unwavering dedication contributed so much to this project from first to last.

Catherine Greer

I would like to thank Stephanie Dowrick for giving me the opportunity to discuss, read and learn from this book as she wrote it—a rare and generous gift. For their friendship, encouragement and support I gratefully acknowledge Janet Anderson and Merrin Masterman, who read early drafts of the manuscript, and Jean Bradshaw, Dorothy Hawes and Nicky Simmonds. Heartfelt thanks go to my mother, Katie Greer, who spent several months in Australia caring for our family; to my sons, Luke and Elijah, for their patience and presence; and, above all, to my husband, Luther Poier. *Thank you.*

Smart Index

Choosing Happiness covers an unusually broad range of subject matter. The titles of each entry are frequently self-explanatory. You will also find summaries of the "essentials" at the end of each chapter. But to ensure that you can locate whatever you are looking for quickly and effectively, this Smart Index offers you access to specific topics *and also* to implicit themes within the book. Written in plain language, and with minimal cross-referencing, this Index is your key to the "emergency services" the book offers as well as a useful resource for browsers.

For each Index category, you will be *referred to the beginning of the entry*. The word or concept you have searched will almost always appear within the entry (or in the breakout below the main entry), but occasionally you may also find yourself reading about the concept more broadly. Of particular interest within the Index are the affirmations and the comprehensive list of questions. The affirmations are power statements or solution phrases to use, modify or hang on to in tough moments in order to create immediate change in the way you experience and respond to a situation. There are affirmations *to deal with* difficult situations, and affirmations *for developing* your resources and strengths. Similarly, the questions that occur throughout the book are indexed to help you gain greater understanding of your attitudes and responses. These questions will prompt you to explore issues of concern more deeply, in both highly original and straightforward ways.

CHOOSING HAPPINESS
LIFE & SOUL ESSENTIALS

Stephanie Dowrick is the author of a number of life-changing, internationally bestselling books, including *Intimacy & Solitude, Forgiveness and Other Acts of Love* and *The Universal Heart.* She has also achieved the rare distinction of writing bestselling fiction as well as nonfiction, with her novel, *Tasting Salt*, topping the Australian bestseller lists in the same year as *Forgiveness and Other Acts of Love*. Her most recent book was *Free Thinking*.

Born and raised in New Zealand, Stephanie Dowrick lived for fifteen years in London, where she founded the distinguished feminist publishing house The Women's Press. Since 1983, when she moved to Sydney, writing has been her principal occupation. She has had many years of experience in a variety of psychotherapeutic approaches including psychosynthesis and object relations. For some years she had a small psychotherapy practice but more recently has focused on giving workshops and spiritual retreats. Stephanie Dowrick has been writing the "Inner Life" column for *Good Weekend* magazine since 2001. In June 2005, Stephanie was ordained as an Interfaith Minister at St. John the Divine, in New York City. She continues to live in Sydney, where she has a son and daughter.

Catherine Greer collaborated with Stephanie Dowrick on the concept, research, and editing of *Choosing Happiness,* and has contributed a series of questions to the book. Born and educated in Canada, where she graduated with a Master's degree in English, she immigrated to Australia in 1998 and started her own copywriting business. She lives in Sydney with her husband and two young sons.

www.stephaniedowrick.com